Lost Faith and Wandering Souls

Lost Faith and Wandering Souls

A Psychology of
Disillusionment, Mourning,
and the Return of Hope

David Morris

LAKE
DRIVE
lakedrivebooks.com

Lake Drive Books
6757 Cascade Road SE, #162
Grand Rapids, MI 49546

info@lakedrivebooks.com
lakedrivebooks.com
@lakedrivebooks

Publishing books that help you heal, grow, and discover.

Published in the United States by Lake Drive Books, LLC.

Paperback ISBN 978-1-957687-00-1
eBook ISBN 978-1-957687-01-8

Library of Congress Control Number: 2022933599

Printed in the United States of America

Cover Design: Jonathan Sainsbury // 6x9design

For all of us, that we might find community.

Contents

Part II. Biographical Analysis

Preface

I DIDN'T THINK I could lose my faith for a second time. I had been through it once before, and thought I knew the pitfalls and how to keep things moving in a constructive direction. I thought I could make it work. But it is such a complicated business.

The first time it happened, I was in college, which might sound like a cliché, a common occurrence in young adulthood. The thing is, a garden variety wanderlust is not supposed to have an element of hurt. It is supposed to give you a break, an open and free space to gain perspective and help you better appreciate the beauty and power of your religion. It is supposed to help you find ownership. What it is not supposed to do is leave you feeling like you've been sheltered, living in a world unto itself, cut off from so much goodness to discover. For me, this time of exploration only made me want to distance myself from something that was holding me back rather than letting me go.

As a psychology student at a large state university in Virginia, like so many of us, I was given an opportunity to look at life more analytically. I was learning about the motivations behind our behaviors, that our brains could play tricks on us in ways the rational mind cannot immediately perceive. It was all obvious stuff once you began to look at it clearly in a classroom setting. Not satisfied with the strictly clinical and experimental side of psychology, I also started taking classes in religion and philosophy, eventually adding a religion minor to my psychology major. I was reading and discussing biblical criticism, sociological theories of religion, a survey in theology, and philosophy. I found it exhilarating, enlivening.

I cannot pinpoint the moment I started feeling sad, feeling the hurt, but I do remember the experience while taking a walk on my university campus. I can only say that I was reflecting on what I was learning in my classes, and had the thought that things were not adding up with life outside classes. For one thing, why wasn't I ever able to think this freely and expansively when growing up? Why wasn't there an attitude of open handedness when it came to the beliefs and identities of the Christianity in which I was raised?

To put it bluntly, I felt as though I was sold a bill a goods that was no longer of the same value. Much of what I was raised to think, feel, and believe seemed so unexamined, so fraught with inconsistency, and so cliché, speaking of cliché. I could not yet put a lot of words and ideas around it, but the feeling was overwhelming. Although I was thinking about the beliefs of the religion of my family and community, the feeling was not directed at anyone, and there was no single memory or traumatic episode (though that's true for others). It was a more diffuse yet palpable sadness in my chest and gut that the religious community that had sold me that bill of goods had prevented me from discovering so much goodness in life.

The undergraduate studies, meanwhile, remained exciting. As I continued, I got it stuck in my head that after my bachelor's degree, I wanted to study both psychology and religion at the same time. I did not necessarily want to be a pastor like my father and grandfather, but I also knew I didn't want to become a cookie cutter clinical psychologist. I wanted to go to a graduate school that would allow me to read and study deeply both psychological theory and knowledge about religion.

To make a long story short, the result of that graduate work produced this book. I do not remember at what point I decided to study the loss of faith, but that's what happened. My graduate work in psychology and religion allowed me to make sense of issues of identity, religion, individual development, social structure, with attention to matters of power seen through issues of race, class, and gender. I wanted to take that analytical work of making sense of my faith crisis as far as I could.

To put it one way, what you will read in the pages that follow is a way of looking at religion that wasn't afforded by my upbringing. Simple as that. What follows draws in some theoretical ideas, but none of this is supposed to be cut off from common sense that anyone might have, fancy degrees or not. This work is no more than an elaboration of common sense, or call it reason, or science. It is simply a participant-observer mindset about faith. You participate in religion, and to some degree you also bring your analytical point of view along for the ride.

With my prolonged period of study and no small amount of distance from religion, I eventually started to see a path where I could get my faith mojo back, to be as much a participant as an observer. My confidence and common sense about church and belief was up, the way you feel physically when you have started exercising again. I felt that I pretty much owned my journey, not letting anyone or anything tell me I wasn't legitimate or on track. I found fresh interest and felt impervious to the sometimes negative aspects of religious life in the US. Little did I know.

For the second faith loss go around, the trouble started somewhere when my wife and I had begun attending a church in Michigan where we had just moved due to a job in evangelical Christian book publishing. After a good experience at a Methodist Church in New Jersey, we wanted something close to our home, something in which our then tenth grader could find a spiritual cohort and see kids who were neighbors or friends at school. I also thought that I had to engage in an evangelical church if I was to be a publisher at a well-known evangelical company.

After a few years, our daughter headed off to a college two-hours away, and my wife and I were on our own at the church. We had made some good acquaintances there, and some of my co-workers attended the same church. Yet even after some years, it still seemed a slow process for us to feel connected. Annoyingly, for example, we kept getting asked if we were new. That was strange, as we attended regularly and were involved in activities outside the main church service.

We had good success feeling connected at our previous church, knowing that it did not happen overnight. We knew it would take time, even when you do not quite feel like going every Sunday. In the case of this new church, however, we really, really did not feel like it. Each ensuing Sunday morning we struggled to get the gumption to go, even though the church was an easy five-minute drive. I could recount the various reasons we felt that way but suffice it to say that at times we felt that the people at that church had little interest or ability in establishing personal relationships, which always struck us as surprising given their emphasis on evangelizing. The place felt fake.

Our leaving this church was a bigger issue than any one political stance or theological belief. Nevertheless, all our departure needed was what mental health counselors would call a precipitating event. The former pastor of the church, the pastor who had started the church some decades earlier, who along with his wife and children had given his best years, kicked him out, kicked them all out. Simple as that. The pastor's son, who was gay, asked him if he would officiate at his wedding (somewhere else), and he of course said yes. As a result, the denomination of which this church was a part, and of which this pastor was no unknown figure, revoked his ordination and asked him to never preach again.

Now Lisa and I did not know this pastor well, but we did have a chance to meet him a few times and have dinner together. He was one of those people that seemed wise, gentle, and passionate. His work in that church and his contribution to that denomination would be difficult to quantify. He'd given his life to this work, and they publicly rebuked and rejected not only him and his wife, but by extension they rejected his son, who was spiritually raised in that church. This is a stage of life when one is supposed to be reflecting on years of good work, actualizing your wisdom, and perhaps mentoring others and giving back to those currently doing the work. So what that denomination and that church did was psychologically egregious behavior, immoral behavior. No equivocation, no further qualification, no more unexamined biblical arguments or arguments from tradition. Whatever happened to common sense? You simply cannot build a community of faith and let good people work there, live lives there, grow up there, and then ex-communicate them and turn them into pariahs. It was just too much for my wife and me.

One Sunday morning, just as it would be time to start preparing for church, we talked it through and decided not to go. Our desire just wasn't there, none whatsoever, and it was time to honor that. Something was wrong, more wrong than simply saying it just wasn't a good fit. Marriage, for example, may not always seem a great fit, but you hang in there, and perhaps you find love despite yourself. But for some marriages, the problem is not that it's not a great fit. Many casual observers might say that this church was friendly and gracious and giving in many ways, but we felt that as an organization, our church was acting in a toxic way, and it was unwilling to be accountable for its behavior. It was time to end the marriage.

We said we were done, and with that came emotions, a whole flood of them: righteous indignation, self-doubt, relief, worry, freedom, a sense of shame. It was a wide rush of feelings, just like you have with any significant decision, justified or not. At times our emotions became more intense, or alternatively, we just felt a little numb, which was the worst part of it.

Did we lose our faith? To say yes no doubt oversimplifies things, but it would be at least partly accurate. We lost something we thought was important to us. We had put five years of church going into this effort. We had indeed made some friends, some of whom we felt we needed to inform about our decision, which brought more difficult feelings. We had found our faith shaped by the place, as spending time in any faith community inevitably does, no matter how much some might argue with what is being said behind the pulpit or the songs being sung. But we were shaken. It was profoundly troubling. While we felt we lost something, we also knew that perhaps it wasn't us that lost faith but that rather the church that had betrayed our trust in a church that would be inclusive, not literalist fundamentalists.

What is more, I thought I was inoculated and immune to this happening again. I had taken precautions. I was equipped with a PhD. I knew what to do. Be involved yet independent. Be yourself, take initiative, and make things happen. Own it. Study and think for yourself.

Talk about clichés, here I was once again feeling isolated, lonely, and depressed. How did I screw this up so royally? How can I possibly be back at the beginning again, or maybe even a few steps back? Why did I drag my wife, who was raised Catholic, into this?

I had reasoned with myself that I could be around people who were in lower faith stages or did not have a religious studies degree, which was a dumb rationalization. Suddenly I was realizing that faith stages are no excuse for corporate discrimination. There is also the matter of common sense. I realized, had to realize, that no amount of wisdom and generosity and self-agency that I had achieved matters when such egregiousness happens right in front of you. These religious people acted the way they wanted to, or failed to act, and it was clear that they could not care less if I thought any different. Even with my conceptual understanding of what was going on, no amount of graciousness on my part was going to make any difference with these white, affluent, educated suburbanites who had created their tribe. I could see more clearly now just how entangled, how entrenched such abusive behavior is with a religious life that seems nice and kind and wonderful.

My wife and I will be fine. We are figuring things out, living in a dynamic fallow time. Where we will end up is unknown. What I do know is that we are not alone. One does not need to work hard to find the often-cited research of the undeniably growing number of "nones and dones," those who no longer claim a religious affiliation or even say they are no longer interested in religious life as we know it. If you do not want to look at the research, just ask any pastor or acknowledge in the churches around you that frequency of attendance is down compared to years gone by. We are all going through change, as we always have. What I also know is that the dynamics discussed in the pages that follow still apply. They served me well the first time I lost faith, and they still apply now.

A Way of Looking at Things

What follows is a way of looking at things, a hermeneutic of suspicion, a psychological interpretation. The language of psychoanalytic psychology presents not just a taxonomy, a breakdown and categorization of the stages of spiritual life. More than that, the language of psychoanalysis provides a participant-observer stance of watching carefully and being better aware of the things that motivate us. It looks beneath the surface. It does not take things at face value, but as representations for so much more—and what a beautiful thing that is. Whatever we are going through, it is packed with meaning. One thing signifies another, and so much of it is based on needs that must be met, identities that must be formed, group coherence that must be achieved.

Perhaps the greatest question of our time is whether we can find community, a place to recognize and be recognized. With so much breaking down in our religious institutions, people want to know what is next. Is it a return to church like we have known it, a reformulation and reformation of church, or is it possible that we will or can find sacred community in a way we've never experienced? So many of us think that we must find some new form of church that looks much like the old form. Yet the very presumption in that question may hold the key to understanding the nature of our problem.

When we lose our faith, our connection, we are indeed embarking on new ground. The loss of spiritual community might simply be a disruption, but a disruption that is bound to happen on the way to what is next. It is not necessarily a progression of theological reasoning, which is possibly how most people express this loss, but a problem with the larger social structure, like the seemingly impenetrable superstructure of white evangelicalism. The question is, how do we understand how hard it is to break free, and what do the healthy steps look like, both for each of us individually but also for how we form the community we so desperately need?

A psychological understanding of religion can be helpful. Speaking purely psychologically, religion helps us find meaning and offers identity. It comprises symbols, beliefs, practices, and the corporate structures that codify and reinforce those things for the individual. Such a definition, for example, does not necessarily mean that religion is any of the multitude of denominations one may choose, especially in Protestant evangelicalism in the US. The sheer number of splintered denominations and churches—doing religion the "right" way—in this context itself lends credence to the idea that religion, psychologically speaking, can be many things. In other words, religion may, and perhaps more than not, be something that could be markedly different than what we think it is. Defining religion strictly in a psychological sense, therefore, opens the possibilities of different kinds of concrete expressions that we might call religious or spiritual.

Here is where an analytical, participant-observer point of view really kicks in, and here is where we can bring in a broader, sociological or a "psychosocial" point of view. For example, we might talk about how American religion is extraordinarily shaped by individualism (hence all the church splits), and how that individualism shapes any one person's identity, relationships, and presenting worries and anxieties. We might also talk about empirical sociological research that shows a quality of sadness in spiritual seekers, and by extension, that sadness is a defining characteristic of the religious self today. Or we could also talk historically about what I like to call "the great inward turn" of religion that happened as soon as Europeans left their homeland in search of religious freedom. Arguably, we've been losing our religion since the days we came to America, constantly seeking, relying on ourselves, sometimes just surviving, never really able to form real community.

How, for example, do a people embedded in a culture of the individualistic, sacred self, who have institutionalized an inward spiritual life, properly mourn the loss of religion and spiritual community? Do we really "go back" to faith? How do we find trust and faith in our worldviews again, without the structures we are accustomed to? The task of our time is to redefine what it means to be religious, to have healthy symbols of ultimacy shared in community. It is a monumental task, but also a dynamic one and at times exciting.

There is no doubt that this exploration showed me some of the keys to finding our way to once again trusting in ultimate symbols, even in community. One of those keys is learning how to own your faith, take responsibility for it, and to slough off heavy-handed high achievers. Then to take what you own and show up in community and discover a sense of play with others. I thought that I could apply these ideas, even if sometimes the "others" were not necessarily playing fair at times. I thought I could accept that. Instead, I found out that the faith community I was in not only did not play fair, but it also was downright hostile. Play cannot happen in that kind of environment.

What I found out, eventually, was that you could put yourself in a new situation, a new playing field, and you might convince yourself that it is a healthy environment (the evangelical church mentioned above did allow women pastors, for example). You could get pulled in and form some friendships and attachments, but then realize just how conditional it was. You also realize that you were seen in a way that was not the full you. The environment could not hold all of you. To be true to yourself, to allow all your theological thinking, your religious experience, and any new experimentation meant that you were going to have to hide. And I could not hide any longer and abide by what was wrong. I felt bad that I was involved. I felt like I led those people along, but also realize they led me along, that we were leading each other along.

All that to say is that there are principles in this book of what a healthy faith looks like, especially in the context of overcoming unhealthy faith. But just because you learn them, it does not mean it will be easy. In a way, that's the whole point. It will be messy, even potentially traumatic. There's no reason to put up with that, and yet when you do try to participate in community, it can happen again. What I hope will become evident is that you can always find a good game, a place to be careful but to try to play along. That's the only way you are going to make progress. Try to find a safe space (and I'm not necessarily talking about a church), and be ready to lose at faith again and again.

The foregoing introduction will explain what is to come throughout this book. There is a lot of background discussion summarizing sociological research, psychological stages of faith, and the basic psychoanalytic stance toward religion. Then there is a prolonged exploration in the psychoanalytic theory that pertains to loss of religion, what can be called mourning religion. The theoretical sections can be demanding and perhaps at times presuming some background in psychology, psychoanalytic theory, and sociology. Hopefully, the theory is not so hard to follow and the jargon not too overwhelming, and hopefully it holds a certain evocative nature for putting a language to the religious identity crisis so many of us feel. And as mentioned above, some of this thinking simply cultivates a discipline of common sense, or reason, and a way of looking at things under the surface. I would also recommend to the reader not to miss the biographical analysis in Part II, as that is where the theory is applied, and the interpretive, analytical stance goes into action.

David Morris, January 2022

Introduction

The Faith Crisis in Our Time

THROUGHOUT THE LIFE of someone in the United States, religious experience seems like a perpetual game of Twister—you're always trying to find some new additional spot to stand on and keep yourself from falling. Alternatively, you just don't play the game, worried you might lose. Either way, it's not easy. Social upheaval, economic fluctuation, a free-flowing world of ideas, and increasing cultural diversity make it no simple matter. It is difficult to form attachments to beliefs and rituals that motivate and bring people together. Change, not stability, rules the day. It is part of our religious DNA.

Our spiritual instability is so common that many of us may wake any morning, like a Sunday morning, and our trust in religion is no longer there, we have simply lost our grip on it, or we work even harder to grasp it more tightly. We have trouble defining spiritual practice, giving it a name, and having it remain something solid that we can share with others. Observe for example the growth of generic, nondenominational Protestant churches in recent decades. Isn't there within this movement an unwanted compromise with passive spectatorhood and a corresponding lack of community or feeling of belonging? Aren't there difficulties in agreeing upon compelling sacred objects, resulting in the big box church experience?

The fluid, seemingly shapeless features of religion, especially of

1

late twentieth and early twenty-first century Christianity in the United States, create what seems to be a difficult challenge to the ways in which we accumulate experience and knowledge of religion. Churches attempt to respond to this challenge but may miss the root causes. Whether the task is beefing up attendance in an ailing, urban mainline church or starting a new "seeker sensitive" megachurch in the suburbs, elusive obstacles lie in the way and the process seems slow if not impossible. A new and improved Sunday morning service or a clever way to repackage a set of doctrines can sometimes seem no more than mere marketing or emotionalism and fail to address the deeper dynamics that keep us always on our toes trying to figure things out.

There indeed are deeper dynamics at work, often hidden from view. Briefly stated, this book is about the overlooked interplay of psychological and social dynamics in the individual journey of faith. Such dynamics are always, always playing a role in how we create and interact with the formal structures of religion, such as its various theologies, symbolisms, and structures. Sometimes God the Father, for example, is far more your real-life father than you've ever possibly acknowledged.

So just what may we say about the individual experience of religion? What is its depth, scope, and power? When does it begin, how strong is its hold, and what effect do its beginnings have on later religious life? What are the consequences of an experience gone wrong? Before answering these questions, let's be reminded, because it is so easy to sweep it under the rug, of the affecting and influential force of the individual experience of religion.

The Power and Influence of Individual Experience

Exposure to religious symbols and religious community, begins in the very early months and years of life. Even the experiences of how a child is handled, greeted, dressed, taught, and developed in relation to a sacred community should, in and of themselves, be inspiration enough for us to undertake careful examination of the lasting developmental effect of religious life. These experiences always remain a part of the individual, regardless of whether he or she still participates in that tradition or believes in its creeds.

Kate Young Caley, in her memoir *The House Where the Hardest Things Happened*, describes a scene from her childhood when she attended the First Church of God in Moultonborough, New Hampshire. She recalls one day when the pastor, Brother Munroe, was preaching with tears in his eyes a message about the importance of the Bible, and how important it ought to be for every Christian:

> Then he is shouting to us, "And if you don't feel this way, then you might as well throw the whole thing out the window right now!" And as he says the words he flings his Bible out into the congregation toward the window where Althea Buckley always sits.
>
> Maybe it is only my imagination, but the Bible seems within inches of hitting me in the face as it flies by. I wait for the smashing of glass at the window, but there is none. Brother Munroe had tied a rope around his Bible, and just as it is about to smash windowpanes he jerks the rope and whips the Bible back to him like a cowboy in a movie.
>
> Thirty-five years later, that sermon illustration is still working its message in me. Part of the message I keep with me is that things can happen in a church you'll never be able to forget.[1]

How is it that this experience has stayed with Caley through all those years? Her memoir lets the reader know that it is memories like these that motivate her to discover a new and different connection to religious life.

Getting beyond an outsized childhood experience with religion may be possible, but to discover a new way of connecting to it as an adult can often be fraught with difficulty. Facing one's symbols of ultimacy means dealing with far-reaching and potent matters. Bestselling author Kathleen Norris describes how she came from a "thoroughly Protestant" background, but during her young adult years fell away and became disillusioned. Nearing middle age, she made attempts to return, but reconciling herself with the symbols, people, and practices of her religion was not easy:

> When I first began going to church, I was enormously self-conscious and for a long time couldn't escape the feeling that I didn't belong there. . . . My attempts to worship with others on Sunday mornings would trigger a depression lasting for days. . . . Gradually, over several years of fits and starts, I was finally able to feel that I was part of a worshiping congregation. But I still had a tenuous hold on belief, and any number of powerful words I might encounter during church—commandments, creeds, resurrection—could send me reeling.[2]

As we hear in Norris's narrative, a falling away from a religious community involves forces that go well beyond any sort of rebellious wanderlust or young adult experimentation. Something in her religious life apparently went so wrong, was so unfortunately mishandled and misguided, that she had great emotional difficulty, marked by a visceral, physiological power, which made it nearly impossible to set foot in a church at all. Again, one might suggest that such a physical reaction to reapproaching one's religious tradition may be a normal response in the life cycle of faith, but to do so would be to underestimate the power of memory or the experience of personal and collective history.

Karen Armstrong, who has authored books on religion for general audiences, says her memoir *The Spiral Staircase* was written as an attempt to accept that she could not, no matter how hard she tried, ignore that she had spent several formative years, beginning at age seventeen, in a convent preparing for life as a nun. This book was not her first attempt at spiritual memoir; in fact, it was her third. Her first, *Through the Narrow Gate*, offered insight into the challenges of her life as a young novice.[3] Her second, *Beginning the World*, was meant to show unequivocally how she had left the convent both physically and spiritually, had completely severed her connection with the rigid and stultifying experiences there, become a new person, and embraced life in the freedom of the 1960s and early 1970s.[4] Armstrong tells us that *The Spiral Staircase* was written to correct the hasty conclusions of earlier writing, as she had come to realize that she could no longer extricate herself completely from nor deny the intense experiences of the convent:

> I have never managed to fully integrate with "the world," although I have certainly tried to do so. Despite my best endeavors, I have in several important ways remained an outsider. I was much closer to the truth at the end of *Through the Narrow Gate*, when I predicted that in some sense I would be a nun all my life.[5]

> [B]eing a nun at that time was not like training to be a teacher or a broadcaster or a doctor, where you learn a skill but your deepest self remains—and personal life remains intact and unaffected. This training was meant to be a conditioning, a conditioning that was designed to last a lifetime, and it did. And when I left the convent, I did not know how to live without these structures. I felt the whole tenor of my life had changed, and yet I was still the same. I was still basically a nun, but in secular clothes, and I needed to train myself to become a secular as rigorously as I had trained myself to become a nun.[6]

In *The Spiral Staircase*, Armstrong seems to be doing important psychological work. With a tragic but hopeful tone, she lays claim to a past that possesses her. By doing so she seems to come closer to something true and genuine about herself that allows her to both incorporate the past and meaningfully pursue the future, regardless of whether she had shed her religious clothing and could call herself a "secular."

While Caley, Norris, and Armstrong have their struggles, for others, the damage of a religious background is so profound, so insipid and abusive, one must wonder that the *only* appropriate response is complete and permanent rejection. In her memoir of growing up in a fundamentalist and racist community, Julia Sheeres describes the emotional austerity of her parents, especially her father, who was prone to fits of rage and violence, often directed at her African American brothers, two boys adopted by the family in the name of Christian duty. Sheeres, along with one of her brothers, was sent by these parents to a Christian reform school in the Dominican Republic, where she was subjected to still more verbal and emotional abuse. Her memoir is rife with bitterness and indignation, yet also with a certain strength, direct engagement, and active interest in the troubles that haunt her:

> Having been brainwashed from birth as a Calvinist, it took me years to shake my religion entirely. . . . I lost my religion by degrees. The first step was witnessing the hypocrisy of Christians around me when I was a child. The second was escaping the rigid subculture I grew up in and meeting secular folks who were much more moral and trustworthy than the Christians I was told to revere.[7]

Sheeres had to divorce morality from the religion that she knew, even from the image of the parents who raised her, to rediscover it in the everyday people around her. A story like Sheeres's leaves us with the question of whether the rediscovery of faith and the symbols that represent it occurs outside what is conventionally considered religion.

It would be easy for some, in evaluating stories like these of those who have fallen away from a community of shared faith, to put focus on "sin," that is, individual failures to follow specific religious doctrines and practices. My focus here, however, will be to avoid observations from within a religious framework, and to take a more empirical, pragmatic mindset. What can we see that can be named in the individual experience of the sacred, including all that works in its favor and all that does not?

What must not be overlooked, for example, is not only personal experiences but also the broadest social factors of contemporary living. In other words, religion is not experienced in isolation—in fact, it is far more socially determined than we realize. Gen-X writer Douglas Coupland, in his collection of short stories, *Life After God*, provides a glimmer of the broad scope of society that impacts the individual sense of the sacred. He writes with an allegorical nostalgia about growing up as "children of pioneers" in a world of suburban affluence and apathy, and the milieu of contemptuousness that it breeds, including a cynicism toward all things religious. He relays a sense of faith lost that encapsulates so much of what is working against the strivings for gritty, life-giving coherence, and a religion that holds it all together:

> I think there was a tradeoff somewhere along the line. I think the price we paid for our golden life was an inability to fully believe in love; instead we gained an irony that scorched everything it touched. And I wondered if this irony is the price we paid for the loss of God.
>
> But then I must remind myself we are living creatures—we have religious impulses—we *must*—and yet into what cracks do these impulses flow in a world without religion? It is something I think about every day. Sometimes it is the only thing I should be thinking about.[8]

As we see in these snippets, religion motivates powerfully. Religious tradition connects individuals to a cause so great that it has to do with the very creation, control, definition, and destiny of their lives. No amount of scientific discovery, commercial success, or satisfaction of physical desires can equal the psychological and social dynamism of religious symbolism. Nothing better inspires or destroys the individual's basic faith and trust in the world, and their connection to community, than the way we use symbols to express ourselves.

So when something goes awry in the life of faith, it is no wonder that it can easily turn into something of great personal cost. When we fail to discover hope despite each new challenge, and when those around us fail to nurture and encourage our relationship to ultimate symbols and community, we fall deeply into despair. Unfortunately, such despair is often kept secret, or it is difficult to find words to describe it. When things are not working out the way they are supposed to, no one wants to talk about it. When doubts, misgivings, or even simple questions arise, there is a natural tendency to dodge them. Instead of dealing with these feelings, one invests energy in distraction, turns inward, or alternatively adopts a belligerent stance. All those things may be necessary, but eventually the motivating unmet needs cannot be avoided altogether, not brought to light. Even in academic research, it can be said that the role of doubt is seldom given its due. Yet it may be that only through understanding this doubt and despair that we will document the spark of religious imagination, the process of spiritual creativity, and the signs of new growth.

Problem and Thesis

The argument I will make works with the assumption that Christianity in the United States today is in a time of change, and that it is always changing just as social constructions of life are always changing. Within that change it is reasonable to assume that some individuals become lost and even suffer at the hands of traditions or situations that adapt poorly to change. Yet, after losing their way and leaving organized religion, certain individuals find their way back, or forward. While a thorough review of the sociological data regarding church attendance trends and patterns is beyond the scope of this book, it is safe to surmise, from the narratives sampled above, that the personal journey of faith in our time—that is, the individual's experiences with religion in the US—can be fraught with struggle, some of which seems to go so far as to cause psychological damage. If we hold the above assumption to be true, at least in degrees, the fundamental question is this: how are individuals able to respond to the challenges of our time and rediscover and reclaim a powerful, life-shaping connection to sacred objects and symbols?

Most research that analyzes the spiritual journey today seems either unwilling or ill-equipped to recognize the suffering associated with religious identity loss and spiritual amorphousness. We find that the struggles of those who have abandoned their religious identity, and yet have made gains in discovering a new one, are analyzed through two basic lenses. On the one hand, developmental, cognitive psychological theory—probably the easiest way to understand it—tells us that people are working their way through known stages of personal development, or in other words, are merely making a journey of faith that has been true for all time and in all places. Each person strives toward a point where cumulative life experience and emotional growth can enable progression toward a more universalized and deepened religious understanding. On the other hand, sociological studies tell us that individuals falling away from religion join the many for whom the religious identity handed them has lost its relevance in today's mobile world, especially among the highly educated, and they return to church because marriage, children, and greater social participation enter the picture. While both approaches bring important insights, they are incomplete evaluations of the fluctuations in faith, neglect the component of the inner emotional life, and especially overlook the effect of religious trauma.

What is often missing is an in-depth understanding of how internal life impacts the coming into relation with social constructions of trust and faith. Why, for example, do people become angry with God or religious leaders, or conversely, why does it drive them to depression? Why are these struggles so difficult and why do they take so long? What can we learn from those who have overcome the feelings they associate with their past religious experience? Do people follow a neat pattern of faith development, or do they grow and mature in some ways while remaining immature in others? What role does trauma play, either on the familial level, or as well on the broadest possible social level? Although there have been a number of church-focused investigations to explain why people leave faith, few go further than applying some combination of the sociological or cognitive-developmental approaches.[9] It can even seem like they are purposely avoiding something.

To grapple with these enduring questions, we must delve into the hidden aspects of individual narrative and explore an interpretive theory that makes it possible to reveal that narrative. Without such an approach, we are at a loss to recommend action that can encourage understanding, healing, and growth.

I propose that to complete the picture of analyzing the individual experience of religion in our time—characterized by dislocation, separation, and trauma—we need to draw insights from psychoanalytic process and theory. I argue that by turning to psychoanalytic psychology as both a theoretical and research tool we can better understand the process of leaving and then returning to a participatory faith. In particular, the application of what we know about the role of religion in psychic life, knowledge taken from the psychoanalytic concepts of mourning, object relations, and creativity, will help shed new light on personal crises of faith. I will offer observations on those who have "fallen away" from their religious tradition, experienced a time of fallowness, and yet made certain gains in overcoming the past and creating the possibility for a future in community. I will demonstrate that the return journey to a community of shared faith is not limited solely to a denouement of youthful wanderlust or stage growth, but also involves a lifelong psychological process of finding freedom from disillusionment and the freedom for discovery.

In Part I, chapter one will begin by surveying the sociological research surrounding the topic of the faith journey in contemporary society. Social analysis has been the primary lens through which academicians have analyzed changes in faith participation over time. Surveying the basic findings in this area will accomplish the twofold purpose of drawing the social context of the individual response to religion in our time and suggesting avenues for new research, namely, a stronger focus on psychological experience. Chapter two will take a somewhat intermediary step toward the individual by summarizing studies that draw on a sociological, psychological, *and* historical approach to the experience of the sacred in our time. It is here that the assertion of the role of dislocation and loss finds its strongest expression. I will show that the loss in any one individual is connected to factors that reach far beyond a snapshot of localized experience and, moreover, demonstrate that overcoming a loss of faith means overcoming these larger factors.

Having drawn the broader context of the challenges to the life of faith in our time, chapter three will offer an analysis of faith stage theory in the widely used work of James Fowler. Like social analysis, cognitive developmental faith-stage theory is another common response when questions of transitions of faith arise. While Fowler's research adeptly describes the structural progression of religion, and helps us understand that, regardless of social contexts, individuals as they mature psychologically will inevitably have different needs and outlooks, I will show that this research has little to offer in terms of understanding the pathology that arises as a response to existential loss and widespread trauma. What is needed, instead, is a language that can help us approximate how individuals experience and then respond to both their personal history as well as the broader changes in society and culture.

To begin that discussion, however, we must first lay out the fundamental interpretive theory of the life of human faith that can show how religion is linked to psychology, a theory that can also accommodate psychological pathology. Consequently, chapter four will summarize the essential psychoanalytic stance on the individual, religion, and society. I will briefly survey two seminal figures in this approach to demonstrate that religion creates symbols that are linked to our deepest, most powerful desires, hopes, and dreams, and that the community in which such symbols are employed plays a vital and indispensable part in actualizing individual faith.

With the psychoanalytic approach to religion established, chapter five will then drill deeper into the psychoanalytic theory that articulates the language of mourning. I will sketch a theoretical position that begins with Sigmund Freud's stance on mourning, contrast that with the work of Melanie Klein, then turn to D.W. Winnicott to show the linkage between the work of mourning, the use of play and creativity, and how these relate to the life of faith and religion. This

core theoretical approach, one that works as a response to the observations of previous chapters, will equip us with a set of hypotheses
with which to analyze spiritual disillusionment and the rediscovery
of hope.

In Part II, the ensuing chapters comprise case analyses of biographical data. Here I will provide in-depth reviews of five religious
memoirs. I will put these memoirs "on the couch," and offer analyses
that illuminate both the contours of disillusionment as well as the
path of returning, that is, stories of individuals who were once active
church members, experienced a time of withdrawal and fallowness,
and then once again felt certain freedoms to become involved in a
faith community. The methodology I will employ will be the psycho-
analytical literary study that delves into personal religious history. By
looking at how people narrate their lives, their context, and their spirituality and religion, we can discern heretofore undiscovered psychological patterns in the return journey to sacred community. I will
assume, as much as possible, the posture of the psychoanalyst, only
in this case I will be working solely with written text, and employing
psychohistory, much in the way Erik Erikson does in his studies of
Martin Luther and Mohandas K. Gandhi.[10] Taking this approach will
connect us with the unconscious, unspoken dimension of religious
experience. As a subject for academic and scholarly inquiry into the
religious life, unconscious territory is not an easily articulated topic.
Inquiries of this nature require much more than a fleeting nod to
personal history. They must consider a variety of trajectories including early family relationships, social milieu, economics, history, and
the way the individual unconsciously processes all these trajectories.
The language of psychoanalytic psychology can be of practical value
in that it uses personal narrative as data. Psychoanalysis explores
overall tone, manifest content, and inconsistencies, and creates a way
for us to listen to the hidden themes that reveal the road to healing.
Memoirs such as these also provide rich self-descriptions that span
the entire life of the individual. Above all, what we also find in memoir are doubts and misgivings that are not so forthcoming in the social scientific interview. Much like the therapist's office, what is

12

revealed is the story people want to tell, and do not mind telling when the fear of rejection or misunderstanding is relaxed. More than that, I will look between the lines of the text to see what interpretations and conclusions can be drawn from each memoirist's journey, showing what they have in common despite being different people. The approach here will not pinpoint a particular faith stage, but rather draw the overall picture of what the ongoing struggles and successes are and how they compare to the others. Moreover, I will not simply explore past relationships with parents or a particular religious community. Instead, a wider lens will be at work, one that considers the cultural-historical challenges outlined in chapter two. How these challenges have been met, in conjunction with the way each individual author has been able to attend a group assembled around ultimate symbols, will be a crucial part of understanding the dynamics at work in rebuilding faith.

After discussing these five individuals, the concluding chapter offers the overall analysis that can be drawn from the biographical content. I will summarize key findings and how they relate to psychoanalytic mourning and object relations theory, outlining both the difficulties as well as the ideal tasks that individuals encounter on the return or forward trip to sacred community. I will also include any new conclusions we may draw regarding that theory when applied to the life of faith.

Defining Faith, Religion, and the Absolutist Mindset

There are many words in the discussion of religion that may seem vague or interchangeable. It is therefore helpful to set forth a few loosely held definitions, especially because I will use variations of these words simply to avoid repetition, but also to allow the words at least some flexibility. First and foremost, I wish to be clear that the word *faith* as it will be used in this discussion means something universal and rudimentary to individual experience, and not a specific religious tradition or even a separate dimension of life. In the same manner one might refer generically to the words *trust*, *hope*, and *to have faith*, faith in the context of the psychology of religion refers to something that could simply be described as the basic desire for living. As Erikson points out in his stages of the life cycle, basic trust and its partner, hope, form at the earliest stage of life and comprise one of the infant's first tasks.[11] What is experienced as faith at this stage is the grand originator of and participant in the symbols and images that reflect, capitulate, and provide the means through which humans articulate their deepest desires and strongest attachments across the entire life cycle. Such symbolic life is, namely, our religion, and it is not ever discrete. Instead, religious expression, and the faith that animates it, is the ultimate and most transcendent symbolism in life, a culmination and recapitulation.

Furthermore, faith is a basic human response, as well as something that is shared and negotiated with others through tradition. In the act of sharing, symbolic life takes on multiple meanings and holds some of the broadest possible powers over the articulation of experience. For the purposes of this discussion, religion will represent symbolic life—objects, rituals, practices, beliefs, and creeds—of a group tradition that is a connective communication between the basic faith of its members. Moreover, and in keeping with Erikson, faith is directly involved in matters of identity. Basic trust, as opposed to mistrust, is a response garnered by how well an infant recognizes itself while at the same time being recognized by the mother. Erikson generally uses this language in connection with matters of identity during adolescence, but the principle of the concept, which echoes other theorists' concepts, one example being Winnicott's "mirroring" mother, has its roots in early life. We may think of faith, then, as the force and drive of religion, whereas religion may be considered as the content of faith.

James Fowler, in the preliminary chapters of *Stages of Faith*, adeptly summarizes these very points. He draws on the following: Paul Tillich's *Dynamics of Faith*, which considers faith as ultimate concern, and religion as the objects of ultimate concern; H. Richard Niebuhr, who sees faith as a search for shared visions and centers of value and power; and especially Wilfred Cantwell Smith's *The Meaning and End of Religion*, which labels religion as the "cumulative tradition" that expresses the faith of people in the past.[12] From one of Fowler's later books, we find this nuanced definition of faith:

> Faith . . . may be characterized as an integral, centering process, underlying the formation of beliefs, values, and meanings that (1) gives coherence and direction to persons' lives, (2) links them in shared trusts and loyalties with others, (3) grounds their personal stances and communal loyalties in a sense of relatedness to a larger frame of reference, and (4) enables them to face and deal with the limited conditions of human life, relying upon that which has the quality of ultimacy in their lives.[13]

All of the above further illustrates the definition of faith and religion that will be employed in the present discussion. Moreover, such a definition points to one of the key assumptions of this study, namely, that faith is communal or participatory. This aspect of the definition becomes important when we survey popular understandings in contemporary culture that faith can be mutually exclusive of community. Furthermore, just as it is impossible to separate one from the other, no rediscovery of religion is possible or complete without a social or institutional component.

Closely connected to the words *faith* and *religion*, one that finds frequent use in common parlance is the word *spirituality*. Today, spirituality often refers to something completely independent of a social component that is practiced on one's own and develops fully on the individual level.[14] While no doubt using the word *spirituality* in this manner has value for those who must create physical and psychological space between themselves and established traditions, the psychological definition of faith and religion leaves little room for a radically self-contained individual religion, free of any shared symbols whatsoever. Therefore, when I refer to spirituality in the pages that follow, I will do so without such a connotation. Rather, spirituality will refer more closely to the concrete individual practices of religion, whether that be prayer, reading sacred text, or attending the gatherings of a religious community. It remains something of a synonym for religion and points away from religion's more institutional and organizational characteristics.

I will also often use the word "imagoes" or "sacred imagoes" to indicate an individual or society's entire amalgamation and pinnacle of what is imbued with deep and multifaceted meaning. The word imago is Latin for image, and it has been used in entomology to indicate an adult stage of an insect. Interestingly, the language of psychoanalysis has also incorporated this word to mean an unconscious idealized image, perhaps especially a parent. So the phrase sacred imagoes offers a certain richness in a conversation about psychology and religion.

Having defined faith, religion, and spirituality, it is important now to offer clarification of a few words that are unavoidable when studying individuals in the United States who have left a religious group, distanced themselves, and then returned. While the psychological processes at work likely apply to most religious experience in the United States if not the entire Western postindustrial world, the memoirs that I survey remain closely connected with American Protestant evangelical or fundamentalist tradition. Staying within this area is important because I hope to demonstrate that it is such traditions in our society that bear some of the most clear and extreme evidence for the psychological dynamics at play. The more rigid and legalistic forms of Protestantism—ones that purport a literal and "inerrant" interpretation of religious texts, and that create communities of exclusionary rhetoric and emphasize a "decision for Christ," often through crisis conversions—will be the focus here. Correctly or incorrectly, these areas of religious life in our society are often described alternately and interchangeably as fundamentalist and evangelical. Both terms include different connotations, have different origins, and even point to different and changing sets of cultural groups both in the United States and abroad. In truth, adequately defining these terms is beyond the purpose of this book. Consequently, I will try to use them sparsely because they lack precision in a discussion about the psychology of religion. Instead, I will employ the words *totalism* and especially *absolutism* to describe a general mindset that is at work in these forms of Protestantism.

Erik Erikson is credited with introducing the word *totalism* to describe "a fanatic and exclusive preoccupation with what seems unquestionably ideal within a tight system of ideas."[15] Robert Lifton expanded the definition, describing the "totalistic environment" as based on an absolute philosophical assumption, exclusivity of truth, manipulating communication, loading language to eliminate ambiguity, imposing a culture of confession, and mobilizing guilt through an imperative to remove internal taints.[16] Where Erikson and Lifton's descriptions of totalism have a stronger external focus on the politics of autocracy, Karl Figlio's use of the related word *absolutism* brings a more object relations driven description. Figlio defines "the absolute state of mind" as a core disposition in society and the individual that involves "a state of idealization of the self, merged with an idealized object as an ego-ideal, withdrawn from external reality. . . ." Absolutists dissolve into each other and their idealized leader. They separate their group from other groups, are easily subject to fragmentation and sectarian splitting in a never-ending quest for purity, and are stalked by a sense of cosmic failure. Self-denigration and a compulsion for unattainable completion drives the absolutist. "The ego, relentlessly and compulsively seeking to identify with the ego-ideal, drives itself out of the bonds of relating to the external world."[17]

Erikson, Lifton, and Figlio all share similar observations that the totalist or absolutist state of mind is at work in our world today, that it is widespread and an indicator of the psychological challenges of our time. Psychologically speaking, we may for example find very little difference between a fundamentalist and an atheist. Despite their seemingly stark external differences, both seek a well-defined, absolute worldview, are driven by demonizing each other, and are struggling equally with uncertainty. While a genuine comparison and contrast of fundamentalists and atheists could be a topic for another book all its own, we can be satisfied with the general idea that both types of individuals are responding to whatever crisis of meaning their world presents them. How they respond to that crisis, one that I argue is defined by loss, is the underlying concern in identifying the dynamics of returning to a community of faith.

PART I
THEORETICAL OVERVIEW

1

The Sociology of
Religious Participation

Stages of Social Involvement

THE COMMON ANALYSIS of religious disillusionment by survey-driven sociological research is to place these individuals within the span of the life cycle and to identify the different types of social involvement that correspond to each stage of life. To varying degrees, the individual is raised in a family tradition, experiences a time of questioning, rootlessness, and experimentation during young adult hood, then settles back into a tradition around the time of becoming married, having children, and entering middle age. Social research has identified some of the external factors present when people return to a participatory faith. Social connection, the feeling of belonging to a group, and the status of being a member in a particular congregation become important factors, as does the desire to discover a stronger, more anchoring worldview than what is offered in everyday life at work or home.[1] Above all, the most concrete motivator observed by sociological research comes from the desire to have one's children receive religious and moral education.[2]

Looking at faith sociologically helps us lump a great majority of those who have fallen away from faith into specific categories. For example, most of them are likely to be young, male, and unmarried.[3] Others are likely to be well educated, having been exposed to different worldviews through an advanced education that often pits their religious upbringing against other traditions, the scrutiny of science, or a deeper engagement with literature and philosophy. No matter what precipitates the challenge to one's religion, apostasy and reconversion are often considered solely a matter of life cycle maturation.

To assign the process of falling away and then returning to religion as simply a youthful stage progression, however, would be premature even from a sociological point of view. While the social involvements at different life cycle stages may change, they do not take place in a vacuum. In terms of life history, there are instances when the loss of faith, and a time of withdrawal from spirituality or religious community, can occur regardless of life stage. A life crisis such as the death of a family member, divorce, or relocating from one community to another can contribute to a time of questioning and withdrawal and can occur at any point in one's life. More to the point, loss of faith can be a lifelong struggle that comes because of broad social factors. A solely life cycle, stage-specific approach is the oversimplification that this discussion sets itself against. It is too convenient an interpretation, too incomplete. That is, an individual's spiritual journey must not be evaluated strictly in terms of whether and how he or she has progressed through requisite life stages, as though the maturation process can in most people proceed without much difficulty. The social environment, personal history, and the surrounding culture are factors that must all be taken into consideration. Historically speaking, each new generation faces its own set of crises, and to do so each must reevaluate and reimagine new cultural symbols. This reimagining process can mean experiencing a traumatic encounter with previous meaning structures, or as Paul Tillich would say, each generation must deal with the "broken myth" of their time and remove it or find its replacement.[4] In terms of the sociological view, a life cycle approach is incomplete without a deep understanding of larger social trends and everyday realities that bear down on the individual, about which there is much to say.

The Larger Social Context

Going beyond stages of social involvement, an exploration of patterns of religion in the United States and of the observations of sociologists studying them yields insights vital to any psychological investigation of religious experience, even to the central theme of mourning. As mentioned, the internal life of the individual does not take place in a vacuum but rather participates in various other trajectories and movements. Struggles with matters of faith and religion are not the same for someone living today as for someone living in another time, or in another part of the world. The United States, in particular, is a country where religious participation is a significant component of everyday life. Most studies agree that a majority of Americans go to church.[5] In terms of reporting individual practices of faith, every so often a major news poll reports that a majority of Americans hold a belief about God, heaven, and prayer.

Yet even while religious participation remains significant, it often tends to be an extension of individuality, motivated largely by social status and lifestyle preferences. David Bromley contends that religious affiliations are defined almost exclusively as individual commitments, and this reflects the diminished role of religion in maintaining cultural integration, and by extension, the decline of homogeneous ethnic communities.[6] The increased rates of geographic and occupational mobility, the erosion of the role of the extended family, and the subsequent loss of local community mirror a restructuring of the place of religion in the social order. This loss of cohesion is a theme that runs throughout much of the sociological literature on contemporary changes in American religion.[7] The decision to attend one church over another, for example, can bear little relation to the local community, religious background, and family. This decision has become a matter of asking which type of belief system makes the most sense, what style of worship feels right, and what type of people are most alike. It represents a change from handed-down religion, where the value of the past and the authority of tradition have been replaced by a practical orientation of what fits the new self-created life.

Two widely read sociological studies of religion in the United States today that help us frame the current discussion, and tell us something about the social patterns and characteristics of religious experience that impact individual experience, are Wade Clark Roof's *A Generation of Seekers: The Spiritual Journey of the Baby Boom Generation* and Robert Wuthnow's *After Heaven: Spirituality in America Since the 1950s*.[8] A brief look into these works will provide interpretive guides to the unique challenges of faith transitions as well as identify the point where sociological analysis ends and psychological analysis begins.

Roof's landmark work describes how so much of religious life today is driven by the interests of the baby-boomer generation—that massive segment of the population that is accustomed to having the world respond to them as a group, and who construct a reality based on their needs, interests, and position in life. They are or at least were the leading cohort, and much of their spirituality defines all our spirituality. This study will not investigate the spirituality of boomers per se, but the questions, biographical data, and analysis that I am raising cannot help but be influenced by the challenges played out in much of boomer culture.

Roof's principal aim is to demonstrate the unique spiritual and religious trajectories of those born from 1946 to 1964. This is a group that came of age during a time of great optimism, when choices and opportunities seemed to far outstretch that of their parents. Yet, particularly during the social strife of the 1960s, this group experienced disillusionment and unrest. Many felt the need and the freedom to rebel against authority and define themselves differently than the generation before. Roof points out sociologist Karl Mannheim's observation that during times of social upheaval, one generation becomes more sharply set off from the other. It develops its own "historical-social consciousness," a philosophical outlook on life that congeals when its members are entering and progressing through young adulthood, a time so formative that the outlook tends to stay with them. Those who experienced the 1960s, for example, always carry the memories they formed in that time into the present. This carryover, Roof argues, has had a deep impact on religion and spirituality particularly as boomers enter middle and old age.[9]

Organized religion became one of the many institutions with which boomers became disillusioned. Religion came to be seen more as a private affair, a matter of personal choice. The last thing today's boomers want, Roof observes, is to let their spirituality be defined by something external to them. The changing social realities, coupled with the freedom and growing affluence of the time, encouraged an experimental spirit. Consequently, the type of community boomers seek is often anything but a large, centralized religious institution, which doesn't really exist in the United States anyway. They become involved in recovery groups, feminist or men's groups, yoga classes, or other special purpose organizations. In these groups, they find a place to share their stories about their internal journeys, to connect with others individually without pressure to conform to a collective, established whole. The key is that their own voice matters, is not judged, and is given the opportunity for expression. They are in the groups for a sense of bonding, for girding up their individual, exclusive identities, and receiving personal support. One might even argue that this individualism is an endemic marker of religion in America.

Boomers are not joining groups that are more inclusive to achieve a "bridging" that ties large and diverse numbers of people together in a concerted effort of collecting and utilizing combined resources.[10] Instead, they engage in social interaction as a practical and even necessary funneling of the individual search for meaning alongside the searches of others, regardless of how discontinuous. One detects within it, as I believe Roof has observed, a note of naiveté, a trade-off with organizational rigor and the absence of the force or power that comes from a more unified, outward directed approach. We must wonder whether there will come a point where this naiveté will have to reckon with certain psychological and social needs. Their eschewing of strong organizational connections, Roof notes almost in passing, leaves boomers vulnerable to a nostalgic interest in religion, stuck in a pattern of hopeful expectation for a sense of spiritual community, yet not achieving it.[11] As these themes are explored, we may indeed find that nostalgia, or idealization, is a characteristic that defines a key dynamic in rebuilding faith expressed in a communal setting.

In the concluding pages of Roof's book, he asks the question of what to do with this inward directed self, often coined as the narcissistic self, most notably by cultural theorist Christopher Lasch in his book *The Culture of Narcissism*.[12] What are the unique ways this brand of self experiences religion? How will that impact religion in America today? Roof points briefly toward psychiatrist and psychoanalyst Heinz Kohut, whose theory on narcissism and its transformations may offer some answers—though does not explain what they may be. He also mentions pastoral theologian Donald Capps, whose work on redefining sin in a narcissistic age also offers some illuminating insight.[13] Both of these directions will be explored later in more detail, where we may find some initial clues on how the individual experiences a return to faith.

For the time being, we can turn to the work of Robert Wuthnow, who builds on Roof's observations and offers a few more ideas on how people are reworking their experiences of religion. In *After Heaven*, Wuthnow explores how developments in public religion are being accompanied by equally profound developments in individual spirituality, that is, the way people bring coherence to their lives. Wuthnow outlines a progression of categories of religious experience that can be generally observed in America. First, so much of our religious past may be described as a religion of "dwelling," characterized by fitting in, being at home in a well-defined group, knowing and playing one's role responsibly. Religion is a given part of life, like an ethnicity. It is not something to be questioned or changed. Identity is less reliant on questions of which faith to choose, but rather how well you practice the one you were born into and make it a part of your everyday life.

Yet the ongoing challenge to a dwelling spirituality has always been found in the individualism that characterizes the American way of life. While one might make the argument that individualism is a clear by-product of a capitalist democracy, Wuthnow, as a sociologist, likewise points to individualism's extreme expression made manifest in the 1960s, when widespread rebellion raised questions about the primacy of a dwelling way of life. The large mass of baby boomers had their faith in handed-down institutions shaken by the realities of the Vietnam War and the Civil Rights Movement. The rise of therapeutic psychologies and the discovery of Eastern religions, moreover, presented the opportunity to explore one's past, to create a sacred symbol of the self. Moreover, in a digital society where economic and social mobility are so fluid, where communication and commerce are so accelerated, it becomes more challenging to settle into a predetermined set of social structures or to find meaning in given cultural expressions.

These developments led to a predominant mode of spirituality now widely known as "seeking." When objective truth comes into question, when the cultural and social institutions that represent this truth fail the individual, and moreover, when the individual finds it difficult to form deep allegiances in a world of constant change, it is no wonder that there is a turning inward for symbols of meaning to guide one's life. It is the inner life that becomes the constant, the authority, and outer experience simply informs and feeds that individual reality. Seeking in religion means shopping around for different religious identities, trying them on for size, retaining what works, and then moving on to look for other symbols to use in a personal syncretism. Moreover, seeking means being on a journey for the sake of journeying. All that exists is the self as a sacred symbol, and the seeker is not so much interested in holding fast to a particular set of beliefs and way of life as he or she is on a quest for experiencing, perceiving, and consuming that builds up and honors the sacred self.

Wuthnow argues that the self that corresponds to this new form of spirituality since the 1950s may be described as the "dispersed self." With the scattered lives that we lead and the way our roles and relationships are in a constant state of change, our self is constituted by "a wide variety of encounters and experiences . . . separated in space and time, with different people, and of varying significance. Although the self is always more than these experiences, it must be understood to reside in them as well and thus to be as scattered as they are."[14]

To underscore his contention about this new self that has emerged, Wuthnow writes: "The dispersed self goes beyond the idea of malleability, which implies a unity of being that is simply able to adapt to new experiences."[15] Instead, the dispersed self is easily separated from its past and from the other roles that define it. It is a self, as I will argue, unaware of the loss it has experienced. A type of mania takes over, and the individual consumes all that is offered by the present moment, taking it seriously, letting it wipe out other experiences, and using it as a defining moment of the self's new makeup. Yet as experiences are collected, and as the self moves from one to the next, pieces are ignored or denied. This process of personal discontinuity is borne out by Wuthnow's interviewees who report experiencing moments of sadness. Here Wuthnow creates an important jumping off point for this study: "We recognize that we are not the same person we were a few years ago, and we lament the loss of part of our self when a loved one dies."[16] Could it be, for example, that mourning is the primary defining characteristic of the self today, and subsequently the key factor of successful religiosity?

Although a dispersed self seeking out new and varied spiritual experiences and belief systems has advantages for coping with a complex and changing world, the major drawback is the loss of stable identity, the susceptibility to live only in the status quo, or conversely the movement toward nihilism. Instead of succumbing to these currents, Wuthnow observed in some of the people he studied that there was a longing for something deeper and more sustained, something that would help them cope and be more engaged in their everyday lives. These individuals discovered what Wuthnow calls a spirituality of "practice." Prayer, meditation, and deep internal reflection are the methods of a practice spirituality, where the goal is to see things more objectively, to gain a grounding perspective on the shifting nature of personal biography. Regardless of whatever religious groups the individual may belong to, there is a discovery of a rich inner life and a sustained practice of self-interpretation about the meaning of personal experiences and history. The seeker, by contrast, would not so readily accept the rigor and devotion required by practice spirituality, and instead would move on to the next greatest thing. And those from a dwelling spirituality, who hold a sense of legitimacy, do not need to work so hard at introspection as modern seekers whose identity is in constant change. Practice spirituality also contains more of a moral dimension, including intense scrutiny of personal habits, an element of service, helping the poor, and putting the individual's spirituality into action. Such a moral emphasis is perhaps one way to create tangible personal artifacts that are every bit as legitimate as any other experience of religion.[17]

Wuthnow also discovers in "practicers" the need to recognize the loss of their past lives as part of the process of self-interpretation. Instead of negating their past and holding up a new identity as is common in a Protestant fundamentalism, grieving past identities becomes a skill that enables a feeling of continuity and, I would add, a feeling of location, albeit within the story of one's history.[18] A practice-oriented spirituality is also more accommodating to and reliant upon tradition, particularly contemplative traditions. Activities include participation in religious retreats, seeking out spiritual mentors, and joining Bible studies and other groups that encourage reflection on personal spiritual matters. The goal is to increase the depth and discipline of their spiritual practice, with less emphasis on moving between different types of experience or a stable social location. Such commitment and discipline create a challenge to modify one's outlook, live more deliberately, and thus eschew certain unintentional ways of living or relationships. However, as one would expect, the experience of a community of shared faith remains somewhat elusive. Oftentimes the subjects of Wuthnow's study report that they perceive their life of faith as totally on its own trajectory, independent and mutually exclusive of any participation in large groups.

The challenge that I would direct at Wuthnow's various modes of spirituality is that they are really not so different from each other. From dwelling to seeking to practicing, each contains a part of the other and each is a necessary component of the life of faith. To separate them or to put them in a progressive schema can eventually seem artificial. No doubt the prevailing modality has become that of the practicer, one that is an important survival mechanism in the face of modernity. And it is without question that achieving a feeling of belonging and a stable identity, however elusive, is perhaps the greatest goal of this modality. However, practice spirituality is as much a progression as it is an isolation of one aspect of religiosity. Even though it is adaptive and perhaps creates valuable localized cultures, practice spirituality will, as an end in itself and isolated from larger communities of accountability, produce certain pathologies and ultimately fail a healthy psychological trajectory. In other words, practice spirituality will prevent the individual from the necessary participation in creating symbols in large, institutional settings. The dwelling component, for example, is not just a modality that has been replaced but one that is in relationship to both seeking and practicing modalities.

In addition, Wuthnow's observation of these practicers reveals a self-assertion that they have discovered their spirituality on their own, even in spite of organized religion. In fact, it seems to Wuthnow that their discovery would not have been possible unless embarked upon outside of their church.[19] Yet a certain pride can be detected in their accounts, perhaps even in Wuthnow's description of them, which belies a regressive though perhaps necessary protest against organized religion for having anything to do with what is presumed independent development. Said differently, there is a note of self-righteousness to this protest, an angry protectiveness of the sacred self. This desire to seek and develop an inward, authentic, but also unassailable self seems an important step in establishing a sufficient grasp of identity, but it may be ultimately unsatisfying. Indeed, as I will argue later, sometimes a feeling of spiritual discovery is only possible through a complete rejection of and perhaps even an aggression toward the individual's original indoctrination. In the case of Wuthnow's interviewees, we can, however, be suspicious that they received more help from organized religion than they are willing to reveal or are aware of. They have often looked to Christian or

Eastern mystics, for example, and sometimes identified with them, or to careful study of the Bible and books often published by religious publishers and written by individuals who are regular participants in church congregations. Far more importantly, much of their practice of faith exists in its present makeup as a reaction *against* the faith in which they were raised. What we are tasked to discover in their stories, then, is what exactly comes on the other side of that reaction. As I will argue, organized religion is in essence a vital psychological component—though perhaps not in the form in which it was previously conceived—of the goal of identity integration. Wuthnow softens his stance in a later book, *Growing Up Religious*, a book about the effect of early religious life on later life, in which he mentions how it is often within a religious organization that individuals are enabled to develop their practice spirituality and at the same time make gains on their more personalized style of faith.[20]

We must also bear in mind that much of Wuthnow's data is no doubt influenced by the prevailing cultural trends of the baby boomer cohort, and his findings contain a sense of legitimacy by the shear unilateralism of the data. Suffice it to say for now, as Roof notes with his concern about nostalgic vulnerability, that boomers very well may have some unfinished spiritual business to deal with as they age.[21] Indeed, as Wuthnow notes, social theorist Peter Berger would suggest that this seemingly internal self is itself a social construction. A self that is completely contained, without a link to society, is a tautology, unable to experience growth and adaptation.[22] Although a discussion about the ontological primacy of self or society is beyond the scope of this book, it is nevertheless important to discover how this internality links to and develops in the world of relationships, that is, the social playing field.

In sum, what we find in sociological research are the broader trends and forces impacting individual religious experience. We find that there is more to the character of religion than life cycle factors. Broad social movements have caused a turning inward to discover the sacred, a need to connect with others on a one-to-one level, and a general distrust of conventional and centralized conduits for religious practice. It may be argued that this inward turn is a necessity for survival in a socially mobile world where technology and mass commercialization bring about a flattened cultural field. Keeping such forces at bay means fortifying the self with an individualized religion. It may also be argued, though not perhaps concluded fully, that this turning inward has become so sharp and pronounced that our community bonds and symbolic richness are in decline. How the individual experiences religion, and how he or she participates in or joins others in a corporate spiritual expression or quest, will be very much shaped by these social realities and their corresponding personal responses.

2
Deepening the Field of Analysis

IN THE PREVIOUS CHAPTER, both Roof and Wuthnow briefly mention a feeling of loss in the lives of the people they had studied. Roof speaks of the nostalgia that characterizes boomers searching for religious bonds. He does so with a tone of caution that boomers may have to go back to tasks they failed to complete in their rush to spiritual freedom at the cost of deep connection and accountability. Nostalgia denotes a wistful longing for things gone by, no longer within reach. It represents an arrested development wandering in a false hope of resurrecting and recreating an ideal of the past. The lost object as defined in the present is merely a presenting manifestation of what was lost. For example, nostalgia for a cherished song, sung by a certain performer, has more to do with a longing for a former identity rather than the song itself. The attachment to the loss is of primary importance; and if this nostalgia is so strong that it prevents a forward motion into the future, to a new identity, then it belies a holding pattern, a stuck point where one is unable to envision, create, or even receive a new object of ideation. It calls to mind the narcissist who is enamored with an ideal self, trapped in an identification with a lost object, and unable to differentiate between external reality and the self. For boomers, the longing for whatever has been lost remains perpetually unsatisfied, perhaps until they reengage that lost object and tend to what Roof calls their unfinished business.

Like the lost seeker who rebels and lives perpetually within the quest, Wuthnow notes that the ever-changing identities we are required to undergo, inhabiting the modality of the dispersed self, also necessitate a grieving as the self moves from one set of experiences to the next. Yet Wuthnow sees the spiritual individual as not so much twisting in the wind, but rather quite able to trust, through personal discipline and prayer, in an unchanging reality that the self, no matter how many external changes it goes through, can always contact and rediscover. Still, one cannot help but read about Wuthnow's spiritual practicers and wonder how they are able to go it alone without the need to be fully committed in community. Isolation still seems to rule the day, and creative imagining and fresh ideation within a corporate context is still out of reach. Whether one is a seeker, constantly questing for new experiences, or the disciplined practicer, who turns inward for personal resources of understanding and guidance, the means with which to create deep and lasting relationships within community remain hidden.

The issues Roof and Wuthnow touch upon in their work are just the ones that demand further amplification and discussion to understand the reasons behind disillusionment, and subsequently, reenchantment, with religious life today. We can take this characteristic of an inability, or lack of opportunity, to form strong ties within a symbolic community still further. Within the antipathy for so-called traditional church life and the complaints about the hypocritical extremes of religious organizations, we can detect not only an inability to make social connections on a broader scale but also an indifference toward them. Indeed, personal choice and freedom are placed above all else. Yet might there be something more going on in this disdain and disinterest in powerful cultural ties? Could there be causes not so much identified by routine complaints about hypocrisy but instead also by internal symbolic brokenness, connected with external ones, which contribute to an unending spiritual seeking? Is it not unwarranted to point to the malfeasance of institutional religion and fail to see the real need for it, though perhaps defined in a new way?

Within the history of psychoanalytic discourse, there has been a conversation that turns an interpretive lens on struggles of modernity highlighted in the aforementioned sociological studies, and more sharply defines them in the context of internal life. We can find in this conversation what is unseen and barely acknowledged, namely, the loss, numbing, and melancholy that accompanies modernity and compounds the problem of the individual's connection to community. What follows in this chapter are three psychoanalytically informed viewpoints—that of Robert Lifton, Peter Homans, and Donald Capps—that contribute to our language of loss and further point toward the process of overcoming that loss. Each thinker's work developed independently of the other, but their similar observations add color and depth to what the sociological field has only laid out in the broadest possible strokes.

Lifton: Broken Connections

Robert Jay Lifton, a psychiatrist and historian, identifies what he calls a "broken connection" in the links of humanity's historical and symbolic continuity. Briefly, his main thesis states that the possibility of race-wide self-destruction, now made possible by our mechanistic and technological societies, creates a massive impairment in conceiving ultimate images of ongoing life. We find ourselves unable to discover what Lifton calls "symbolic immortality," the process of creating symbols that place each of us in an ongoing narrative that began long ago and will continue indefinitely, a process that I would argue cannot be understated.

Lifton particularly emphasizes the psychological effects of the use of the nuclear bomb. Although some of Lifton's observations about the relevance of the bomb must be augmented by the fact that the Cold War ended, his argument that individuals feel disconnected with a sense of continuity because of destructive threats rings true today as well. The nuclear threat still lurks; we've witnessed an unprecedented pandemic; we live in an age of terrorism and dangerous populism; and perhaps even more importantly, there are escalating concerns about environmental sustainability. Feelings of fragmentation and dislocation come not merely from a world of great social and economic mobility, but also through a breakdown in the overall human story brought on by the lethality of our own technological advances and overuse of resources. Fear of seeing the end of that story brings on apathy, indifference, a defensive flight into worlds of distraction, and an unending search for freedom from the restrictions—and responsibilities—of a binding cultural identity and moral consensus.

Ours is an age marked by increased disruption, and Lifton helps us understand the psychological dynamic that arises in response to a broken individual identity and shared cultural narrative. Lifton certainly observed this sharp loss of continuity in the extreme circumstance of postwar survivors of the nuclear bombings in Japan. The survivors suffered extraordinary guilt for being alive when so many of their family, friends, and nation had perished. Their unconscious perception of failing the dead led them to wish to be among the dead. Their abject confusion and lack of connection to the world they inherited, so radically altered from the one they knew before, led to a profound numbing and self-alienation. This breakdown of symbolization caused the old ways and traditions not to be a source of vitality but a burden, a reminder of a world they once knew.

The task set before each individual, Lifton argues, is to become a "creative survivor." Such an individual can pick up the pieces and begin to build new forms of collective tradition, and create a new story that memorializes the past, objectifies it, and incorporates it into a completely new vision.[1]

Devising a new way of placing significance on the present world, however, is not possible without much work and the passing of time. There are many pitfalls along the way. Lifton observed a duality with which the individual struggles in the effort to reclaim a new narrative:

> Dislocation creates a special kind of uneasy duality around symbolization: a general sense of numbing, devitalization, and absence of larger meaning on the one hand; and on the other, a form of image-release, an explosion of symbolizing forays in the

struggle to overcome collective deadness and reassert larger connection.[2]

Caught between a deadening inability to connect with past symbols and manically achieved, artificial, rootless new ones, the individual falls into a "protean" mode of living and becomes skilled at moving between and experimenting with multiple and even divergent sets of beliefs and relationships. Everything becomes possible, and a sort of indiscriminate image-hunger emerges, echoing Wuthnow's description of the perpetual religious seeker and dispersed self. The extreme of proteanism can be dangerous, leaving the individual unable to discern right from wrong.[3] Lifton also notes that the fragility of this protean self creates a vulnerability to rigid, authoritarian religions that offer an unambiguous belief system, clear answers to the world's woes, and a sharply defined social group. Such a brittle coherence can offer tremendous relief from the multiplicity of options and even a sense of uniqueness within a broad, pluralistic society.[4] Charles Strozier, likewise an historian and practicing psychoanalyst, and a student of Lifton, brings additional evidence. He points to additional threats such as urban violence, poverty, and disease, and shows how they foster an apocalypticism that fulfills unconscious wishes for transformation split off from true engagement with the problems in everyday living.[5] Philosopher Martin Jay makes a similar connection between the apocalyptic mindset as an avoidance of depressive anxiety and an avenue of manic release, drawing on the work of Melanie Klein, which will be taken up later.[6]

In sum, Lifton postulates that dislocation reaches much further than the simple vagaries of social mobility, and that it includes challenges to the continuing creative narrative of the human race. An ensuing psychological result of this deep loss and disintegration, we may deduce, is the creation of manic religious ideation and structure, which we can find in the United States in the Religious Right of the 1980s and 1990s, or conversely of the New Atheism in the first decade of the current century, or even in the more recent, religiously tinged nationalism. It is not enough, then, that individuals should rebel against these manic structures. Instead, they must acknowledge the deep dislocation they experience and the tendency to react to them in ways that are functionally equivalent to what they are supposedly rebelling against. A solely inward sacredness, a mutual exclusiveness between internal and external, is often likely a spiritual numbing and deadness, rather than a thorough and responsible social engagement.

Homans: Individual and Collective Loss

Peter Homans, a preeminent contributor to discussions of the psychoanalytic movement and its relationship to religion, addresses the symbolic breakdown of which Lifton speaks, and does so by looking at the practice of mourning itself in his insightful and far-reaching essay, "The Decline of Mourning Practices in Modern Western Societies: A Short Sketch," part of the anthology *Symbolic Loss*. Taking a still wider and longer view, Homans posits that along with the fragmentation brought on by modernization—namely, the political and scientific revolutions of the West over the last several centuries—there has been an accompanying decline in the role of community, what he calls a "common culture." This decline has particularly been evidenced by the community's diminishing role in mourning. Homans argues that mourning is fundamentally a social and symbolic process where the community bears the burden of the loss, thus helping in the process of individual suffering. Grief, by contrast, is an emotion that starts with the individual, who needs support. Mourning is an action, a public ritual that takes on the grief and helps bear the pain and despair of grief. Thus, "mourning is a grief-infused symbolic action."[7] But the consequences of modernization have privatized certain social experiences. More as an observation than an opinion, Homans argues that what were once public experiences of processing loss have become personalized. And with the onset of therapeutic psychologies, the responsibility of mourning has been taken out of a wider, common community and isolated to the worlds of individual experience and professional counselors.

In earlier books by Homans—*Jung in Context: Modernity and the Making of a Psychology* and probably his most definitive work, *The Ability to Mourn: Disillusionment and the Social Origins of Psychoanalysis* —he offers penetrating studies on the social origins of psychoanalysis and underscores that symbol creating as a social function has become, with help from psychoanalytic discovery, increasingly internal. He proposes that social science theory itself functions as a new mourning structure, and a subsequent creation of new meaning, in the wake of the loss of common culture brought on by the industrialized world.[8] Psychoanalysis, as alluded to indirectly by others such as Phillip Rieff and Christopher Lasch, created a language for describing, representing, even memorializing personal, inner life.[9] In other words, concepts such as the unconscious, repression, the ego, id, and superego, and the interpretive method of psychoanalytic therapy itself is the work of mourning the loss of the role of community and its accompanying rituals, rites, and beliefs. No doubt the inward turn Roof and Wuthnow have observed is borne out, as Homans would argue, in the need for an interpretive process or a hermeneutic of internality such as that offered by psychoanalysis.

For Homans, loss happens not just on the individual level, but also on the collective level. Whole societies and cultures experience deep and sometimes horrific loss. Like the individual, groups must mourn such losses, and they must do so collectively, often through the creation of memorials such as monuments, art, and literature. Homans highlights studies that document twentieth-century instances of collective loss and the inability to work through such losses.[10] Alexander and Marguerite Mitscherlich, working from a psychoanalytic view in their *The Inability to Mourn*, look at postwar Germany's denial of its compliance with Nazism. They point to Germany's postwar economic and industrial fervor and conclude that the loss of the ideal of Hitler was so sudden that Germans responded to the pain with a flurry of activity, or what Klein would call "the manic defense." In *Melancholy and Society*, Wolf Lepenies, an intellectual historian, identifies apathy in the eighteenth-century German bourgeoisie and late nineteenth-century Russian aristocracy.

These were groups of elites that lost their public significance and sank into a boredom and ennui, from which they had difficulty arising. Henry Rousso's *The Vichy Syndrome* considers how postwar France feverishly bestowed heroism upon the Resistance movement, even alongside disturbing revelations about its collaboration and cooperation with the Nazi occupation. Finally, in an example that by contrast demonstrates real attempts at collective mourning, Homans highlights Jay Winter's *Sites of Memory, Sites of Mourning*, which discusses the lives of soldiers in the First World War. Winter's analysis focuses on the creation of monuments after the war, and how such objects created ways to subsume grief into social construction.[11]

Homans mentions these studies to show that communal symbolic life contains within it the place of mourning. In this case, he is demonstrating that mourning is sometimes not just an individual experience to be taken on by the community, but also a collective one, that is, that the community itself struggles with its own instances of collective loss. He wants to show:

> how a people can create ceremonies, religious beliefs, monuments, and art in response to their shared loss, and how the workings of the culture they have created can represent and to some extent heal the wounds of loss and the sufferings it causes.[12]

It would be helpful to pause at this point and reflect on the central idea of this book, namely, that individuals go through a mourning process, or there is an ongoing dynamic of mourning, in the growth of faith and the continual reengagement with shared symbols. By looking at the changing, creative role of a self that in present day is turned toward inner realities—and by looking at the very fact that mourning is a social symbolic process—we may assume that the recent spirituality is also, regardless of its seemingly inward turn, a social process. While the danger of today's spirituality may lie in a narcissistic fixation of the inward turn, it must nevertheless be considered a genuine attempt to mourn past social structures. Consequently, we may look at people who are rebuilding their connection to faith in community as people creating symbols that are both inward and also eminently public. Indeed, we may look at the creative response of the individual as a commentary on current social and political pressures. It is not difficult to hypothesize, for example, that the rigid conservatism and ideological totalism running through certain segments of American religion is an attempt to create steadfast social structures and individual identity in a world leveled out and depleted of authentic living. Going one step further, the individual work of overcoming that conservatism may likewise hint at ways of memorializing and moving beyond such loss, especially on a social and cultural level. In other words, our conversation around how we describe our inner lives becomes a social conversation, and the more we streamline this conversation and widen it in community, the more we create a new shared, symbolic community, namely, a new religion.

Capps: Melancholy and Self-Depletion

A more specifically theological response to the challenges the individual faces in today's world is the work of pastoral theologian Donald Capps. In his book *The Depleted Self: Sin in a Narcissistic Age*, Capps likewise takes up the problem of the inward turn and the emergence of the narcissistic personality. He does so with a recommendation on how the theological community might better apply the word *sin* and better structure institutions to make them less autocratic and more open to individual responsibility and creativity.

Capps argues that the experience of sin or wrongfulness in contemporary society is no longer connected to guilt and communal morality, that is, an injustice that must and can be corrected. Rather, wrongdoing is a matter of personal shame, marked by an anger turned back upon the self for which there is little possibility of reparation. Capps likewise points to Christopher Lasch, who asserts that the modern self lives in a bureaucratic society bereft of individual initiative. Motivation comes only through coercion and manipulation, instead of through loyalty and the deep attachments of a powerfully established and well-connected identity. In such a world, approval and praise from a direct authority maintains self-esteem and defines the individual's worth, rather than a sense of participation and individuality recognized within the whole. Highly bureaucratic institutions rely on and encourage the narcissistic response, where motivation comes through an infantilized power relationship with authority rather than through independence and critical mindedness within community.[13] I would add, taking a cue from Erik Erikson, that such narcissistic self-esteem is compounded by the deeply ingrained idea of the American Dream, and the perception that the individual is "self-made." Existing within a rigid bureaucracy, the self-made illusion merely feeds the insatiable desire for acclaim created by autocratic authority.[14]

Drawing on a well-known case study in the *Harvard Business Review* that shows an interaction between a manager and his employee who indirectly asks for a raise, Capps explains that those in positions of power maintain their authority through aloofness, calmness, and reverse or indirect responses that put the burden of a problem back on the employee. This is an autocratic, manipulating authority, dispassionate and noninvolved with the employee. There is no sense of mentoring, caretaking, or mutual understanding, and the employee remains stymied, frustrated, even enraged. More importantly, this behavior of the employer only reinforces in the employee a sense of an unsatisfied craving for affirmation. The boss's aloofness causes the employee to feel ashamed of a personal desire for growth and praise, and even worse, to be ashamed of their shame.[15] In such a situation, there is no ethical contract or few ground rules for interaction, and consequently the individual never develops a critical capacity to feel either good or bad about their actions. Instead, such powerlessness creates a perpetual, inward shame.

Underscoring the idea that the individual is trapped in a world of shame, Capps notes that in the late 1950s and early 1960s, psychiatry began to sense a new type of illness in its patients. He writes:

> The classic neurotic patient, beset by obsessive and compulsive behaviors attributable to a punitive superego, was being replaced

by patients with characterological disorders. Initially viewed as antisocial personalities, suffering from a weak or nonexistent conscience, they were subsequently diagnosed as suffering instead from a weak or fragmentary self-structure that manifested itself in a variety of defensive maneuvers, the most notable being the resort to unrealistic self-inflation.[16]

Capps looks for answers in the work of Heinz Kohut, who places the developmental origins of this new narcissistic diagnosis as pre-Oedipal, that is, the time prior to age three when children become aware that the world is not constructed solely for them and are beset by their first feelings of persecution. This initial "narcissistic injury" leads to a defense reaction known as splitting, the primary feature of which is the emergence of two personalities: a grandiose self and a depleted self. As a defense mechanism to trauma, the grandiose self compensates for a lack of affirmation, while the depleted self is a defensive overreaction to trauma.

Kohut calls this exaggerated narcissism "secondary narcissism," which is more severe among those who have experienced inadequate parental attention and are emotionally understimulated. Aloof, uninvolved parents, lacking in empathy, can be seen as a likely part of the narcissistic individual's past. By contrast, a healthy narcissism develops under the care of parents who reliably respond to, or mirror, the child's initiative and autonomy, that is, to return the smile of the child. Failure to do so is often the result of the parent's own shame and inner depletion.[17]

Individuals experience shame when they do not live up to the ideals they believe are expected of them, however obscure or mercurial those ideals may be. They feel depleted, exhausted, drained, demoralized, diminished, and depressed. With guilt, by contrast, they feel anxiety as a consequence of clearly defined wrong actions directed outward toward others. The anxiety can be assuaged by the opportunity to confess a wrongdoing, offer reparation, and to feel enhanced because one has overcome. But with shame, the feelings of wrongdoing are turned inward: "We *perform* guilty actions, but we *are* our shame."[18] Capps explains that shame in an age considered narcissistic causes us to be divided against ourselves; we do our best to maintain amnesia about our shameful experiences, which are difficult to externalize and release. Defensiveness is also a defining characteristic, where individuals who harbor shame see themselves as victims who have not done anything wrong or who are even capable of wrongdoing. This lack of personal culpability becomes particularly problematic when one deals with shame by shaming others rather than encouraging and mirroring their positive initiatives.

Capps describes the self in a narcissistic age as a depleted self. For Kohut, self-depletion is a less severe form of pathology than the self-fragmentation experienced by the borderline personality disorder, a condition richly identified by Kohut and self psychology. The borderline personality is not hallucinatory and is indeed very much in touch with reality. Yet unlike the borderline, whose total self-fragmentation is an ever-present danger, the narcissist can function and lead a productive life, particularly in a rigid bureaucracy. In certain situations, for example, in a work environment that offers the potential for adulation and acclaim, the narcissist might easily thrive, though all the while feeling empty inside and unable to form intimate lasting relationships within or outside of that environment. The key in treating this condition in therapy is for the therapist to encourage and nurture in a client a healthy attachment to the therapist. This attachment is accomplished by consistent and positive mirroring of the client's inner initiative and creating an accepting though not necessarily affirming environment for the client's grandiose tendencies. The goal is to have the client take on a personal effort of positive self-mirroring and to develop the ability for each pole of the fragmented self to see how it needs, accepts, and even loves and nurtures the other.[19]

Capps makes the connection that a theology of shame, based on an authoritative religion, is ill prepared to encourage positive self-mirroring in our time. Instead, it encourages fragmentation and a certain amnesia and loneliness. Defining sin in a system of rigid rights and wrongs merely intensifies the feeling of shame. Individuals may carry around the feeling that they are not acceptable in God's eyes. Guilt for not living up to certain standards is less the issue than the shameful feeling that one *is* wrong, that there is some fundamental, irreparable defect or unfulfilled deficiency within the self. Such a sense of wrongness, when affirmed by the proverbial "guilt trip" laid on by religious authority, feeds into narcissism and the craving for recognition. A theology that responds to the problem of shame, by contrast, encourages individual autonomy and initiative. Such a theology would respond to the times that produce the depleted self with encouragement of independent belief, self-reliance, and intellectual freedom, but also public accountability. The development of such capacities allows the individual to make mistakes and creates the possibility of learning from mistakes, increasing understanding, and not repetitively internalizing a sense of shame.

Capps takes issue with the perception that such independence and freedom—what has been lamented as individualism—is a threat to social institutions, of which religious organizations are a crucial part. Capps holds that the argument accusing individualism of being harmful to religious communities—a view promulgated most famously by Robert Bellah's *Habits of the Heart*—is a scapegoating of individualism and actually reinforces isolation. By not being permitted to think critically and independently of the social institutions one belongs to, the individual is locked in the cycle of shame and craving for approval. Capps writes that "unlike the rugged individualist, who *has* a cause, the new narcissist *is* his or her cause."[20] If Bellah and his colleagues were arguing against ideological and ritual narcissism, they confuse that with the philosophical stance of individualism, which Capps traces most especially to the work of Ralph Waldo Emerson. Capps does not necessarily take up the cause of rugged individualism, but rather the idea that individual freedom and expression, and the opportunity to fully develop one's own ideological initiative, has been driven out of many religious institutions, which assume an "ontological priority over the individual."[21] Capps argues that only by having such ideological freedom can individuals break the narcissistic cycle of shame and find authentic relationships.

A theology that is responsive to our time is one that encourages individuals to have faith in themselves. When we are beset with an experience of shame, Capps argues that we must assign it a certain unreality, as if "waking from a bad dream."[22] The bad dream comes at the hands of a unilateral, absolute authority often represented by a single individual, rather than an authority vested in a group of leaders who provide checks and balances. To wake from the dream, the individual must discover that they have assigned their allegiance to a false God, reframe their experience, and take an alternative life course.

Capps does not, however, explain much about how the individual can accomplish such a reframing. Moreover, I wonder whether assigning the experience of shame to unreality or a dream state might only amplify the individual's perception that he or she is ontologically illegitimate, that the trauma experienced, even if sometimes self-inflicted, is somehow not real. As we will see in the biographical data in Part II, shaming experiences and the victimizing trauma are not so easily shed. Overcoming such shame is a long-term commitment for both the conscious and unconscious mind, one requiring much work and not a one-time act of will. To be fair, Capps acknowledges that the discovery of the false God, or the loss of the ideal God, is a difficult and painful experience.[23] Yet the implication that overcoming a false God can occur as simply as waking from a bad dream is somewhat misleading. The waking up process Capps refers to may be analogous to Freud's observation that in normal mourning the energy directed at the lost object eventually becomes spent and the individual is suddenly free to move on to other objects. I will discuss Freud's approach in more detail in a later chapter. For now, it is enough to mention how Freud observes that any such process of mourning or overcoming is not sudden but painstaking and slow. To fill out Capps's analogy, we should rather say that it is a long, difficult dream from which to wake; it is the dream of the mourning process.

Whether overcoming shame is a sudden process or a slow one, Capps argues that, to work through mourning and wake from the dream, the individual must have faith in the self. I would additionally argue that to maintain this sense of self-assurance amid a shaming environment, one must *lose faith* in the autonomous authority that is promulgating the shame, even enter a period of anguish where loss is palpable. In the case of those who feel discredited and dissociated with the religion of their upbringing, having faith in the self means recognizing both the loss of key relationships, and the loss of the noncorporeal objects and religious structures that held these relationships in place. In doing so, as Homans would add, the individual must confront not only a collective loss the former group fails to confront, but also a personal loss.

To conclude, the work of those like Lifton, Homans, and Capps offers us the chance to see how the social life of the time and place in which one lives is inextricably connected to individual psychology, and in turn has specific psychological effects. Where sociological analysis identifies current pressures of contemporary living and the way individuals behave in the social arena, psychological analysis offers insights into the inner responses that go along with such pressures and what motivates behavior. Where sociological analysis might lend recommendations on how to reshape social institutions to respond to the times, psychological analysis offers ideas on how to encourage individual healing. What we find in the work discussed in this chapter is that the individual partakes in collective struggle to overcome a loss of meaning in a world whose images of continuity, location, and connection face serious challenges; and such loss often causes an inward turn that sets up a cycle of shame and depletion. It need not necessarily go this way, but to break out takes time, and will involve some form of collective conversation about the inner struggle.

The key observation to note for this discussion is that the struggle to come to terms with a loss of faith does not take place in a vacuum. The decision to eschew institutional religion, for example, or more specifically to disconnect oneself from the tradition one was raised in, can prevent the productive, collective work of mourning. Such a process takes place on two levels: 1) mourning the loss of the individual's connection to existing traditions or the traditions of their

LOST FAITH AND WANDERING SOULS

personal history, and 2) mourning the losses that go along with a changing world. Working through these two levels of mourning will bring both individual and social change.

Although I have offered these broad, psychologically informed thinkers in this chapter to set up a later, more specific psychoanalytic understanding of the mourning process in the life of faith, I have also placed it at this point in the book to provide context to the next chapter, which is a critical discussion of faith stage theory. Such a discussion is unavoidable in a study that addresses the changes in the life of faith throughout the life cycle. It is my hope that in the following chapter the direction of this book will become undeniably clear.

3

The Uses of Faith Stage Theory

TAKING ON THE QUESTION of how to rebuild the life of faith cannot be accomplished without an appreciation of developmental theory in general and faith stage theory in particular. Regardless of circumstances such as social location, religious background, and parental relationships, a person's faith, belief, and involvement in a religious community are all colored by the stage of life he or she is in. Children, though their observations on life sometimes surprise us, nevertheless understand things differently than young adults, who in turn have a view different than someone who is middle aged, and so on. Each stage brings a new set of abilities and tasks. Life in a faith community for the very young is mainly a matter of education and social involvement; for the middle-aged, a matter of growing involvement and participation; and for the very old, a matter of being a source of wisdom and ballast. Throughout each stage of life there is the possibility of a profound struggle with doubt and loss of faith in community. Nevertheless, most of such losses or crises occur in the young adult years. During this time self-critical, independent thinking comes into its own. As has been previously noted, the young adult years are a time when the seemingly wide-open world of social possibility offers a myriad of choices. Often young adults enjoy a moratorium from handed-down mores and values and are encouraged to experiment.[1]

Although a developmental understanding serves as a baseline for analysis, I will also argue in this chapter that it would be a mistake to assign all such crises solely to the young adult stage or any other stage of life. Matters of faith are indeed remarkably bound up with one's family constellation, economic position, and social and cultural milieu. A crisis of faith may occur, for example, even in the infant who is somehow abused or neglected by its parents, or the elderly individual forgotten by friends and relatives. Moreover, making a sweeping statement about when a person's crisis of faith may occur can at times have a judgmental tone to it, casting off the individual as someone who has forgotten or rebelled against tradition, has fallen away from the right way of believing, or is mired in a perpetual adolescence. In this book about the road back to a world of participatory religion, it is important to understand that matters of faith—being able to creatively symbolize one's sense of ultimacy and to share it with others—never really lose their prominence in any stage of life. The potential to lose faith, to experience a "dark night of the soul," is always present.

The concerns I am expressing here are caveats to consider when incorporating the developmental view of faith. We must be prepared to answer the inevitable question, is not someone who is struggling with their faith simply going through a stage, one that they will eventually grow out of? This question is one you might anticipate coming from those within religious traditions who are unable or unwilling to see the many trajectories faith and religion may take. The question is, nevertheless, a relevant one. Faith stage discussions often ring true, no matter which side of an argument you might be on. What we must ask, however, is do they say enough?

Fowler's Stages of Faith

The work of James Fowler provides the most cited work in the developmental view of faith. It is indeed difficult to speak of transitions of faith without referring to Fowler's classic book, *Stages of Faith: The Psychology of Human Development and the Quest for Meaning*. Fowler's approach to matters of faith and meaning is predominantly structural; that is, it seeks out the formal, cognitive structures of faith whose job it is, in the most ultimate sense, to bring together disparate realities and seek out equivalencies in meaning. Throughout various stages of life, Fowler traces the potential ways that faith performs this function.

In early life, faith is strictly undifferentiated. Although Fowler devotes little specific attention to early life, he does argue that the individual experience of faith has its beginnings in infancy. Fowler defines faith as "generic, a universal feature in human living, recognizably similar everywhere despite the remarkable variety of the contents of religious practice and belief."[2] Faith is an ability to trust and devote oneself to a pursuit of transcendence, or the increasing understanding and approximation by thought and feeling, with all the assigned meanings, of "shared centers of value and power."[3] Creating concrete, shared expressions of trust, hope, and faith becomes the arena of religion. The work this requires, Fowler asserts, can be categorized into six successive stages that correspond to stages of cognitive or functional development, which I list and paraphrase here:

1) Intuitive-projective (ages three to seven): a fantasy-filled imitative phase in which religious imagination is relatively fluid and uninhibited by logical thought, and where the child is powerfully influenced by internal thoughts and emotional responses to the visible faith of adults.

2) Mythic-literal (school age): beliefs, stories, and observances are appropriated in more coherent, albeit literal, meanings; there is a curbing and ordering of wild religious imaginings, and fairness and reciprocity are the prevailing meanings drawn from religious stories.

3) Synthetic-conventional (adolescence): faith meets broader and more complex viewpoints and levels of involvement, is conformist and acutely sensitive to others' judgments; the self becomes aware of a personal myth journey and stages of religious development.

4) Individuative-reflective (young adult): the individual

51

experiences a burden of responsibility for religious commitments in the tension between staying true to self versus group; there is greater critical reflection, but it is not likely to consider unconscious factors.

5) Conjunctive (adulthood): integration of suppressed meanings, a critical new reworking of the past, a more porous ideology, and more universal sense of justice, including a capacity for irony and paradox, or in other words, participating in one's most powerful shared meanings while recognizing their incompleteness.

6) Universalizing (adulthood): an overcoming of the paralysis of paradox and taking risks, of "spending and being spent" for the cause of transcendent reality, even to the point of shaking up the status quo and an inattention to self-preservation.

According to Fowler, each successive stage incorporates, overlaps, and recontextualizes its predecessor, as wider and wider realms of experience are cognitively connected and appropriated. He suggests an image of an upward, conical spiral, which bends sideways in its midsection as the life of faith strives toward individuation at midlife. In addition, most individuals, regardless of their age, remain in certain stages and never find their way to later stages. Fowler cites a particular study of how elderly individuals best described by stage three, synthetic-conventional, tended to evaluate their experience of aging differently than those in higher stages.[4]

A side observation worth noting, with regard to the stage of faith that encompasses early childhood, Fowler writes that children who are asked to take on the faith identity of an adult suffer from what Philip Helfaer calls "precocious identity formation."[5] The danger here is that if too strong an attachment to a specific identity has been formed, then when the child becomes an adult, there is often a rigid, brittle, authoritarian personality.[6] To this end, one must wonder about the evangelical emphasis on requiring children ages four or five to go through a conversion experience from being "unsaved" to "saved." Such a requirement begs a question about the deep and perhaps ongoing psychic difficulties of those who have found it necessary to consistently rebel against their faith tradition.

For now, we should consider the larger question of whether individuals who have experienced a falling away from a practicing faith are simply going through a phase. Where, for example, would they typically be positioned in Fowler's six stages of faith? Perhaps those who have left their faith communities are coming out of a stage three synthetic-conventional phase and perceiving major contradictions in their faith group's ideology and practice as they leave home and experience a wider world. Without question, late adolescence is a period of change and experimentation, when parental supervision is no longer so acute, and a radical questioning of tradition takes place. Yet if falling away from faith were purely a developmental matter, then one would think a return to faith would be just as automatic. Such a unilateral return, however, does not necessarily match the facts of decreased mainline church attendance in recent decades, the well-documented increase of the non-affiliated, or the widespread feeling of the many fully grown adults who seem content being simply "spiritual, not religious." It is also likely, using Fowler's terms, that many who come to the end of the synthetic-conventional stage find there is nowhere for them to go. Discovering little cultural coherence, they stop attending a faith community and subsume themselves into something else, developing little interest in worlds or people beyond their own discrete circles.

Instead of disaffiliation occurring primarily in adolescence, perhaps it comes with stage four, individuative-reflective faith. Here, a much stronger distinction between self and group identity is drawn. The independence of the more mature adult increases and critical mindedness deepens. There is the potential to stake a claim for a worldview that is in concert though not necessarily in complete accord with immediate others or a larger group worldview. However, as Fowler argues, there is as yet little attention given to the wide array of inner contradictions and unassimilated social pressures that impinge upon this new independence. On the downside, there is a potential for "an excessive confidence in the conscious mind and in critical thought and a kind of second narcissism in which the now clearly bounded, reflective self overassimilates 'reality' and the perspectives of others into its own world view."[7] The words Fowler uses to describe stage four, especially "narcissism," give us pause to reflect on what stage may dominate faith today. If we live in a narcissistic age, is there a quality of excessive critical thought? Furthermore, is it possible that such a narcissistic age, caught in its own criticisms, is stalled in a stage four individuative-reflective faith? We may likewise speculate that those who leave their faith tradition, experience a time of fallowness, and then return, have indeed struggled with a similar rigidity and narcissism. Fowler notes that the need to progress out of a stage four faith comes with the upsurge of unconscious "anarchic and disturbing inner voices." And there is a "gnawing sense of the sterility and flatness of the meanings one serves."[8] Here a stronger sense of disillusionment with the self's presuppositions and logic forces a progression toward the next stage.

Conjunctive faith, stage five, involves a recognition of both the suppressed inner contradictions as well as the social unconscious— its myths, ideal images, and prejudices. It is at this point that the individual may develop a "second naiveté," as per Paul Ricoeur, in which a greater emotive charge is assigned to symbols that have now become better united with cognitive meanings, both socially and psychologically construed.[9] As previously mentioned, contradictions and paradox become more tolerable. There is the rise of the "ironic imagination," a capacity to exist within one's self and within one's groups and religious traditions, while also recognizing inevitable distortions and incompleteness.[10] The danger of this stage—and it is certainly one that defectors may fall prey to—is paralysis, complacency, and an inability to act and to allow oneself to submit to a potent and productive ideology and faith.

Yielding to paradox and risking religion is, of course, the action required for moving into stage six, universalizing faith. Said to be a rare stage, reserved for the likes of Gandhi or Mother Teresa, universalizing faith tolerates and even thrives in the paradox of the equality of traditions. Living within a tradition and taking action based on the deepest callings of that tradition means maintaining the greatest integrity even when it requires risk to one's personal safety. Consequently, seemingly few are willing to take this path or discover its necessity in the faith journey.

For those struggling with their relationship with an organized religion, we may speculate that many reach an ability to see paradox and contradiction, but that is right where they stop. Some quit their religious social involvement and are vulnerable to an overly confident stage four faith where other outlooks or traditions become attractive and are overassimilated. Conversely, there may be others who are able to move beyond this stagnation and indeed engage their own ironic imagination. Even while involved in a group that generally appears in a lower stage, it is possible that such individuals can move forward and enjoy shared symbols, although the way they draw meanings from said symbols may lead them to different conclusions. In the observations made in this discussion, we may perhaps find that the experience of the broadest, yet most simple symbols and everyday theologies are heightened and deepened in the individual who has made a journey forward to a new shared faith. For him or her, a sense of mystery comes to the fore, one that is not so much confounding and frustrating, but full of paradox, beautiful, and invigorating.

The Limitations of Faith Stage Theory and Conversion Theory

The popularity of Fowler's schema may be attributed to the fact that it is generally easy and seemingly tangible to see faith as cognitive or as progressively logical and ever-expanding in the ability to incorporate greater and broader worlds of experience. Such a stage-growth schema sits well with our rationalist-enlightenment mind that presupposes religion to be mostly about a set of beliefs. Yet it is difficult to confine such phenomena in a static, controlled experiment, and detect clear linear patterns. The universality of Fowler's theory only goes so far, and the context he uses to make his conclusions appears mostly limited to conscious ideological descriptors and neglects the ever-changing, unconscious, paradoxical relationship between the self and society. In other words, mature mental health and good social adaptation may not necessarily correlate with the stage of faith in which one finds oneself.

We must ask the question, what do you do with such a deeply cognitive way of evaluating faith development? How is it helpful? No doubt it is beneficial for those in the pastoral professions to understand that each person they counsel exists in a stage with particular needs, perceptions, and abilities. We must also ask, however, whether there is a point where a cognitively informed stage theory encourages a value judgment and as well a teleological imperative that is neither transcendent nor psychologically beneficial. There very well may be a benefit to broadening horizons in a world where there is so much cultural diversity, though we may also wonder toward which worldview we are leading people. Are they being asked to join in with a sense of universalism and deny their particular traditions? Indeed, there are those who have raised objections that a liberal or utopian ontology lurks beneath Fowler's schema.[11] Fowler writes "I claim that stages in faith development are hierarchical, sequential, and invariant."[12] In addition, there seems to be an absence of grace and understanding in a schema so defined by cognitive aptitude, even possibly a certain callousness to affective needs.[13]

One of the most intriguing sections of *Stages of Faith* comes toward the end of the book, where Fowler points out that although a change in the contents of faith may correspond to a progression in faith stages, the two are not necessarily dependent upon each other. On the one hand, there may be faith stage change but not conversional change, as in the case of someone who is born into a religion and remains there. On the other, conversion may take place but not faith stage change, where one makes a lateral shift between traditions of faith, exchanging one set of symbols and values equally for another. Marriage provides one example of the lateral shift, as does relocation to an area where symbols and values are vastly different, and an adjustment is necessary. In still other cases, this conversional change may also be a way to avoid the difficulties that can come with faith stage change. Once again, we must think of the spiritual seeker who moves about from one set of symbols to others, never really grappling with the ultimate meanings or social ethics of any one system. In addition, there may be conversion into a new religious context that precipitates faith stage change, and equally, faith stage change that precipitates a need to find an entirely new set of contents, or a rebirth and deepening of one's attachments to already familiar contents.[14]

The mere use of the word *conversion* raises an important issue regarding its definition. Conversion may mean a shift from a loosely defined worldview for a concrete and ritualized worldview, or vice versa. Or it may mean rebuking one set of symbols and practices and replacing it with functional equivalents of another. Within these discrete definitions it may be possible to sketch various stages that show the step-by-step processes involved. Lewis Rambo's *Understanding Religious Conversion*, for example, observes a series of steps that begin with a crisis, such as a mystical experience, an illness, or philosophical questioning. The crisis takes the individual out of their cosmological context and sends him or her on a quest for something new. Next there is an encounter and deeper interaction with a new system, and experimentation with relating to others both in and out of that new system. Finally, the individual commits to the new religion, reconstructs the self within it, and over time evaluates the consequences of the decision to convert.[15] Going through these steps may bring, as Fowler likewise observes, psychological progression or regression.

Yet what do these definitions accomplish in terms of a practical theology, or conversely, a constructive therapeutic? Psychoanalytically speaking, it is difficult to trust that any one conversion, however defined, has corresponded to change in the relationship to inner meanings and life-long attachments. Such a distrust is somewhat shared even in Fowler's assertion that there can be a change in the contents of religion, but no faith stage change. The description of a conversion as a reorientation of the individual's personality is often transferential, describes what may be real but mostly external changes, and does little to identify the unconscious and social dynamics at play in the conversion. We must also ask ourselves, as does William Meissner, whether such stage-specific descriptions of faith growth and conversion, regardless of their purely empirical intent, reveal an unchecked progressivism and encourage in their subtext either a utopianism, as in the case of Fowler, or a rationalization of boomer proteanism, as in the case of Rambo. In any event, speaking of conversion and faith stage often ignores the affective dynamic, and begs the question of what to do when an individual's connection to tradition begins to break down for reasons that have little or nothing to do with psychological growth.

Should conversion be defined narrowly to an external change in the contents of faith, or does it have meaning as a process of progressing further into the knowledge, understanding, and practicing of one's current religious tradition? Change is not simply a matter of an immediate and all-encompassing lifestyle and ideological change, but also a more gradual process of deepening in a tradition. To their credit, among some "evangelicals" who study conversion—despite their tradition's singular emphasis on a personal creedal decision and crisis conversion—there is a recognition that conversion is an ongoing process and not a once and for all event.[16] Consider the person who readily enters into a tradition with which they have had little previous experience or knowledge. A convert like this, in the strictest sense of the word, has indeed changed the contents of their religion. But how much personal transformation and how much change has there been in the way he or she thinks, perceives, and behaves? Has there been an equally striking movement from one stage of faith to another? Such a conversion could be no more than an example of the ever-questing religious seeker.

For those who are rebuilding their faith after having experienced a falling out with their religious tradition, our best approach will be to take the longer view of the growth process, not settling for describing the temporary circumstances surrounding a quick change of religious clothing. There is so much compacted meaning when describing the individual faith experience that taking a stage approach brings disadvantages. While we speak of the contents changing or of a progression through stages, there is little room for discussion of why the contents should fail us. Instead, to achieve growth, we must sometimes struggle deeply and downward with extraordinarily interpersonal objects, our own demons so to speak, and with the manipulative behavior of others that must be resisted. In terms of Fowler's theory of upward progression, there is little room for the "return of the repressed," the unconscious ways of thinking and feeling that can bring one's faith down each and every day—sure as the setting sun—to its lowest common denominator. Individuals fully engaged in their worlds and not isolated from psychological, social, historical, or economic challenges, are always at risk of disintegration, even in a later stage in life. Regardless of faith stage spiritual growth, everyday life often involves a daily reencounter with these problematic, changing externalities.

While stages of faith development offer us a descriptive convenience, and while we cannot deny that there is cognitive progression, none of this occurs outside of a contextual matrix. There are always discontinuities and nonsequential dimensions introduced by the context. As Romney Mosley, an early colleague of Fowler, writes:

Faith is always more than its empirical stages. This "more than" quality, the "surplus of meaning," has to do with the paradox of seeking the eternal in the temporal. Whatever is identified as a stage is and is not yet. If there is any normativity to stages of faith, it is this paradoxical quality.[17]

Mosley asserts that our concern should lie more with understanding the role of faith in a transcendent relationship between the self and the world that is a teleology or therapeutic, rather than with encouraging an ideal universal community of stage six individuals.

Literary analyst John Barbour's *Versions of Deconversion* explores the narratives of known spiritual autobiographers from Augustine to Sartre and describes their experiences with losing faith in a way that sounds more circular and horizontal, and not necessarily as an upward spiral. He writes:

> In one sense, every conversion is a deconversion, and every de-
> conversion a conversion. The "turning from" and "turning to"
> are alternative perspectives on the same process of personal met-
> amorphosis, stressing either the rejected past of the old self or the
> present convictions of the reborn self.[18]

If indeed there is a rejection, there must necessarily be an acceptance. Epistemologically speaking, the transition may be one
marked by a new wisdom, something wrought through experience
and knowledge, as Fowler would argue. Phenomenologically speaking, however, the rejection will also be caught up in the emotion
laden vicissitudes of loss. To any extent there is a rejection, there is
also the task of incorporating that rejection within the integrity of the
self in such a way as to minimize any overbearing divorce between
sacred allegiances past and present, or in psychological words, the
"me" and the "not me" that nevertheless was. The fault lines of any
former self create a paradox that requires transcendence, rather than
a manic proclivity to rewrite the beliefs and attitudes of the former
self out of personal memory. Precisely in the task of incorporating a
former self into the present do we find reason to speak of faith as
something that is always there. A basic sense of trust, regardless of
the pathos it may contain, is neither something we can wholly turn
away from nor return to.

Perhaps the most reliable variable we can count on is that there is
nothing reliable in the life of faith. Doubt, misgivings, even shame
and abuse can at one point or another be tied to an individual's life
of faith, either formally within an institutional context, or on an interpersonal, or *intra*personal level. When something goes terribly
wrong with the connection between the individual and a personal
attachment to faith, and as well with a community of shared faith,
there may not be a matter of growth at stake, but simple survival.
The recovery of faith and reparation to the damage to faith is just as
much the task at hand as the need to encourage growth.

4

The Psychoanalytic Stance

THUS FAR, we have surveyed several fields and lines of inquiry in terms of creating a framework within which to place those who have experienced marked shifts in their life of faith. They include the sociological view, which identifies some of the broader forces to which individual spirituality and organized religion must respond; the socio-historical-psychoanalytic view with theorists who point out still deeper challenges to individual meaning making; and the cognitive, faith-stage view, which places faith development in a set of progressive intellectual stages. At this point, I would like to place this discussion more firmly within the interpretive psychoanalytic stance on the individual experience of faith and religion. If there are dynamics at work that affect far more than can be evaluated based on sociological and cognitive constructs, then it is valuable to continue this discussion by taking an in-depth look at those dynamics. It is here we turn to the study of personal history, the pathology that results from trauma, and the theories formed around individual narrative, that is, formative experience, as an object of analysis. Taking an in-depth look at individual meanings and the interpretation of the inner symbolic life is the domain of the psychoanalytic enterprise.

I will discuss briefly how private symbols and the meanings assigned to them are identified via the psychoanalytic viewpoint in such a way as to shed light on the difficulties inherent in overcoming religious disillusionment and disaffiliation. Psychoanalytic theory can help us discover the components of a vital life of faith, which, as I will also argue, include the ability to reclaim and reinvest oneself in what is an eminently public phenomenon. Put another way, the sacred other is not just the God image, but the God community. The ensuing chapter will, therefore, explore the hypothesis that there is indeed a communal aspect to individual faith that is not as optional as is popularly argued by an inwardly turned seeker society, and that faith is only fully expressed, and its potential fully realized, when in a communal setting. I also wish to be clear that in taking the position that faith does not come into its fullness unless lived in community, I am not advocating for a self that is fatalistically determined by society. Instead, I would argue that the self is vitally bound by society, as a self in relation, but has the capacity and opportunity to transcend it, transform it, and be transformed by it. My view is one informed by psychoanalytic tradition, specifically Erikson's idea of "the sense of 'I'" as "a center of awareness in a universe of communicable experience, a center so numinous that it amounts to a sense of being alive, and more, of being the vital condition of existence."[1] The self, and its capacity for transcendence, exists within a universe of experience, and must have that experience in order to exercise such capacity. In other words, the self is not complete without society, and consequently, faith, trust, and hope are not fulfilled without community.

While there is a large body of work that addresses the psychoanalytic evaluation of the role of religious life, I will confine myself to a brief discussion of two similar but contrasting seminal thinkers—Freud and Erikson—to highlight the psychological connection between individual faith and community. We'll move through their points of view quickly.

The Freudian View: A Royal Road to the Unconscious

For Freud, the primary role of religion represents the "fulfillments of the oldest, strongest, and most urgent wishes of mankind."[2] Religious belief and practice commutes feelings of unexpressed guilt, confusion, and frustration, and sets up a moral value system that can be easily tied to the authority of parents. The image of God for any one person is, for example, imbued with unresolved, mostly unconscious feelings toward primary experiences with parental figures, and most especially, Freud argues, the father. On a larger scale religion is, as Freud explains in *Totem and Taboo,* and then again in *Moses and Monotheism,* a collective agreement to establish a universal group symbol that assuages our earliest and most primeval anger toward and guilt about a fatherly force we have both rebelled against and felt estranged from.[3] Having committed some crime or transgression against such limits to our sexualized, driven nature, we are forever striving to restore the symbiotic union with an all-encompassing, protective, limitless power and paradise we once experienced as infants.

When it comes to Freud on religion, the method of psychoanalysis as a "talking cure," can be best thought of as a process that helps the individual recover, understand, and excise the meanings and feelings that he or she has previously given over to religion—to make them conscious and to feel free to experience life's challenges without any need for religion. While Freud recognized the usefulness of religion over the course of human evolution, he is famously known as a staunch opponent, always intoning that religion is undergoing a withering process that will one day give way to a scientific worldview. What those who either support or criticize his condemnations or manifest reductionism often fail to appreciate, however, is the possibility of an underlying teleology in Freud's thinking. He's an iconoclast, and that's a healthy role few of us are willing to play.

For Freud, any image of a deity is subject to projection, whether your epistemology calls that transcendentally inspired or not, and particularly in connection with the sacred imagoes (more than mere images) we construct. In other words, our concepts of God are often more tied to our parents, our social arena, and our political structures more than we are usually willing or able to admit. A psychoanalytic hermeneutic offers a warning to purge one's faith of anthropomorphist accretions. To the point, including one's religion among the data that may be used for psychosocial evaluation and interpretation makes for an extraordinarily fertile ground. Religion is indeed the royal road to the unconscious. Such a purging process leads to a closer and purer understanding of the transcendent.[4]

Contrary to Freud's critics, and arguably contrary to Freud himself, if the analysis ended with conclusions that religion will one day lose its efficacy and usefulness, it renders impossible *any* discussion of the use and efficacy of culture—which includes art, theater, literature, *and* articles of religion. We would have to conclude that there is no place for a collective, ritual nature of symbolizing. Yet at the same time, it is also difficult to take Freud's seeming antipathy toward religion seriously. To be sure, much of the professed intention behind his discussions of religion is to prove that it is unnecessary, beginning in so-called primordial times and ending in the age of reason. Nevertheless, the quantity and quality of Freud's protestations leads one to wonder about his sincerity, that they belie some hope and fascination with the power of religious symbols. Consider Freud's fascination with the subject of religion in his writings, which was part of his repertoire even in his last major publication at the end of his life, *Moses and Monotheism*. Paul Ricoeur in his landmark commentary on Freud, *Freud and Philosophy*, underscores that there is no psychoanalytic principle that would lead Freud to exclude the possibility of religion as participating in Eros, the power of conciliation and love that transcends the compulsive and palliative potentials of religion.[5] For Freud, religion is most eminently worthy of study, and yet he is unable to knowingly make a turn from iconoclasm to the freedom to create new sacred symbols. For the theologian, there is more to do than sit on the sidelines as did Freud and embrace a functional approach to religion and not also assume a substantive approach.[6] There is instead the opportunity to discover meaning in religious symbols, and not necessarily reduce them to artifacts of an outdated society. Used in a true archeological effort, symbols of religion provide a means by which to obtain a deepened understanding of our story, who we are, and what is most important to us.

These are conclusions that do not come with much difficulty to the longtime student of psychology and religion. They are borne out most definitely in the work of ensuing waves of psychoanalysts and students of psychoanalytic method and religion. What I am most interested in highlighting along the way is the value of the story of the individual, and how the self is placed within a larger grid or matrix, how it is linked to many events and trajectories. To see one aspect of life at the cost of the other makes it impossible to see an individual as more than the sum of parts and to understand how the self transcends context. The value and force of narrative suspends the need for atomizing in a phenomenological study. Like an editor of a novel wanting to transform words and sentences into an impactful drama, the analyst of religious experience connects the separate components of an individual's life to see the signature make up and areas for growth. The comprehensive meaning of a narrative is not so much dependent upon any group of factors, but upon its entire composition and the meaningful takeaway within.

The Eriksonian View: The Psychosocial Matrix and Ritualization

Within the field of psychoanalysis, and arguably social scientific study in general, the work of Erik Erikson provides the most satisfying, comprehensive, and versatile body of knowledge with which to understand the place of faith and religion within human development. Erikson's theorizing and the ways he applied his theory, particularly to historical figures, are so broadly constructed that his work is often unpalatable to many in academic disciplines and are too removed from the clinical environment for those in psychoanalytic therapy. And yet Erikson's work may be credited for capturing much of the imagination of a generation of students, practitioners, and scholars who came of age during his prominence. The force of Erikson's observations as a whole had a broader impact and somehow held more meaning for a greater number of people than elite academic circles. This fact alone raises a question of the power, responsibility, and usefulness of social scientific inquiry, that it may serve as an interpreter of the times we live in, a "culture maker" as Homans would

LOST FAITH AND WANDERING SOULS

say, and an impetus for change writ large.

In short, the defining article of Erikson's theory is his life cycle sequence of development. Erikson observes that development is epigenetically based, that is, any one stage contains within it the past stage. The epigenetic principle, borrowed from embryology, states that each organ has a hierarchical order in which growth must take place. Just as each organ has a time when it must arise without disturbance, so also are there psychological formations and structures that must arise at certain times, and must develop fully, for the rest of development to take place normally. Erikson was also among the first contributors of what became known as the school of ego psychology. He positions his personality theory on the growth of the self in relation to others, or more specifically, on an ego that functions as relationally adaptive, rather than an ego that negotiates with internal libidinal forces, as Freud argued. Erikson's most significant difference with Freud, however, is his assertion that formative psychological challenges occur not only during the intensive years of early childhood, but also significantly in adolescence, through adulthood, and even into old age. To manage these challenges, ego adaptivity becomes the crucible for psychological health. Whereas Freud stressed revealing unconscious desires that grew out of early life experiences—to put ego in place of id—Erikson pointed toward ongoing challenges throughout life, likewise repressed into the unconscious, that add to the instances where trauma happens and psychological growth may be impeded. With each stage there are developmental tasks for the individual to master that contribute to an age-appropriate adaptivity. It is not a forgone conclusion, for example, that wisdom will come with old age, as so much is dependent upon formative tasks located in mid and later life.

If we can agree with Erikson that there remain vital components of development beyond early childhood and adolescence, it adds unquestionable significance to the struggles faced by those who feel out of touch with their faith and cultural milieu. A disaffection with one's religious upbringing, or even the form of religion in one's surroundings, points to a very real problem, one that is related to adaptivity

66

and development at any point in the life cycle. Through religious culture we find the broadest and most penetrating forms of meaning making in everyday life. Leaving such culture or losing faith in it because of its own brokenness is not simply a matter of lifestyle choice. Disaffiliation sometimes holds keys to the quality of psychological equanimity, to self-image, and perhaps at times, survival.

For Erikson, faith is a vital component of human existence from the earliest days of infancy to the final moments at the end of life. Psychological maturation becomes more than a matter of finding gainful employment, intimate relationships, housing, and the birthing and caretaking of children. Life is also a matter of finding significance within everyday relationships. Our desires are not completed with possessing the means to satisfy hunger, find shelter, and propagate ourselves. We can do without some of these things and find immense satisfaction and pleasure if we are able to achieve goals that do so much more. Erikson builds this sense of existential concern into his theory as a clear component of his overall impetus to define development throughout life.[7] He adds to each stage of his famous life cycle chart just such a component—one that involves the search for meaning and symbolism that will help us solve a stage-specific task and propel us to the next. Such a search is encapsulated in what Erikson calls *ritualization*. Moreover, as with much of Erikson's way of thinking, there is a bipolar construction—"syntonic" and "dystonic" opposites—in each of the stage-specific characteristics of ritualized life. In this case, there is ritualization, and then there is its opposite, pseudoritualization or *ritualism*.[8]

Below I offer a summary of the meaning making, existential, or spiritual component of each stage of Erikson's life cycle matrix. My intent is not to use this matrix exclusively in the later chapters of this book, but rather to bring forward language of religion while very much grounded in human living and development. This language builds and informs a point of view, if you will, that is no doubt more phenomenologically oriented, or what in other words might be called non-confessional. Yet it is language like this that is sorely missing from a "religious discussion" about the healthy journey of faith and religion. More than ever, we can benefit from strengthening this language in our everyday ways of talking about our spiritualities. Pay particular attention to the stage of adolescence and the psychology of totalism, and the importance of this language becomes evident.

By contrast, I did not offer this in the above summary of Freud's stance on religion. Freud's stages of development, while provocative and deep, put the focus of unconscious drives on the experiences of early childhood while Erikson's matrix opens things up to the entire lifespan. This shift in view no doubt allows for a more robust discussion of religion.

Erikson's Life Cycle Stages and Religion

The continuum of life begins in infancy where we first experience a sense of the *numinous*, first articulated in the highly ritualized caretaking of mothers, who instill in the infant a "sense of hallowed presence." It is the stage where the individual first experiences the vital components of hope and trust. The numinous fulfills a dual function: a feeling of transcendence between subject and object in that it "assures us of *separateness transformed* and yet *distinctiveness confirmed*."[9] When this double dynamic fails, or when it fails too often, the numinous becomes perverted into *idolism*, an illusory attitude of adulation and a narcissistic image of perfection.

A sense of play and imagination in the process of mutuality and ritualization is key for Erikson. In his therapeutic work with young children, he discerned in their patterns of play thematic elements that could be connected to challenges or traumas in their childhood. Play constitutes a reenactment of life history, and is productive, therapeutic, and fun when it contains a surprising, creative element or twist of meanings.[10] In a subsequent chapter where I will discuss the work of D. W. Winnicott, we will find a similar isolation of the quality of surprise. For Erikson, the element of surprise leads us to a discovery of the numinous. We interchange, cast off, renew, and combine meanings that give us a feeling of newness and freshness, as though we are connected in thought and feeling to a "hallowed presence" that is both within and beyond us.[11] But when we lose our connection with the numinous, we lose our ability to play. Our most basic, pervasive desires attach themselves to idols—objects we presume to contain omnipotence and goodness. As with all idol worship, we are not genuinely participating in creating such objects. They are not our own, but someone else's, and will nevertheless fail us if, as infants, we lacked a playfulness with our caretakers.

The second phase of life, early childhood, is characterized by autonomy, the ability to stand and crawl, and the desire to assert one's will. When the child begins to assert independence, he or she also, and just as acutely, discovers boundaries. Rules for what is acceptable and what is not, and the reinforcements and consequences that follow are what Erikson terms the *judicious*. When such rules are taken on with too much emphasis, or even when they are given with too little emphasis, there is the danger of *legalism*, where a connection to true moral liabilities is lost and substituted with rigid adherence to uncompromising laws. For Erikson, this stage also holds the ontogenetic source for the negative identity. Here the divided self emerges, an image of everything one is not supposed to be and yet is capable of being, where certain wants and desires are attached to feelings of shame and guilt. The divided self also forms the basis for a divided species. In legalistic communal rituals we are engaged in a process of "eliminating" the negative self and species, often with anger and condemnation. We may see, for example, in the person who has fallen away or left organized religion, a taking on of the negative identity, having now become an outsider.

Such absolutes of right and wrong become somewhat suspended and elaborated upon in the third stage of childhood, the preschool age. Good and bad find more complex representations, such as in children's storybooks, playacting, and pretending, which are placed on the stage of a child's imagination. Play is dominated, at least in the case of boys, by "the impersonation of victorious self-images and the killing off of weak and evil 'others.'"[12] Identification with the hero of the story and the vanquishing of the evildoer manages feelings of guilt resulting from a divided self. The child's initiative develops in the ritualization of the *dramatic*. He or she becomes confident in roles that engage a widening sphere of meanings, and in which there is an increasing understanding of the sanctions for finding one's own way. The danger, however, comes in identifying too strongly with an over-idealized hero, or alternatively, giving up on the hero, finding it too burdensome. Taken to an extreme, to the degree of "dead earnest-ness," such identification becomes the ritualism of *impersonation*. Play becomes stilted and uncompromising; it loses adaptability, creativity, and innovation. As a result, play becomes difficult to make happen with others, who now find it unattractive and lackluster. Their par-ticipation in creating the rules and boundaries of play is unwelcome, and enchantment for the group is lost.

As a child enters the school age, an element of "methodical per-formance" emerges as part of life's ritualizations. Marked by a sus-tained discipline through predetermined sequences of certain acts, the task at this stage is to achieve competence in given behaviors that allow participation in any one of life's systems, whether economic, technical, or even cultural. These are *formal* acts, where ritualization becomes cooperative, such as in the interplay between a pupil, class, and teacher. The child gains a sense of industry, of having contrib-uted to something greater by following given rules and guidelines, for which there will be a reward. Conversely, a failure to reach these competencies results in a sense of inferiority, which can contribute to a rush toward perfectionism and empty ceremonialism, or what Erikson calls *formalism*. Instead of mastering rules and guidelines to achieve some dependent benefit, the rules and guidelines themselves become the focus, while appreciation and enjoyment of what they are supposed to produce are beyond reach. It is this compulsion to-ward the formal that often becomes the subject of the psychoanalytic analysis of religious life, that is, the argument that religion is simply a means through which to obtain a sense of control over uncontrol-lable variables. In the formalism of religious life there is a strict ad-herence to the letter of the social contract, and a deadness to the intention driving the agreement. In the endless search for profi-ciency, there is a denial of the context within which the proficiency was developed. If for example that context changes or a need arises that had not been originally accounted for, the immutable proficiency can become dangerous, and harmful to those who are deemed out of the norm.

The fifth stage of ritualization is perhaps more than any other stage the culmination of everything that has gone before—numinous, judicious, play, and formal—and anticipates much of what is to come. Here the individual reaches adolescence and very early adulthood, at which time he or she looks forward to and begins participating in the world of work and productivity, having mastered certain skills and competencies. Yet, as Erikson explains, this is also a time of great upheaval, and perhaps the most pivotal point of the life cycle (contrary to Freud). Childhood is left behind and the plateau of responsible adulthood, along with the conformity it requires, looms ahead. The previous stages culminate to produce a new, seemingly complete coherence. A more complex amalgamation of ideas come together to form a specific component of ritualization Erikson calls the *ideological*. Rites of induction and confirmation enjoin adolescents to become full members of a social and cultural ethos and to share a reasonably well-defined worldview. Ideally, they become part of a "pseudospecies," a localized sphere of individuals who share similar goals, interests, customs, and language. The psychosocial task is to claim an identity within this group, to assert one's own contribution or role and to simultaneously feel affirmed by those around them.

When this process breaks down, identity confusion ensues and the adolescent searches around and experiments with various counter or negative identities. To some degree, this is a healthy and normative process, even prescribed and encouraged in some groups, and moreover formalized in certain rites of passage in others. Erikson terms this the psychosocial moratorium, where the adolescent is permitted a certain leeway and devotes him- or herself to extended periods of experimentation. In this way, a negative identity is useful. It creates a countervision, which is a necessary element in the transmutation that goes on between generations. The young adult must form

71

a new identity in a new time, in a new context, and thereby will necessarily conflict with most of the handed down and sanctioned identities. The danger of this period is, however, that certain negative identities may linger that have no dynamic countervision.

If there is a failure at this stage to incorporate an ideology that honors the past, energizes the present, and looks to the future, then in its place certain ideas and views form that are idolistic and legalistic. They are the by-product of detached, objectified impersonations, and not the ideas of creative actors involved in an ongoing story, and they are formalistic, unable to point toward a higher goal to which certain skills and competencies aim. Ideological failure results, says Erikson, in a ritualism of *totalism*, "a fanatic and exclusive preoccupation with what seems unquestionably ideal within a tight system of ideas."[13] For Erikson, the adolescent need for identity with its accompanying ideology is sometimes exploited by older generations to achieve certain goals, for example, in the creation of the Hitler youth by the Nazi Party. In the Vietnam era, such exploitation backfired, and a strong and prevailing countervision formed among a critical mass of youth. Religious leaders, locally and nationally, past and present, are and have been only too aware of the ripeness of this stage for gaining strong allegiances among adolescents and young adults to specific worldviews and traditions. And the efforts of such religious, or even political leaders, points as well to the spiritual maturity of the leaders, if not the maturity of the society and culture.

While Erikson places most of his emphasis on the elements of ritualization in the first five stages, he completes them with three more. The fifth stage gives way to the sixth when commitments in work, friendship, and love become more intimate and sustained—what Erikson calls the *affiliative* ritualization. The opposite would be participation in a "shared narcissism" and the resulting *elitism* of exclusive groups. The next, seventh stage, brings authoritative roles of parent or teacher of some knowledge or skill. The individual seeks to mentor others and be confirmed as "a numinous model in the next generation's eyes" and a "judge of evil and transmitter of ideal values." Conversely, the seventh stage's ritualism is a "self-convinced and yet spurious usurpation of authority" or what Erikson calls *authoritism*. In the eighth and final stage, the individual reflects back and hopes to see a life lived with integrity and meaning, without experiencing despair and disgust. Rituals are *integral*, or what Erikson later called the *philosophical*, such as ceremonies recognizing lifetime achievements and roles as elders in certain groups, which affirm life's significance even in the face of physical decline. The ritualistic danger, however, comes when only a pretense of wisdom and integrity are attainable, which Erikson first called *sapientism* and then *dogmatism*, which when combined with institutional power can become coercive and ultraorthodox.[14]

Always with Erikson, elements of earlier life are present in later life. In every ritualized moment throughout the lifespan, there are many, if not all the accumulated experiences of past ritualizations at work. Even later life ritualizations may be present in earlier life, if only in a nascent form.

In sum, what Erikson's stages of ritualization offer the student of religion is a set of analytic guidelines for understanding the psychological composition of an individual at any point in the life cycle and the corresponding roles that religion plays. It avoids reductionism as it simply makes no claim about whether beliefs are true, or even developmentally immature, as in the case of Freud. Instead, Erikson's theory puts the observer in the middle of the many trajectories that make up a life, and demonstrates just how powerful, far-reaching, and central faith and religion are in a specific psychosocial context. What could be less reductionistic? It is extraordinary to think that the life of faith is full of symbolic meaning that has its origins in the early years, interacts with the sacred imagoes of others, and develops through the seasons of an entire lifespan. At any one moment, a basic trust and faith pervade everything we are and do, whether we lay claim to a specific religious affiliation or not. What is more reductionistic is to imply that faith and the symbolism used to express it is simply propositional, a matter of an ideological profession or a specific set of words and phrases, repeatedly affirmed, without regard to whether they incorporate and nurture the whole, changing person.

A key point to appreciating Erikson's stages is that they are not, from a normative or ethical point of view, progressive. Each stage of life has its developmental task to complete, and the failure to do so creates the potential for pathos. By contrast, a general reading of Fowler's stages of faith gives the impression that faith is a successive process of building a cognitive apparatus, achieving greater and greater moral acuity and spiritual enlightenment, with the highest stages only being achievable by a few great individuals. Such a schema leaves little room for the great dark night of the soul that can descend without warning at any point in life, sometimes testing the fundamental nature and power of religious symbolism borne out in everyday life. Even someone such as Mother Teresa has admitted that God at times seems absent and deeply struggled with holding on to hope.[15] Erikson's stages, each with a syntonic and dystonic pole, allow for such variances, and incongruities that can exist even in the most rigorously devout.[16]

In the struggle of practicing faith in today's world, we may situate an individual within Erikson's stages without making any moral judgments about the richness of that symbolic life. We already know it is quite rich. Instead, we are enabled to articulate personal difficulties in detail, pulling out enduring elements of personal history, and social and cultural-historical themes. We may look for one or more ritualisms that may be related to a present life stage or a failure to master a previous stage. We can situate those ritualisms within a specific local context, but also draw historical observations about the broader needs and desires those ritualisms may serve. We are thus better able to make a therapeutic, redemptive interpretation that drives inward into personal history and outward onto the larger society. Such an effort is transformative for both individual and society, binding together themes that creatively point toward something new.

What does Erikson's life cycle theory say about the person who has left a communal expression of faith? We may draw several conclusions. First, we may point to both the syntonic and dystonic poles of ritualization that may apply. If a person who has left a particular faith community is foundering, he or she may need to return to a certain task for new growth to emerge. They must repair what was damaged and recover what was lost or given up. If, for example, a school-age child was led to a "decision for Christ" and asked to pray a "sinner's prayer," he or she may not have achieved competence with discovering the power of a religious symbolism on their own and in true cooperation with a community. Having been pressured to assume the mark of a fully qualified believer, regardless of whether there should be a recognized difference between children and adults, the child can develop a feeling of failure and inferiority, that is, knowing that they do not measure up to expectations. Such are the downsides of a precious identity formation. A social contract has been entered into, and the child feels compelled to follow it to the letter—a forever unachievable goal—while at the same time never grasping, incorporating, or enjoying the spirit of the agreement. To repair such a trauma, an individual may need to break the contract, with no small amount of difficulty, and enter into a newly drafted agreement that enlivens and reconstructs a genuinely dynamic relationship between self and sacred other.

A complete reconstruction of one's relationship to transcendence takes work. The outer appearance of such work may even appear as the opposite of progress. Indeed, a negative position may dominate, where the individual goes on a search—sometimes one that may teeter dangerously on self-destruction or permanent harm—to find tangible evidence of meaning and worth. Such a destructive impetus may involve a great inward turn, or it may seem vehemently outward directed. This mighty battle takes place perhaps especially in the use of religious symbolism. If only there were a language to describe this battle, we would perhaps be better positioned to help manage its course, prevent its extreme appetites, and encourage an outcome that brings salvation to not only the self, but also the other. That language, as I will argue in the next chapter, is the language of mourning.

5
Mourning and the Faith Journey

I HAVE SO FAR SAID that transitions of faith involve much more than what is immediately observable. Personal belief, for example, in creating a powerful single-mindedness, sense of purpose, and communal participation, can also be seen as a mere manifestation of changing social and historical factors. Even politics and power play a role in the sets of beliefs one chooses. A belief held and expressed in certain words and ideas formed in a specific language does not exist solely in transcendent purity; rather, it is a part of the time and place one lives in. In addition, we have also seen in our brief look at religion and psychoanalytic theory, that religion is the ultimate ground for experiencing and developing the numinous. Creating a set of symbols, individually or collectively, brings form and adds substance to the basic trust and hope required for everyday living. Moreover, the way an individual connects to the symbolic content of a certain time and place proceeds in stages throughout an entire life span. However, following Erikson's approach, these stages are mere descriptors of a multifaceted struggle with ultimacy at every stage in both the conscious and unconscious mind. With each stage comes a task fraught with peril, and the pathos of such struggles cannot go unheeded if there is to be an understanding of the failures to engage one stage or another.

To better grasp the depth of this struggle, to explore its ever-present potential in the life of faith, and to better appreciate the full poignancy of those who experience transitions of faith, I now turn to an exploration of mourning theory. The language of mourning theory not only makes logical sense, but it also has immediate therapeutic value. To suggest that someone who has lost their religion—whether that be through social and cultural dislocation or having suffered some trauma within a faith community—is experiencing a loss that must be mourned has immediate resonance. A death has been suffered, and the reaction to that loss of religion has parallels to the death of an individual loved one. But what has been lost? In the case of losing the connection to symbols of faith, there are additional concerns that in important ways make this loss even more difficult or prolonged, more subtly painful, and requires special work.

In this chapter we now come to the center of this study, namely, applying the psychoanalytic language of mourning to the suffering involved in the loss of religion. We will begin with Freud's famous 1917 essay, "Mourning and Melancholia," which sets the stage and offers some clear and relevant observations. Then the work of Melanie Klein, which takes Freud's loss language and reaches some different conclusions, will likewise add depth. Where the mourning theory of both figures ends, the observations on creativity and play by Winnicott begin, and move the discussion of rediscovering faith and religion forward. After exploring these avenues, it will be easier to ask the critical question discussed throughout this book, that is, the foundational challenges to the life of faith in our times as identified by those such as Roof and Wuthnow, and Lifton, Homans, and Capps: How do those embedded in a culture of the sacred self, who have turned their spiritual life inward, properly mourn the loss of faith, and seemingly without a communal component?

Before we begin in earnest, let's consider for a moment the epistemological presupposition that is made when going about the business of applying knowledge gleaned from one type of endeavor to another. Many of the thinkers I bring into this discussion are theoreticians who draw their observations from clinical work. It is from these observations that psychological categories and descriptors are derived. With some important exceptions, these theorists begin their work with little thought of the applications to the life of faith and religion. Indeed, one may argue, that the two areas are at cross purposes. However, as I have argued in the previous chapter on the iconoclastic and interpretive character of psychoanalysis, it is the very principles discovered in the clinical situation—particularly the emphasis of psychoanalysis as a "talking cure"—that can help with the barriers to a life of faith in religious community. An impetus to create symbol and language, in its most ultimate forms, encourages the freedom and ability to talk through and past these barriers and reestablish religious creativity and imagination.[1]

Delving into the specialized language of psychoanalysis can at times seem tedious and overreaching. Consequently, I plan to emerge at the end of this chapter, with generalizable principles that can be applied to the concrete experiences in the life of faith and, moreover, be transformed into an original language that points to restoration and rediscovery.

With the discussion in the previous chapter on the role of faith and religion, we may take this archeological direction without any concerns that we are unnecessarily disturbing hidden holy relics. Indeed, an archeological approach is the point: uncovering relics to inform and even inspire us about the life of faith today.

Freud on Mourning

In the opening paragraphs of Freud's famous "Mourning and Melancholia," he begins with a statement that offers immediate support for this discussion: "Mourning is regularly the reaction to the loss of a loved person, or to the loss of some abstraction which has taken the place of one, such as one's country, liberty, an ideal and so on."[2]

For Freud, normal mourning involves coming to terms with the reality that the lost object is no longer there. The libido (or love) attached to that object must be withdrawn so it can be free to reattach to new objects. Yet this is not a change that happens all at once. A longtime attachment to a close family member, for example, may never be fully mourned insofar as the cumulative memories associated with that person are so infinite and complex. The work of mourning involves remembering what was lost—so much of which is delegated to the unconscious—and bringing those experiences into conscious reality using the symbols of language where that object no longer exists. The more this work is completed, the more freedom the ego (our conscious, processing self) possesses to transfer libido onto other objects. A necessary and easily observable part of mourning is the inability to think of anything else but the loss. This dwelling upon the loss represents the attempts by the ego to fully realize and complete an identification with the lost object in such a way as to permanently memorialize it in the ongoing construction of personal history. In this way there is a building up of ego structure.

We can easily observe that a period of grief and mourning ensue upon the loss of a loved one, but what Freud also asserts is that loss extends even further. We also know that when Freud refers to country, liberty, and ideals, he does so in the context of surviving the ravages of the First World War in Europe. As he indicates in his short essay "On Transience," such ideals become all the stronger during the tempest of war. These ideals became symbols of great pride for his own country during the war: the beautiful countryside, buildings, works of art, and the like.[3] Such abstractions hold extraordinary power in the life of the mind. Yet not only do ideals possess the power to unite a people amidst the destruction of the world around them, but they can also inspire the formation of great societies, help us reach the pinnacle of achievement in competitive sports, build large corporations, and bring aid to millions of people across the globe. For the individual, ideals are the driving force behind everything from overcoming overwhelming odds to a lifelong work centered on some purpose. The question for this discussion, however, will be to ask ourselves, just what is involved in experiencing the loss of something abstract? Freud provides us clues, particularly in his summation of melancholia, which points to the pathological or negative side of mourning:

The distinguishing mental features of melancholia are a profoundly painful dejection, cessation of interest in the outside world, loss of the capacity to love, inhibition of all activity, and a lowering of the self-regarding feelings to a degree that finds utterance in self-reproaches and self-revilings, and culminates in a delusional expectation of punishment.[4]

Freud goes on to note that in normal mourning all the above attributes are present except for "disturbances of self-regard." Melancholia, insofar as it can be distinguished from mourning, exhibits a loss that appears trapped in the life of the mind, in a world of ideals. It can relate to the loss of a loved one by death, but also may include losses along a wider spectrum, such as someone who has been engaged to be married who is then deserted by their partner, or in a more traumatic sense, a parent who dramatically fails a child in providing necessities of love and protection. Or perhaps it is a loss of a community and the culture that bound it together.

In mourning there are feelings of ambivalence toward the object of loss. There is both the wistful longing for the lost object but also a whole personal drama of disappointment, a feeling of being slighted or neglected, and even anger and rage. In melancholia, however, the internal attachment to the lost object now becomes for the individual a foreign object, supposedly no longer one's own creation. Having perceived a slight, recriminating thoughts may quickly turn inward, attacking and blaming the internal, unconscious identification made by the ego, which permitted an attachment to the lost object in the first place. Not only is self-recrimination evident in melancholia, but there is also little concern over or even awareness in expressing the self-recrimination to others. If indeed self-derogatory statements were truly to express a humbleness, they would not be so readily offered. Instead, these statements are aimed at the lost, betraying object, and, in fact, individuals suffering in this way can make a great nuisance of themselves, seemingly able to complain without end.[5]

The psychological difference from mourning is that in

melancholia the loss is denied or not perceived or fully experienced. If the object had been loved freely, unconditionally, and without any hidden expectations in return for the love, then the individual would presumably be able to take that love and, after a time of mourning, transfer it onto a new external object. Such unconditional love is not always possible, of course, and there are usually internal connections to the love object—that is, object ideals—that were compensatory for hidden, unmet, or untempered needs and desires. The loss of an object that was artificially employed by the ego to satisfy these needs is a loss that is likewise driven into the unconscious. Freud refers to this as a loss of the ego, in contrast to the loss purely of an object of love, when he writes: "In mourning it is the world which has become poor and empty; in melancholia it is the ego itself."[6] This depletion of the ego in melancholia expresses itself in dissatisfaction, with a strong moral shading, that piles on fears of worthlessness. Instead of libido being freed to be invested in another object, it is withdrawn into an identification, a repetitive clinging, with the lost object. In *Group Psychology and the Analysis of the Ego*, Freud goes further and observes that the identification becomes what he calls an "ego ideal" that wars with the ego. The ego ideal is the lost attachment not mourned but maintained and kept artificially alive in the unconscious. In contrast to the superego, the ego ideal is likewise critical, but it is relentlessly and unjustifiably so.[7] On the one hand this battle results in the degradation of the ego, and on the other, the two may become fused in a manic triumph where there is little or no self-criticism. In a group situation, the follower assumes the part of the degraded ego, and it is the leader who embodies the overbearing ego ideal and enjoys the manic triumph and absence of self-criticism.[8]

Unlike healthy mourning, both melancholia and mania, Freud writes, "are wrestling with the same 'complex,' but in melancholia the ego has succumbed to the complex whereas in mania it has pushed it aside."[9]

As mentioned, an alternative to a melancholy of self-reproach is for the libido to turn outward into a powerful, energetic state of mania. Confronted with the inability to transfer a libidinous attachment

81

to the lost object onto another object, the ego makes a ravenous run at completely obliterating the lost object by immersing itself in some seemingly new choice. Instead of grieving over the lost object, and bringing that loss into the light of awareness, the ego goes in search of a new object, one that can be controlled, and upon which internal, unrealized libido can pivot. The fact remains, however, that there is no give and take relationship with this new object, which is an object that is completely foreign to the world of the lost object. It is like how a lover "rebounds" from a lost relationship immediately after a loss, regardless of its waywardness, and not as a new, authentic relationship.

One caveat worth mentioning is that mourning and melancholia are not mutually exclusive dynamics. Even the most healthy-minded individuals will suffer through feelings Freud attributes to the melancholic. It is also important to distinguish the general vicissitudes of overcoming loss, which play out in the life of the mind, and the struggles of those deeply mired in a pathological process of depression, which may stem from somatic causes. For the purposes of this study, while biographical analysis may touch upon the symptoms and dynamics of serious personality disturbances, deep trauma and anxiety, the concern here includes common unconscious, psychosocial challenges we all face, and which impinge upon our sense of faith and religion.

While suffering through a loss of faith may not result in serious psychological illness, there are nevertheless powerful symptoms that may occur, including depressive features. The memories and reflections on the journey of faith are often painful and reveal difficult and prolonged struggles. Having left a faith community, there is a fear of reprisal, or the reticence to face the social ostracization or stigma that has ensued, whether real or perceived. Manic and even aggressive features often emerge in the form of ideological bickering with parents or siblings. Of all the struggles, self-recrimination is perhaps the most prevalent. Freud's mention of this feature of melancholia tells us that it occurs most specifically in the case of an ideal loss.

Extending Freud's thought on mourning and ideals, we may ask the following: what more pervasive and widespread trigger might there be for self-recrimination in melancholia than a loss associated with a *religious* ideal? Consider especially the Calvinistic emphasis on total depravity; it is a doctrine that can be used to turn the ego back on the self, leveraging original sin to reinforce compliance. When one retreats from a religious community there is in essence a variety of losses. These losses include the power and force of a shared religious ideology, a shared historical identity, and a social and familial identity. People are left to their own devices, and as long as no new group force comes into play, there will always be a struggle with what was lost. Such a struggle takes on a moralistic sheen, as one might see in complaints against a condemning, authoritarian church. Over time an individual may have no engagement with communal faith what-soever and is mired in personal internal fantasies of what religion is like. As long as this is the case, the anger directed at religion is merely a manifestation of one's own lack of ego strength, a debasement, and rage against the self, or in other words, an introjection of one's sinful nature. Moreover, the more the anger is driven inside, and the more suppression there is of the desire for the love and affirmation of community, the more protection is set up against a full realization of the loss and against the possibility of any future attachment.

In modern society, as Homans has argued, there is the tendency to take loss upon the self, to internalize the causes of the loss, albeit unknowingly, without the help of the community. The responsibility of the community becomes so obscured that at times the depression that comes from loss may be classified as a medical condition. Capps argues that, in our need to free depression from social stigma and deem it solely a physiological problem, we lose the symbolic aperture of depression, that it is, to varying degrees, also a sickness of communal culture building, or a social-symbolic disease. The moral imperative would be to identify the deeper cultural pathology. Capps notes that in past centuries an individual in a melancholic state would be identified as being possessed by an evil being.[10] Today, the only forms of professionally recognized symptoms having to do with religion are those delusions of a clinically diagnosed schizophrenic or a chronically depressed person. Yet prior to the 1900s and going back throughout history, religious melancholy was a recognized subset of melancholy itself, as a distinct disease. For those today who suffer feelings of persecution, of being possessed, or that God was making them feel guilty and they had penitence to pay, we are ill equipped to dignify their experience. Helping such individuals requires creating a mourning space for their illusions to be held to the light and given the opportunity to build new personal symbolism, and hopefully transcend, not deny, their melancholy.

Freud concludes his essay by summarizing that in melancholia there is no simple relationship with the object of loss. Conflict and ambivalence complicate every aspect of the relationship. The causes of melancholia, therefore, have a much wider range than those of mourning. Freud writes:

> In melancholia, accordingly, countless separate struggles are carried on over the object, in which hate and love contend with each other; the one seeks to detach the libido from the object, the other to maintain this position of the libido against the assault.[11]

These struggles twist and turn in a never-ending series of unsatisfying internal object relations within the ego, never finding a suitable object through which they can be transmuted. External relationships, whether they are one-to-one, with significant others, or in the identification of the self with a community, are limited insofar as these internal relations are unresolved. It is for this reason that early experiences in relationships are called formative, and to them one must return, as one returns to an old and decayed, long-buried artifact, to reconstruct the past and reformulate one's understanding of it. We may likewise find that to the extent one returns to the attachments of early childhood, especially as they relate to the construction of faith and symbols of ultimacy, the better one is able to overcome the conflict and ambivalence that blocks avenues to a renewed faith in community.

Klein and the Depressive Position

Let's now turn to Melanie Klein, an Austrian-British child analyst and originator of the object relations school of psychoanalysis, to see what language her personality theory lends to a discussion of psychology and religion. Where Freud's picture of development centers on the father during the early years of life, for Klein, it begins with the mother in the first year of infancy. Well before the father becomes a significant force, the mother occupies the status as the sole source of gratification and frustration, and it is thus she who becomes the target for infantile emotions. In infancy, the child is unable to comprehend that the source of feeding, comfort, and warmth is also the same source that denies care at the onset of the desire for pleasure. The infant is unable to associate different stimuli with the same object. As a result, Klein posits that the child splits the mother by associating all that is pleasing with the "good breast" and all that is not with the "bad breast." It is the task of the mother to meet the child's needs so that the rage of frustration does not overpower the overall developmental experience. When the mother fails the infant in too many instances, the rage or imaginary attacks not only protect the child against further sensations of frustration but also impede the growth of relationship to a good and whole object. Klein calls this infantile emotional stance the "paranoid-schizoid" position, or what she elsewhere calls a transitory manic-depressive state. The infant projects its inner experience of frustration and anger outward onto the "bad" object it has imagined and splits it off from the good object that is likewise imaginary.[12]

When the normally developing infant perceives that the mother is not two persons but one, it becomes terrified and confused that the very hand that feeds it is the same one which fails to feed it. The realization that the mother who gratifies and the mother who frustrates are the same person gives the infant its first, most powerful experience with loss. No longer is that wonderful source of comfort and warmth without shortcomings, failings, and perhaps even malice. The bad or persecutory breast that the infant has invested so much energy in hating and raging against is also the very source it has idealized and loved. The infant has not only lost that sense of the ideal but also discovered that it has wished destruction on that good mother. Along with the experience of loss comes guilt and the desire to restore the good feelings or make reparation with the mother. In the work of overcoming the guilt and making reparation, the infant experiences its first feelings of sadness and the subsequent desire to restore the connection to the mother, or what Klein calls pining.

Such is the origination of Klein's theory of mourning. It begins in this early stage she terms the "infantile depressive position," where the primary task is to develop internal objects and fantasies about the mother that can incorporate both the good and the bad and ultimately, love the mother as a whole.

This deep inference about human development, which Klein makes from her clinical experiences with children and adults, offers up some simple metaphors for faith. If we can surmise that faith development begins with assigning to the holy Other all that is good, benevolent, and providential, it is then possible to see that what we carry at this early stage is merely a part object. The discovery of a holy Other that does not provide good, that allows evil, for example, forces the work of the depressive position. If our developing visions of what is ultimate are not encouraged with broader and more encompassing symbols of the holy or the divine, we might have trouble integrating the two images of both a God who provides good but sometimes does not. In such instances we are unable to experience the loss of objects of ultimacy, of what we can trust most implicitly, and are trapped in excesses of rage against such objects.

For the infant that experiences trouble working through the depressive position, Klein discusses two polar yet related defenses that come into play, "idealization" and "manic denial." Idealization serves to insulate against anxiety by creating a fantasy about the mother that is faultless and makes it unthinkable to want to destroy it. Such rage then becomes split off onto other objects or even the self. The infant sees itself as unworthy of the mother's attention in order to justify the lack of attention it is getting in the first place. Alternatively, the infant, which first becomes a child and then an adult, comes to find fault in other objects that cannot possibly take the place of the mother, even though they may be sources of sustenance and protection. Conversely, manic denial defends against depressive anxiety by denying any need for the mother by creating an internal and omnipotent scheme to control the mother, who is now an object of contempt.[13]

There are two key points for the present discussion regarding Klein's innovations beyond Freud on the subject of mourning. For Klein, she observed in the dreams and associations of her patients that the mourner is constantly susceptible to a feeling of triumph over the lost object. In the case of manic denial, such omnipotent fantasies of control over the lost object defend against the sensation of sadness and loss. Yet even in the journey of normal mourning, the feelings of hatred that the mourner had associated with the lost object will erupt in the unconscious—as a feeling of having triumphed. An acknowledgement and acceptance of these feelings gives rise to the guilt first experienced in the depressive position. Klein differs from Freud in asserting that the working through of idealization and control fantasies connected to any new loss not only recall memories of the lost object, but also reactivate the associations with the loss that were established during the infantile depressive position and then added to and modified throughout life. One's entire catalog of losses, and the ways in which they were overcome, enter the drama of mourning.[14] It is for this reason that the mourning process is so slow and painstaking, which Freud observed but could not easily explain. More than just recalling the memories of the lost person and subsequently introjecting them within the ego, mourning elicits memories of the experiences associated with loss throughout life. The usefulness of such recollection comes through piecing together the memories of how loss is overcome, how the good object is found, and creates a context for understanding new loss, which enriches the experience of loss.

Klein would call such recollecting, whether conscious or unconscious, a return to the infantile depressive position that enables the individual to find the way toward a gain in the midst of the loss. Reentering the depressive position means reactivating, through the prolonged work of mourning, the ability to discover the good internal object despite a mixture of idealistic and persecutory feelings about the loss. It means overcoming the guilt regarding the anger directed at the lost object, feeling sadness, and discovering the desire to repair the relationship. In the case of the lost object that is no longer there, it means arriving at a broader and more objective externalization, but that now there may be a possibility to find new objects onto which affections may be directed. Klein discovered that in her patients' dreams, struggles, and likes and dislikes were wishes related to parental figures, archaic experiences that the mourner goes in search of to find help with overcoming a current loss.[15] The process of mourning begins with manifestations of these deeply buried, early experiences of loss that are often too difficult to relay directly. Some psychological defenses come into play, such as self-directed anger or manic behaviors, and often impede the individual from experiencing the feeling of loss. As the mourning process continues, further emotionally difficult experiences throughout life are recalled. It is when the overcoming of these earlier losses is re-remembered or recovered, that is, the hope that comes from the possibility of reparation, that the mourner begins to shed the defenses of idealization and manic denial and recall the good and positive moments associated with the object of loss. Pining for the lost object comes to the fore, not just as sadness, but also as hope for something new. Being able to experience sadness creates the possibility for joy. The individual is once again free to experience the desire for new things, to want to go in search of new love, to create new joy that is enriched by the entire continuum of loss throughout life. Furthermore, it is in the wake of such painful times that the mourner often discovers new gifts, such as the desire to paint, write, or engage in some other creative activity. As Klein writes, and as perhaps most creative artists know, "suffering can become productive."[16] Indeed, as analyst Peter Shabad has observed, symptoms in themselves offer a creative path through which trauma may be transformed. They are "communicative actions intended to build a lasting monument for one's experience of suffering."[17]

Bearing in mind the person who has lost a strong connection to a communally defined religious life, we may ask, what process, according to Klein, might this person undertake? At first the loss should be considered one that creates a great challenge to and a large degree of confusion for the mind, as both the conscious and unconscious levels will have not yet had the chance to thoroughly perceive what has just happened. The loss is immediately followed by a period where it is not acknowledged, or even perceived. The individual simply falls away, disappears from religious life, which for him or her may have also vanished completely from everyday awareness. This is a time before one can muster any strong defenses, which no doubt takes some time to develop. Only the shock and confusion of the loss prevail.

What has been lost is *both* the relationships of the group as well as ideal attachments to the symbols the group shared. For this reason, people who have left or have been asked to leave a church community as a result of conflict often describe it as very painful. Even for members who remain, the subject of those who are no longer part of the group is a difficult and troublesome one. What makes the relationship aspect of the loss different than that of a typical mourning situation is that the individual has lost not just an existing relationship, but one that could still have corporeal potential. In the case of a lost relationship due to death, the potential for a further relationship with that person is gone. With relationships in a faith community, the impact is much more troublesome in that it represents an interpersonal failing. The expectations of the relationship were presumably unrealistic and went unmet. This failure occurred in connection to ultimate symbols, rituals, and interpretations of the meanings of religion around which the relationship was built. I believe that this one factor in the loss of faith is the most profound and debilitating and makes it psychologically more difficult to navigate than the death of a lost one. When an individual converts from one type of faith to another, by contrast, they are exchanging one set of relationships for another, which continue to meet, by and large, the same ongoing needs. Meanwhile, the change of ideology, however sharp, is not so difficult or traumatic insofar as the strong relationships are there to cement their formation.

Losing potential relationships is similar to the challenges of losing an ideal that Freud finds so closely linked to melancholia. In rejecting, or being rejected by, a faith community, one has the potential to lose so much more than in the death of a loved one. No longer will the individual have group affirmation, whether explicitly expressed within the group, or implicitly given through participation in agreed upon rituals and beliefs. It is, in essence, a crisis of identity, a breakdown of the mutual recognition between the self and the group. Only in this case, it is a crisis of ultimate symbols as they are mediated through relationships.

If indeed what happens in the initial shock of the loss is a crisis of identity, we very well might expect the arrival of certain defenses, and subsequently the blocking of an ability to return to new relationships within a faith community. Returning to Klein, the first major defense against a loss of faith would come in the form of idealization, where the individual insulates against the anxiety of the loss by creating an ideal picture of the faith community to which they once belonged. Such a defense hardly seems probable given that in many cases what we are talking about is someone who has rejected and left their faith community. Yet there is much more than meets the eye in the process of rejection. For one, the community itself could have failed the individual, having not offered a sufficiently cohesive and personally supportive environment. In such cases it is not surprising that among what seems to be a rejection of a faith community there is nevertheless a very real, albeit unconscious, pining for some group entity of spiritual support. Moreover, inherent in any rejection is not just a reaction *against*, but a hope *for*. An idealized fantasy of the lost community exists even in rejection, which is usually completed only with great effort. In the idealization, however unconscious and powerful, the individual insulates him or herself against the anxiety of the loss by constructing an idolatrous image of the faith community as faultless and beyond reproach, or alternatively, as hypocritical and autocratic. The person who has fallen away fails to develop and find comfort in direct, clear observations about what was wrong with their former faith community. Yet the sense of loss is still there, and the anger and rage that results from the inability to reconnect becomes split off onto other objects.

The stricter the faith community and the narrower the worldview, and the more demands that are made upon the believer to be subsumed to the external authority, the more likely any rejection of that community and subsequent unconscious idealization will result in turning that anger upon the ego. As Freud would indicate, regarding mourning an ideal, it is not the world that has become colorless, but the ego itself. The libido that needs to find new external objects for ultimacy and faith remains unrealized and unfulfilled. The ego turns this energy back onto itself in the form of self-hatred. Such self-recrimination becomes a pervasive and ongoing theme, albeit unknowingly, all in the name of distancing oneself from the ideal faith which cannot be attained. Without an ability to engage and even confront the people and beliefs of their former faith community, such an individual is easily seen by those of the former community and even him or herself as spiritually immature, when in actuality he or she is dealing with an inner chaos—and the promise of a reborn life of faith—that the uncritical believer may not appreciate. Nevertheless, there is truth in the accusation of immaturity because the idealization defense not only guards against the anxiety of the loss but also blocks any new growth beyond the loss.

Along with idealization in the estranged believer we also find the psychological defense of manic denial. In such instances the need for a belief in God or community of believers is perhaps adamantly eschewed. Objects of ultimate concern are unconsciously withdrawn, and the individual consciously considers themselves independent from any expressed belief system or group. When Klein speaks of omnipotent control, the infant has taken the good mother into the ego and created an internal object that can be controlled at will and whenever the infant so chooses. However, when this happens the infant cuts itself off from the chance to experience external warmth and potentially even physical nourishment. For the adult who has internalized and created ultimate imagoes that are strictly internal, he or she likewise commits the self to independence from others, a seeming triumph of the ego, and subsequently a reliance on personal and private experience as the sole authority. External manifestations of ultimacy become objects of rage and contempt, over which a victory has been gained. Manic denial in this case leaves a person in a poverty of symbols and in a state of increasing meaninglessness as he or she withdraws further and further into a triumphant yet necessarily isolated internality. Ironically, a parallel process can be seen even among the most pious and fundamentalist believer. Just the same as the atheistic choice involves an omnipotent control over internal imagoes and contempt over external representations of those imagoes, so with the fundamentalist there is an internal, unilateral control over faith imagoes, often achieved by stripping them of their complexity and reducing them to mere propositional statements and codes of behavior. Such internality, especially when accentuated by an acute sense of sinfulness and shame, cuts such a believer off from a dynamic relationship with those symbols as well as the relationships that help define and mediate them. For both the adamant nonbeliever and strident believer, external manifestations of religion are carefully controlled and constricted to only those forms that comply with a certain ethos and will easily turn a derisive eye toward all other forms. It is a part-object theology, or part-object atheology, lacking any generosity toward inclusivity.

For those who have left a faith community, there is often a flight into unbelief, or expressed atheism. Whatever the external label we may apply, there are certain observations we may make. Such a person becomes withdrawn because of having lost a sense of belonging. Life becomes a lonely, individual pursuit, with challenges of forever clinging to the internal ideal of the group and an inability to find a place in any new group that measures up to the ideal. Ironically, in the very midst of the withdrawal, there is rage, directed at the ideal group, which acts as a block to participation in other groups, or at least similar groups. Moreover, the individual's ideal of the group remains static while the original group may indeed change over time. The rage, therefore, is against the unconscious, internal object created to represent the group.

In the application to the person who has rejected an absolutist group, we may infer that the loss will entail more than what one might experience after having lost a healthy group environment. Just as the person who has trouble leaving an abusive relationship has little psychic structure to use in a forward progression, so does the person who is attempting to shed a restrictive group has little usable internal objects to form new group relations.[18] We may conclude that the process of withdrawal and rage will be all the more accentuated when the individual protests against the manipulative elements of the faith community and attempts to find new primary identifications.

This component of anger and rage in mourning a loss of religion, however, must not be taken too lightly. We must resist the temptation to label atheism or outspoken bitterness toward organized religion as a mere stage of an immature faith, or as a posture that has not been able to enter into mourning. For Klein, rage is a necessary part of the process of dealing with loss and reactivating the depressive position. Too much repression of anger merely blocks any chance for the motivating guilt that leads to making the necessary reparation to the lost object. British analyst John Bowlby joins Klein in emphasizing that aggression is a necessary part of healthy mourning. When aggression is conscious rather than displaced, repressed, disassociated, or turned against the ego, it can be the first step in recognizing the true nature of what has been lost. Where Klein views aggression as a result of an inborn contempt, paranoia, and desire for triumph over the object, however, Bowlby views it as merely a natural reproach and protest for having been abandoned by the object. For Klein, it is the guilt that motivates one to repair the relationship through identification. But for Bowlby, aggression need not arouse guilt if the object, whether internal or external, can receive the attack and protest without retaliation. Anger toward the lost object is a sign of an objective relation, and neither an idealization nor a withdrawal.

Guilt comes into play only as a neurotic phenomenon, according to Bowlby, when such feelings of rage are not accepted either by the self or by others. If the anger and aggressive affect can be expressed without undo censure, retaliation, or fear of retribution, it will subside and the ability to experience the sadness and pining of loss will open the door to healthy mourning.[19]

In dealing with a loss of faith, Bowlby's observations imply that mourning such a loss will indeed contain components of anger, and that normal mourning will not take place until that anger is given expression. For Klein, the anger arises from the existential world of bad objects, wrought from trauma, which are seeded early in life and necessarily lead to guilt, and the guilt to pining and reparation. By contrast, while such pathology is a part of every individual to varying degrees, Bowlby states that anger at a loss also involves a protest over abandonment, and whether that protest is met with grace and mercy, theologically speaking.

To summarize what we learn from Klein's object relations theory, we may surmise that the individual must work through relations to various bad objects, experience guilt, and seek reparation, but along the way discover acceptance. After having wrestled with defenses of idealization and denial, and discovering anger, the individual will likewise pull out of not only the loss they feel most acutely, but also go in search of the good, repaired objects that were the result of losses throughout life, and particularly from early life. These objects were the result of the most primary experiences of the good mother—the infant's first experiences with ultimacy—and of the father, the young child's most significant encounters with power and morality. First experiences with community, such as in the nuclear and extended family, and the symbols they hold dear, and first experiences with ritual in a communal setting, will become necessary to the rebuilding process. When the individual reactivates the experience of overcoming loss in earlier life, they create an avenue to work through the current loss. At this stage they are able to objectify it, memorialize what was good, diffuse anger and triumphalism, denial and self-deprecation, and regain a fondness for the lost object. For the person who has fallen away from a faith community and its ideals, this means allowing the anger to dissipate and finding a way to remember these imagoes with kindness, joy, and love, even if it is no longer possible to enjoy the same life of faith in the form it took previously. Sadness then becomes possible, and a pining for something good replaces anger. Finally, in the ability to feel the sadness, free of antipathy or idealization, comes the opportunity to introject the lost object, own it, love it with detachment, and go in search of new objects onto which hope and desire may be placed.

The Kleinian Approach to Groups

The leaders and followers that make up a group all use and often exploit individual psychological needs. The shift away from Freud's drive theory to a focus on relationships consequently brings us to the arena of group psychology. Freud's approach to group psychology extends from the Oedipal metaphor. In *Totem and Taboo*, for example, he outlines an argument that begins with the conflict of the primal horde, that is, the competition between the brothers, and between the brothers and the male patriarch, for the women of the horde. Out of their jealousy and anger toward the father, the brothers band together to destroy him. Yet in the aftermath of their triumph, which includes a cannibalistic incorporation of the father, guilt motivates them to honor the father with a totemic representation. This totem, along with ensuing rituals and taboos or prohibitions, brings the controlling authority of the father symbolically into the present. In place of a continual killing of the father, other ritual sacrifices are made, and rites are completed, which also have the effect of quelling restlessness in the group.

Although we may not need to take this fundamental phase of human behavior literally as the beginning of all group relations, Freud would most certainly have us take it seriously as a metaphor. In particular, the inferences about the primal horde offer an outright if not perhaps altogether disturbing iconoclasm, which was clearly Freud's intent. Likewise, his much later discussion in *Civilization and Its*

Discontents positions group morality as a collective superego that counters and maintains control over libidinous drives. The rules of society are a necessary evil, as in the case of religion, which serves the purpose of providing cosmological structure and comfort. Alternatively, civilization can also be the place where conscious reasoning comes to the fore. Instead of acting as an authoritative superego, it can be the reasoning ego, and subsequently the hope of Enlightenment rationalism in which Freud was so clearly invested.

The groundwork Freud lays allows us to see the dynamic of love and hate within all group participation, and how that dynamic is mitigated, matriculated, and manipulated. Although Klein makes no direct application of her theory to group behavior, various social theorists have seen the value of the bipolar dynamics of group participation.[20] Klein's unique contribution introduces the idea of a continuing stream of internal objects onto which the ego attaches libidinous drives that give rise to love and hate, idealization, and contempt, beginning with the mother and continuing to Oedipal conflict and beyond. The group environment provides yet one more set of objects with which unconscious feelings of satisfaction and frustration come into play. The group that is loved is also the group that is hated. It demands that group members learn to respond reparatively to their individual feelings and come to see the group as not perfect yet serving an important, vital purpose. Without a way to bring together both the good and the bad, and to consciously assert the self within the group as an independent evaluator of its relation to the group, the ego relinquishes its role and allows the self to be absorbed into the group. Conversely, the ego clings exclusively to its internal objects and feels rejected by the group. The real danger—and point of psychological malaise—in any total acquiescence to or rejection of the group lies in the aftermath of idealization and manic denial. Having severed any view of culpability and responsibility of the individual's participation within the group, the individual's rage, contempt, or frustration with the group's failures become transferred onto external threats. The targets of such contempt often take the form of individuals or groups outside the group. Contempt also and perhaps more frequently manifests in anger toward other group members, due in large part to proximity, just as a married couple might bicker or siblings fight. Patricia Davis, a pastoral theologian, offers us an example of Kleinian group analysis in her study of James Dobson, the psychologist and evangelical radio personality, and his view of women. Dobson's picture of women, Davis contends, is schizoid, separating them into good ones who stay at home with their children and live in submission to their husbands, and bad ones who work, refuse to have children, despise those who do, and hate God and religion. Dobson, on the one hand, advocates that women, through their work in laying the foundations of love and care in their children, play a crucial role in the furtherance of a moral, civilized society. Yet on the other hand he concludes from this premise that it is only the mother who can provide such nurturance and that the mother's place is solely in the home. In response to a woman who once complained to him about a system that "saddles" women with all the menial tasks of childrearing with no help from her spouse, Dobson writes, "But that's the way the system works."[21] Dobson overlooks the mothering role of the father, even at the earliest stages of life, and instead takes a heavy-handed argument against women who work and decide not to have children.[22] In Davis's view, Dobson is simultaneously activating deep passions about teaching children strong values through motherhood and also leveraging Kleinian ambivalence about mothers by splitting them into two very different kinds of mothers. Dobson's alarmist and paranoid tone about feminists who scorn motherhood and the "traditional concept of femininity" belie an unfounded persecutory fear, one that activates in his radio audience rage against the bad mother.

A sociological way of looking at Davis's argument is to ask whether Dobson's duality between the idealized Christian mother and demonized feminist is a refusal to face social realities. For many families, the need for two incomes is often a necessity. Whether that is a consequence of a cost of living driven too high by a rootless, consumerist society, or by genuine economic challenges, the hardship for some families is real. Returning to the arguments of Peter Homans, we are led to wonder whether the splitting of women—with at least some measure of veiled rage and contempt—is not a refusal, and perhaps a patriarchal one at that, to face the reality of a lost common culture. As Karl Figlio would argue, following Klein, leaders such as Dobson seek a "feeling of certainty [that] is driven by the need to get to the root of the object in order to secure itself against loss—against depressive anxiety."[23] What we may conclude is that a religious group can, though not necessarily will, take advantage of and form its existence on a defense against the world of bad objects. Such a conclusion supports a key emphasis of this current discussion that overcoming a loss of faith is not merely a matter of working through personal idealizations and denials, but also overcoming unhealthy blocks to growth that are codified and reinforced by a socio-cultural milieu. If a religious leader such as Dobson were to turn his efforts to the social challenges families face, then implicit in such efforts might be a recognition of the losses of the family unit, a healthy mourning of it, and the ability to reparatively pine for that lost social object.

This reparative action is indeed the work this study suggests is necessary for the person who is overcoming a loss of a faith community. Overcoming such loss means breaking free from a group that refuses to assume the depressive position and plays upon fears and even idealizes a lost past. An example comes in the form of the best-selling historical fiction marketed to evangelical Christian readers from authors such as Janette Oke, Gilbert Morris, and the Amish stories of Beverly Lewis. One does not have to work too hard to find present day conservative evangelical sensibilities, such as the traditional submissive female archetype Dobson advocates, being superimposed on a fictional colonial or a frontier America setting. Another area of books come from the "dominion theology" or Christian nationalist movement of recent decades, whose proponents overlay contemporary, conservative evangelical theology on the founding of America. Indulgence in such idealized images of the past reinforces the "depravity" of our world today and becomes a compulsion that makes it impossible for any new collective psychic structure to develop, that is, the ability to recognize and experience the losses of our world, discover sadness, and do the creative work of mourning.

Winnicott: Object Survival, Concern, and Transitional Phenomena

D. W. Winnicott, a protégé of Melanie Klein, stood within the British school of object relations theory. Like Klein, Winnicott believed in the decisive importance of early childhood development. He furthered the idea that what a child fundamentally seeks is a relationship that can contain and hold instinctual wishes, rather than to fully realize them. We are primarily relational beings, and it is through relationships that we establish the symbols—in what Winnicott calls the transitional space—for extending those relationships into wider and wider spheres.

Although Winnicott does not explore the topic of mourning directly, he most certainly presumes the developmental principle of it in his work. Winnicott's paper, "The Manic Defense" elaborates on Klein's concept of mania where avoidance of feelings of emptiness and sadness is possible with the creation of fantasies of elation and joy—as a facsimile of true happiness.[24] When Winnicott observed the daydreams of his patients and their implied or explicitly expressed wishes, he saw a connection between the amount of omnipotent control expressed in those fantasies and the degree of trauma suffered in the internal milieu of good and bad objects. A relationship to an external object is used in the manic defense, but is ultimately unsatisfying, as the capacity for object love is underdeveloped or in disarray. Mourning cannot be experienced until wishes of destruction are made available to the ego that can then objectify bad internalizations, let go of obsessive externalizations, and be liberated to go in search of good internal and subsequently external objects.

Winnicott briefly elaborates on a handful of characteristics of the manic defense, which lend clarity to the dynamics of mourning faith. The characteristics include: 1) the denial of inner reality, which is only clinically observable as the elation that is related to the denial; 2) flight to external reality from internal reality, such as the person "who exploits every possible aspect of sexuality and sensuality;" 3) holding inner reality in suspended animation, in which inner bad objects are controlled and dealt with yet never confronted or overcome, thus preventing the formation of new relationships; and 4) denial of the sensations of depression through seeking their opposites—for example, movement, humor, and harmony when it would be more appropriate to recognize and confront the stillness, seriousness, and discord.[25]

Winnicott makes several additional remarks that are provocative for understanding the person who is caught in an absolutist religiosity, such as the conservative fundamentalist who strives for "God's glory," when he writes:

> It is just when we are depressed that we *feel* depressed. It is just when we are manic-defensive that we are *least likely to feel* as if we are defending against depression. At such times we are more likely to feel elated, happy, busy, excited, humorous, omniscient, "full of life," and at the same time we are less interested in serious things and in the awfulness of hate, destruction, and killing.[26]

If the absolutist stance is more than just a developmental stage of faith, as I have argued, and is instead a reaction to the lack of communal connections and loss of shared symbols, and if it is marked by an unnatural sense of joy—to the extent that one feels social pressure to join in such joy whether it is genuinely shared or not—then it is fair to surmise that such a stance is an elaborately encoded, jointly invested denial of sadness. To the absolutist of whatever stripe, for example, it would seem impossible that sacred texts that encourage love, togetherness, and strength of character are the same texts that should also acknowledge despair and sadness.

Further along in "The Manic Defense," Winnicott clarifies for us that denial not only causes avoidance of the bad but a devaluation of anything good coming from the self. There is the artist who feels as though a picture were painted by someone else living inside of them.

More to the point, there is the religious person who attributes good that has come from them as coming solely from God.[27] Not taking credit for one's contributions can go too far and can become prohibitive to developing individual potential. In a group setting, the individual may disavow their individuality for the sake of the group, which may be more interested in exploitation, distortion, and control, rather than encouraging the strengths of the individual. For the person transitioning out of such a group, as in the case of the absolutist religious group, it can be difficult to reestablish self-agency and individuality. Being able to challenge, question, and encourage change to the ideas about a deity and the values and mores surrounding it would require tremendous ego strength. Membership in an absolutist group conditions a certain self-distrust. In the case of Protestant fundamentalism, strong emphasis is placed on humanity's ultimately sinful and depraved nature, that nothing good can come of our lives. It places a strong emphasis on the sinfulness of pride, leaving little room for taking satisfaction in the fruits of one's own labors.

Winnicott makes an additional observation within this paper that Christian symbolism and rituals surrounding Good Friday, the crucifixion, and resurrection, contain a strong "depressive-acensive" significance. By this he means that there is an interplay between bad and good—in other words, between a death instinct and a libidinal drive, or between withdrawal and relationship—that allows good to prevail. The Easter customs enact on a grand scale the titanic inner battle between good and bad objects. The remembrance of Christ's death indeed can include much opportunity for the worshiper to experience sadness, despair, and loss. There is even room for anger and confusion over feelings of abandonment, even from Jesus' own lips in the last moments of the crucifixion story. The ensuing celebration surrounding the triumph over death represents a transformation of the loss into a gain, particularly in the significance of Jesus' fleeting reappearances and then also the Pentecost, the moment when the spirit of God descends and bestows gifts. It is interesting to note—and here I am speaking from personal experience—that in American

Protestant fundamentalism, there is a neglect of the depressive or decensive aspect of this ritual. Compared to Roman Catholicism, for example, nondenominational, grassroots Protestant communities in particular offer little ritual or ceremonial elaboration on the decensive importance of Good Friday; instead, the splendor and glory of bodily resurrection gets all the attention. It comes as no surprise, then, that many who leave such communities have often found solace and meaning in a comparatively more elaborate ritual structure, which more clearly articulates both decensive and acensive dynamics.[28]

Winnicott merely reminds us that the reenactment of the depressive-acensive dynamic is an important psychological aspect of ritual symbolism, and it raises questions about any experience of religion that might neglect this dynamic. In the case of the person removed from an absolutist milieu, for example, the experience of sorrow and gloom may awaken a less narcissistic, less anthropomorphized, and even stronger, more robust identification with the Christ figure. The focus changes from a celebration of a bodily resurrection and triumphant ascension, to objectifying the loss, making reparations, and gaining a stronger understanding of Christlikeness that no longer requires the actual person of Jesus to develop and grow. Without a capacity to experience sadness, there has not been an assimilation of the guilt for complicity in the persecution of the savior. To the extent that any new community of faith can dramatize this dynamic, it will likely be better equipped to answer the needs of the person seeking a reengagement with practicing religion.

What we find in Winnicott is not only an amplification of the dynamics of good and bad objects, and the repetition of denial, omnipotent fantasy, and withdrawal, but also an elaboration on the ways in which mourning creates the impetus for hope, overcoming, creativity, and play. Klein asserts that in the process of normal mourning, the individual goes through a process of rage toward the lost object and takes hold of past feelings of destruction wished upon the lost object, which have now found expression. Once recognized, there is the motion to make reparation, once and for all, and a resultant sense of pining for the lost object; that is, the desire to somehow restore it, not as a narcissistic or idolatrous identification, but as a useful outgrowth of understanding and wisdom born of experience, one that is connected to the earliest and utmost feelings of love and hope. However, like Bowlby, Winnicott puts it slightly differently, but in such a way that further enables us to identify the internal journey of faith. Three concepts put forward by Winnicott are applicable to the discussion of mourning as a developmental process: object survival, the capacity for concern, and the transitional object.[29]

In "The Use of an Object and Relating Through Identifications," Winnicott makes a frank admission that one of the most valuable lessons he learned as a psychoanalytic psychotherapist was to simply weather the transferential storms of his patients. If he responded to anger and misgivings with clever interpretations, an experience of abandonment would ensue rather than an experience of a "holding environment" in which the analysand may work through the anger and allow it to dissipate. Only once the destruction of the analyst, as a representation of internal objects, has been attempted can there be the chance for the analysand to see that objects may survive. It is as if the analysand says, "Hullo object! I destroyed you. I love you. You have value for me because of your survival of my destruction of you."[30] It is at this point the analyst has been placed outside of the analysand's world of omnipotent control, and room is provided for new knowledge of the analyst.

Winnicott theorizes differently from the Kleinian view by saying that the object is not reconstituted solely based on reparation of guilt, which is more internal, but by the simple survival of the now better recognized and externally understood object.[31] This is what Winnicott sets as the goal of therapy: for the patient to be able to *use* the therapist. The destruction plays a part in making reality, and the patient's ability to create this reality is dependent upon the therapist's capacity to survive. Aggression in classic psychoanalytic theory is thought of as something that must be replaced by conscious reasoning in the face of the reality principle. By contrast, Winnicott asserts that aggression, or rather the wish for the destruction of the figure that represents the thwarting of libidinal impulse, is the very impulse necessary for coming into relationship with reality. Unconscious associations to certain objects must be allowed vigorous expression in the realm of everyday relationships for the individuals in those relationships to experience love. According to Winnicott:

> Without the experience of maximum destructiveness (object not protected) the subject never places the analyst outside and therefore can never do more than experience a kind of self-analysis, using the analyst as a projection of the self. . . . [T]he patient may even enjoy the analytic experience but will not fundamentally change.[32]

This letting out of anger directed at the analyst within a safe space such as the psychotherapeutic environment constitutes an attempt to create and objectify reality. Without such expression, the analysand may never learn to use the analyst, and the treatment may go on interminably. If the therapist can limit the individual's attempt to control and manipulate without losing the rapport that has been established, and resist rushing treatment, then there stands the chance for initiative and growth.

In the realm of religion, similar anger dynamics work on the content of faith. An absolutist experience of religion often includes a humbleness and politeness that acts as a smooth veneer covering and containing any possibility for anger and initiative directed at ultimate objects. The same veneer also acts as a shield against the pressures and contours of outward reality. Such a hard-shell religiosity nevertheless indicates a repetitive-compulsive faith turned in upon itself, occupied with uncritical, omnipotent self-projection that is never satisfied. There is indeed an anger, but it is kept unconscious and only finds its way out in uncontrolled outbursts. Such a covering of civility is far from enabling a facilitating environment and affords little room for doubt that springs from letdowns and disillusionments. The resulting anger toward symbols of ultimacy and those who promulgate tightly managed sets of symbols finds few avenues for expression.

If, however, the anger that results from the clash with externality may also and especially be directed at symbols like God, the church community, and even the cross—and these symbols and people survive the anger—then a larger, more potent, more objective view of religion becomes possible. For anyone experiencing a decentering of religious life, such feelings of anger permeate any new attempts to reengage participatory religion, particularly if it is near to one's original tradition. Winnicott would not necessarily encourage the expression of such anger, but instead create an environment for those struggling to reengage religion where the crushing power of absolutism—such as biblical literalism, eschatological exclusivity, and the hammer of original sin—can be evaluated critically, even disparagingly. Such disparagements would not, however, be commended by the facilitator.

The second Winnicottian concept regarding mourning can be found in "The Development of the Capacity for Concern," which discusses the observation that if guilt can be tolerable and containable, it will form a capacity for concern in the relationship with the significant object.[33] On the one hand, guilt born of unconscious wishes of aggression may, as in the manic defense, be driven back upon the denigrated ego, or it may manifest in even greater aggression and projective retaliation. If, however, in the clinical situation, guilt can be "held" or "mothered," it will become a catalyst for the perception of the loss of the idealized object and bridge the gap between infantile gratification and broadened reengagement with the other. The goal of clinical work is to encourage the individual to discover awareness of their own aggressions and even better, the guilt that they feel over their desire to lash out and hurt others. If they can indeed make their guilt conscious, it will result in their own ability to elicit feelings of concern for others.

Thirdly, and most importantly, Winnicott's most provocative contribution for the discussion of mourning, and for the combined fields of psychology and religion, is his concept of transitional phenomena. Beginning in early childhood, Winnicott observes that objects such as a stuffed animal or the corner of a blanket become substitutes for the mother's breast. He places these objects "inside, outside, at the border,"[34] as neither internal nor external, but at a borderline between the two. Such objects represent both the solidifying internal representations of externality as well as the external objects themselves. Transitional objects occupy what Winnicott calls the "potential space" that becomes the arena for the interplay of subject and object. Psychological health is dependent upon the individual's entry into this "intermediate zone," with confidence that he or she will creatively find new, interesting, even fun ways of engaging subject and object.[35] A playful, game-like balance is struck where the subject *finds* the object, or the subject is *found by* the object. As a both/and dynamic, the transitional space allows for both the feeling of being cared for and the feeling of ownership and proficiency.

While the language of mourning does not explicitly find its way into Winnicott's discussion of transitional phenomena, he does observe that over time the transitional object serves its purpose of helping build the internal, mothering fantasies of the child. The experience of separation, and the momentary loss of symbiotic union, creates distress within the infant as the image of the mother fades. The mother that returns in a reasonable amount of time relieves and mends the stress.[36] Throughout childhood development, the parental task is not just a matter of providing nourishment at the appropriate times, but to do so within the time frame that the child can tolerate—to do so in such a way as to not overestimate the child's ability to sustain the symbiotic fantasy, and the ability to create transitional phenomena. In this sense, mourning begins as soon as the distress sets in, yet is not quite overpowering. Mourning is built upon the trust and confidence that the lost object can be creatively sustained in fantasy.

When the mother does not return and mend the distress, however, the child experiences trauma, an anxiety that thwarts the possibilities for play and creativity surrounding the loss. Such trauma marks the point at which the ego, lacking enough good internal objects, begins the process of turning the needs for relation back upon itself. Instead of extending and elaborating the transitional phenomena, trauma results in the creation of defensive mechanisms, and the result is objects that become rigid, compulsory, and unusually driven. Existentially speaking, the experience of trauma is unavoidable. Mourning, then, becomes not just a linear developmental task, but rather an ever-present tool for overcoming trauma through creating more elaborate and highly developed representations of both the inner and outer worlds.

For Winnicott, healthy living, vitality, and joy come from the ongoing ability to find adaptive representations, that is, playful, exciting uses of objects that mediate between subjectivity and objectivity. While in childhood they may begin with a favored toy or blanket, in adulthood they extend to music, art, and in an ultimate sense, religion, which composes a whole cultural field of transitional phenomena. These creative objects serve as vehicles for overcoming loss, finding understanding, momentary release, and reengagement with whatever new realities emerge.

A characteristic of transitional phenomena that Winnicott identifies and that brings additional focus to this discussion is that the phenomena themselves need not be mourned. Instead, during normal development they are replaced with stronger encapsulations and broader representations:

> It is fate to be gradually allowed to be decathected, so that in the course of years it becomes not so much forgotten as relegated to limbo. By this I mean that in health the transitional object does not "go inside" nor does the feeling about it necessarily undergo repression. It is not forgotten and is not mourned. It loses meaning, and this is because the transitional phenomena have become diffused, have become spread out over the whole intermediate territory between "inner psychic reality" and "the external world as perceived by two persons in common," that is to say, over the whole cultural field.[37]

It is important to note that symbols themselves, Winnicott would argue, need not be mourned. Winnicott's theory suggests that what must be mourned is the object of loss that symbols represent. Thus far I have been suggesting that the language of mourning offers strong insights into the dynamics of those who have lost their religion and have fallen away from a faith community. So much of the experience of losing one's religion resonates with psychoanalytic observations of mourning: it is a painstaking process; and there is denial, anger, self-recrimination, even depression or, conversely, mania. The lost religion may at first seem to be the very object that must be mourned. The concept of God or certain creeds and ritual observances are what people often point to when they account for what has been lost, what they are reacting against, or what they wish to somehow reclaim. However, Winnicott's observations would suggest that it is not these objects themselves that must be mourned. Rather, it is the loss of the link between symbolic objects and the ideals and relationships they represent. Relationships, social structure, and a broader environment that creates for the individual identity and purpose are what must be mourned and created anew. When the world in which the individual resides does not measure up to the ideal of the "good enough mother," the potential space of symbolic life suffers. For the individual on a journey to reengage a participatory faith, he or she must start the task of meaningful social integration. The pain of the loss is not caused by the symbols themselves—the words, objects, and rituals—but by the connection to the worlds with which one must interact in the use of such symbols. Sadness over losing the rich traditions of the past is the manifest content of the symptoms of loss. Such traditions may indeed be carried over into the future, but they will by necessity be changed, perhaps not strictly in form, but certainly in the meanings conveyed.

Without question, the loss involved in losing religion is very much one of losing an ideal, in contrast to the palpable and immediate loss of a close loved one. It is an ideal formed through years of identity shaping, interactions with others, and is ingrained in the very language one is accustomed to hearing and using. Such loss is difficult to identify. One may be removed from a community that encouraged a certain set of religious ideals, and that loss may seem concrete and specific. Yet the ultimate nature of religion dictates that the symbols of faith should be transferable from one situation to the next. For the person who is reentering a faith community, for example, there may be a great deal of confusion as a process begins of realigning the meanings of certain symbols. The previous use of these symbols somehow no longer seems to apply. They may seem at best ineffective, or at worst incorrect and even harmful. Such a realignment seems painstaking and slow, and it will bring with it all the characteristics of mourning. Yet, as we learn from Winnicott, the attachments to these symbols are more properly understood as attachments to the people, situations, and environment that are no longer useful as associations around ultimacy. One may cling desperately to a ritual object of some form that seemingly does not provide a sense of integration, but it is the ideal objects of the former self and the relationships that created the attachment to the ritual object that are of concern. Whether we are speaking of those who have transitioned from an absolutist faith to something more flexible, or more broadly of someone who has lost the significance of symbols that have become outdated through the gradual passage of time, it is the self attachments that need to be mourned, not the transitional phenomena themselves. It is not, for example, the contents of faith that people ultimately become angry at or despondent over, but rather the world of experience that surrounded those contents that is no longer alive.

Play, Creativity, and Religious Imagination

Having established the ideas of object survival, the capacity for concern, and transitional objects within the object-relations approach to the life of faith, we now can bring added emphasis to one of the core characteristics of Winnicott's theory: play and creativity. As the primary goal of this study is to identify key psychodynamic elements involved in the resolution of struggle in the life of faith, then Winnicott's observations on the role of play and creativity helps us set our sights on the ways of healthy religiosity. Such a discussion brings us to what can be considered the positive, upbeat spirit in Winnicott's writings, something often seen missing in seminal psychoanalytic theorists. Epistemologically speaking, what Winnicott offers on play and creativity creates serious problems for hastily made accusations about psychological reductionism and functionalism. Winnicott is a psychoanalyst and psychotherapist and has very little in his writings to offer beyond that professional experience. And yet in reading him, one finds a sense of trust in and respect for symbolic life, as expressed both individually and collectively.

Play for Winnicott is not merely another avenue into the unconscious, that is, material that may be used by an analyst for interpretation. He writes, "Psychotherapy has to do with two people playing together."[38] Play is the goal of therapy, and only in playing is therapy possible. Interpretations and observations, classically and prescriptively understood, are secondary to establishing a world of play in the clinical situation. If play can be established—and sometimes that is the initial and solitary goal of therapy—new personal and shared symbols may emerge that bring order and meaning to the disorder and meaninglessness of inner life.

Winnicott says that play, like transitional phenomena, occurs neither exclusively inside nor outside, but instead occupies the potential space between baby and mother, or subject and object. In play, the two are merged in such a way that it is exciting, contains the possibility of surprise, and is dependent upon the trust and confidence that the participants each will take part as agreed upon. In the case of the infant-mother dyad, it is the mother's job of "making actual what the baby is ready to find."[39] The mother, while keeping the infant's frustration at a tolerable level, allows for the emergence of transitional phenomena, whether sucking the thumb, playing with a toy, or discovering new sounds. Successful play with various phenomena is indicated by the ability for the object to be "repudiated, reaccepted, and perceived objectively."[40] Play is precarious in that it must provide the experience of omnipotent control but not so much that it shuts out all relating to external objects. Likewise, external objects must not overpower internal ones. It is in the interplay, the give and take of meanings, that both the subject and the object create mutually beneficial meaning. This interplay is the primary parental responsibility, as well as the task of the therapist and, in an ultimate sense, the work of religion. During child development, it becomes important to be able to "be alone in the presence of someone," namely, being able to establish an experience of play based on the assumption that the reliable other will participate in the play, regardless of whether the other is there. Being able to maintain a psychic space of one's own requires creating degrees of internal play and learning a level of independence. In addition, children will develop a "capacity to like or dislike the introduction of ideas that are not their own."[41] In this sense, the child is encouraged to become an individual, with a critical capacity that becomes necessary for more and broader forms of play. Again, play is not beholden to the subject's sense of omnipotence, nor is it under exclusive control of the external object.

Play does not occur without much practice. Playing is "spontaneous and not compliant or acquiescent," and, as mentioned, it is intensely exciting, and "cannot be easily left, nor easily admit intrusions."[42] Play requires a necessary amount of exclusive attention, of total absorption of consciousness. In the therapeutic situation, creating an exciting game of meaning making—however challenging that might be—brings about healing.

To this game of meaning making, however, I would offer a point of clarification that Winnicott seems to imply elsewhere but ignores in his discussions about play. If playing means entering a potential space to bring meaning to unconscious pressures and chaos, it will indeed be intense and exclusive, and yet it will also at some point run its course or serve its purpose. There will be the denouement, the end of the game, closure, and clinically speaking, termination. Winnicott himself alludes to this when he discusses the "significant moment" when the child surprises him or herself.[43] Here the psychoanalytic interpretation becomes secondary and is guided not by what the play reveals but rather by what new ego strength or understanding it inspires. Without this sense of surprise and discovery, interpretation merely becomes—to use Winnicott's word—

indoctrination. In the case of the individual who has not yet achieved play, interpretation may only cause confusion, that is, it makes illegitimate the objects that are brought to the play, and introduces new objects that are not legitimate, and cannot be reasonably shared except through coercion.

Turning attention to the life of faith, play likewise becomes a critical component. From one person's cultural viewpoint, the rituals of another culture may seem foreign and absurd, perhaps even childish and silly—and vice versa. Yet such rituals are enacted with the utmost seriousness. The clue to the difference in such perceptions is the element of play. Knowing the rules of the game, so to speak, means discovering the ultimate meanings attached to certain observances and symbols. While the physical components may seem vastly different from culture to culture, or era to era, the psychological components are the same. Play and creativity become a question of how the physical symbols mediate between the objects of the inner world, the shared objects of the community, and the environment in which that individual and the community live. The symbols that fill the potential space are transitional phenomena and are powerful only as they can be suspended from linear reality and enact allegiances and centers of value in a widening sphere where everyone can be included. This requires increasingly elaborate forms of play, and a rich creation of rules and guidelines, such that the feeling of ultimacy, or individual omnipotence, is given its due and yet is not allowed to overpower the same in others. If such mediation breaks down, it becomes rigid and exclusive. The rules become inflexible and distorted and fail to consider the particularities of its participants. Teaching starts to sound more like propaganda rather than the sharing of wisdom and understanding.

Religion that becomes organized and institutionalized is always in danger of losing play and creative imagination. One does not have to think too hard of instances and experiences where religion in our world today or in history becomes absolutist and ignores the playful, dramatic, and interactive dynamics of faith. If we now live in a time of a lack of common culture, and must meet the challenge of rapid change, pluralism, and technology, the question that must be raised whether are we responding well to such a loss, and in which circumstances does this response become rigid on a macro scale, thereby causing trauma on a micro, individual level? On one hand, we can look to the seeker-oriented, protean impulse and see how it might become so enamored by individual choice and the addiction to experiencing that it becomes, ironically, its own rigidity. On the other hand, we can observe that the fundamentalist or conservative evangelical hunkers down and attempts to hold on to what are considered clear and matter-of-fact forms of faith that are clearly fetishes and idolatries. In certain forms of Protestantism, one finds a deep aversion to symbolic play, a suspicion of art and, as mentioned earlier, an incapacity for the decensive aspects—or the pathos—of biblical narrative.

When someone is raised as a child in an absolutist mindset of whatever orientation, they are being set up for a most extraordinary case of confusion and struggle with illegitimacy as they move onward in life. In the early years of individual development, the environment is easily controlled. Information may be carefully channeled and directed, communication and experience closely monitored. Religious symbols become shibboleths that create strict boundaries and dichotomies for a child's primary objects of faith. Certain ways of speaking, a style of living, a cultural identity and its ritual observances and articles of faith reflect strong attachments to an exclusive community and ways of relating to parents, relatives, and friends. If, however, as an adult there is exposure to worldviews quite different from their own, they may also find that the identity they chose as children and young adults—or the one they were coerced to choose—does not allow them to affirm other identities while also being affirmed, which as Erikson suggests is vital to adult development. It is at this point and for this type of individual that an understanding of the mourning process may provide insight. We are enabled to understand that a struggle ensues as either a manic flight returning to a rigid, exclusionary world, or as a case of profound confusion, withdrawal, and anger for having lost that world.

113

The False Self

One final Winnicottian concept that furthers this present discussion is that of the false self and the concealed true self, discussed in the paper, "Ego Distortion in Terms of the True and the False Self."[44] Everything in Winnicott's psychology extends from the metaphor of the mother figure who mirrors the child's emerging personality. In this game of recognition and response, symbols find their birth. In health, such symbols effectively mediate between the child's need for omnipotence and the outside world. Needs will be met in a bearable amount of time, and the developing capacity to meet one's own needs, through transitional phenomena, is encouraged and allowed expression. When this process fails, as it inevitably will in varying degrees, the child falls short of full self-recognition, and lacks confidence and the ability to convey its own desires. Transitional phenomena take on a rigid quality, and the ego-defense creates a gradual structure of a self that is built solely from identifications, that is, features of others that are not integrated. The result is a "false self" that is compliant to the environment instead of participating in it as a compromise. When such defensive structures break down, the "true self," the individual's unique creative qualities, become exposed, invalidated, open to exploitation. Functioning on a level solely devoted to identification with an object ideal, the individual roams about looking for copies of others, to protect the true self from the naked, powerless experience of misrecognition. The false self becomes an actor, pretending, in the extreme, "*as it would be if it had had existence.*"[45] Even in the analytic situation, a false self personality may interminably stand in for the true self, as Winnicott explains:

> It is as if a nurse brings a child, and at first the analyst discusses the child's problem, and the child is not directly contacted. Analysis does not start until the nurse has left the child with the analyst, and the child has become able to remain alone with the analyst, and has started to play.[46]

When the false self does its work of concealing and sheltering, there is a prevailing complaint of having never begun to exist. It is not until this nonexistence is recognized that the true self may begin to assert itself. The mark of the true self, according to Winnicott, is spontaneous action and creative expression that is not an act of compliance but compromise.[47]

Extrapolating Winnicott's explanations of the false and true self, we may say that in the case of an absolutist religious group, compromise that is replaced by compliance offers little room for the spontaneous gesture of play. What the individual internalizes is an inner world of imitation that creates a false sense of omnipotence as defined solely by the group. Moreover, as aggression is turned inward, I would argue that the true self finds substitutes for spontaneity and transcendence in the construction of a wicked, counter self. Anonymity and deadness are the identifying characteristics of the outer self, of someone who is unable to openly express feelings. The feeling of being a phony, imposter, or actor prevails as the false self maintains control. True engagement with symbols of ultimacy and the opportunity to use aggression against the objects of ultimacy is thwarted. In theological terms, a life of faith based on compliance brings only small awareness of our own destructiveness, our hidden proclivity to destroy the Christ.

A Summary of the Language of Mourning Applied to Religion

Having explored the work of Freud, Klein, and Winnicott, we have been provided with a powerful inventory of descriptors that can be applied to the struggles in the journey of faith. They are dynamics that operate on both a conscious and unconscious level and exist in varying degrees depending on the individual. As it can be misleading to describe them in stages, a point I have argued throughout this discussion, I instead choose to call it a *bipolar dynamism*. At any moment in the struggle of the life of faith, any one psychological aspect or set of aspects may be at work on either a progressive or regressive trajectory. This dynamism is an ongoing, never-ceasing process that must be entered into over and over, particularly as the individual's life circumstance, social, and cultural contexts change. Such a bipolar pattern denotes motion and return to primary experiences in such a way as to participate in the necessarily ongoing adaptations in symbolic life. Combining the various thinkers and themes discussed in this chapter, let me briefly summarize this dynamism.

Mourning in relation to the life of faith means mourning an ideal, and more accurately, the experience of relationships that the ideal represents. It is a much more prolonged, and nearly interminable process because ideals are by and large noncorporeal. One of the clearest indications of pathology in mourning an ideal is, as Freud mentioned, self-reproach, self-recrimination, or a "disturbance in self-regard." Such a disturbance can simultaneously manifest either in a deepened idealization or nostalgia of the lost beliefs or faith community, or a fervent or manic denial of the loss. Where the idealization forces an inward turn that results in self-persecution, the manic denial forces an outward turn that persecutes artificial external objects, such as stereotyping all pastors as corrupt or all congregants as hypocritical. Both idealization and manic denial, however, are reacting to the setting up of an unattainable ideal in the unconscious mind, or in other words, a sense of perfectionism regarding the life of faith. Here the individual is trapped by their inability to come into true relation with externality. One becomes caught in a colorless, suspended animation, has foreclosed initiative, and is at odds with a false self that is always in search of any way of borrowing other people's feelings and experiences.

What becomes necessary is a process of remembering the experiences and relationships associated with what was lost and discovering the deep sadness that comes in the recognition of the loss. Often this process of remembering includes returning to life's earlier and earliest experiences of loss and using those experiences to help memorialize the present loss. First, however, sadness is mainly accomplished through a descent into the anger over abandonment. Once the anger has been given recognition, and if the true object of anger has survived, then there is the opportunity for deep sadness. Out of

116

such sadness initiative is restored and a subsequent pining to make reparation and to rediscover the object and find new ones becomes possible. Within this pining grows a capacity for concern to come into relationship with the object. Such a relationship is accomplished through creating a space for playfulness, and the possibility for surprise that is not heavy-handed and is instead owned by both the individual and the object or faith community. A structure is put in place where feelings of discovery, newness, and excitement amidst the unexpected and even dangerous, all make possible new ways to relate to the object.

Having sketched this model of mourning in the life of faith, and worked through so much fertile psychological language, we may now turn to discover how such a language may be applied to life story.

PART II
BIOGRAPHICAL ANALYSIS

TAKING A CUE from Robert Wuthnow's observation that contemporary practice spirituality is characterized by deep internal reflection,[1] the second part of this book will draw biographical data from what is perhaps the most well-developed form of personal introspection: the spiritual memoir. Each of the five memoirs that follow happen to be written by representatives of the middle-aged, white, boomer generation, and it could be said that each is an attempt to share stories, find community (among readers), and "come to terms" with an individual journey of struggle. Rather than chronicling what might be called developmental tasks of faith or exploring personal experience to reveal the truths of theological themes, these spiritual autobiographies each tell a story of overcoming the past and finding meaning in the present. Instead of doctrinal statements, the world of relationships in communal faith is the driving force behind these stories. If it can be said that these memoirs reveal an ethos-specific practice of personal introspection, it can also be said that whatever we find may also provide clues to the difficult challenges to faith and religion in our time and creative ways to overcome such challenges.

I have selected these memoirs because each writer details in some way a struggle with an absolutist faith, sometimes in the extreme. Such stories of struggle insofar as they offer resolution and approximate successes will reveal in a clearer light the dynamics of pathology in the life of faith. We will find in them uncanny resemblances to the process of mourning as described in the previous chapter, as well as an important observation that augments mourning theory particularly regarding communal and symbolic loss. As Freud noted, the process of mourning is a painstakingly slow and largely unconscious process. Because these memoirs often sketch a journey that spans decades, we are given the chance to see just how long this journey takes. Moreover, such memoirs offer evidence of the direct connection between loss of common culture and absolutism in American religion, as well as help us draw the psychological map that shows the way out of this loss.

As a methodology, analyzing and interpreting autobiographical data is a well-worn path in psychological and psychoanalytic studies. From William James's *Varieties of Religious Experience* to Erik Erikson's seminal works *Gandhi* and *Young Man Luther*, a life story expressed in written accounts is ripe for psychoanalytic interpretation. Especially in autobiography, we have access to early childhood experiences, repetitive storytelling patterns, dreams, and knowledge of the experiences and beliefs the writer holds most dear. Short of entering therapy with the author, and better than a relatively brief structured interview, memoir that is rich with description can reveal a great deal of insight about which the writer may not be aware, simply through an attentiveness to the choices of words and the feelings they express. What we find in memoir is indeed something akin to the psychoanalytic clinic. Psychoanalysis, famously known as the "talking cure," is in its essence a safe environment where the analysand and analyst together attempt to make meaning of the analysand's struggles. The goal is not so much the detached, omniscient interpretations of the analyst, as Winnicott noted; rather, the goal is for the analysand to learn to "use" the analyst as an interlocutor onto which aggression, bitterness, and hurt can be displaced and as an object that can survive such emotions and still offer support and love.

In the memoirs that follow, each writer has made the composition of a book their therapeutic environment. Their interlocutor is their reader, who is essentially a blank slate. Granted, the interactive dynamic—what in analysis is called the transference, or in ethnographic research is called participant observer—is not as prevalent, and no doubt in some cases authoring a book can be a near-perfect narcissistic acting out. However, the writer knows that an editor will have to approve the book, certain friends, and family members—some about whom the memoir is written—will read the book, and buyers of the book will also react. Also, as a participant in the religious struggles each of the memoirs discuss, I will interject observations and information that will show my partnership with and empathy for each of these authors and my hope to let their stories serve as examples of healing. In the end, it will then be possible to make a few conclusions about whether there had been change in the writer's life, and whether the writing of the memoir itself meant the author has built up new ego structure and no longer needs as much therapy, regardless of the things that may remain unresolved.

6
Finding a Safe Place: Kate Young Caley

COMING BACK HOME despite having forever lost that home is the paradoxical theme that pervades so much of the narrative regarding returning to faith and religion. It is a loss experienced in discrete, temporary moments and yet extends throughout the eternities of a lifetime, a journey of pining that may neither be abandoned nor completed. In the case of Kate Young Caley, we find a quest for a safe place, a search for freedom from the threat of external betrayal and the internal, nagging feeling of not belonging. Where Caley accomplishes such goals, she will find freedom for the rebirth of her religious imagination.

In her memoir *The House Where the Hardest Things Happen: A Memoir about Belonging*, Caley describes her childhood years growing up during the mid-1960s in the rural town of Moultonborough, New Hampshire. There she lived in a close-knit community and attended the First Church of God. The church service involved enthusiastic preaching from the Bible, hymn singing, and dressing nicely. Sunday school was a matter of attendance records, Bible stories, and memorizing the names of the books of the Bible. Church was also a place of intense togetherness, where she had the confidence that she was loved by all and that "everything was all right." The preciousness of that time for her is summed up in what she calls her favorite part of church, the altar call:

The preacher would invite us all to bow our heads and close our eyes. He would say that he knew there were those out there who did not have Jesus in their hearts and who wanted to start a new life that very morning. He knew Jesus was reaching out to us even as he spoke. The piano player seemed to know too, and would begin the soft and loving chords of the invitational at just the right moment each week. We would join in and softly sing, "Just as I am, without one plea, but that Thy blood was shed for me, and that Thou bidd'st me come to Thee, O Lamb of God, I come, I come."

I was so moved by it all—by the preacher's ability to see into our hearts, the lull of the chords, and the promise that we get to come just as we were—that I would ask Jesus into my heart every single week, just to be sure it took.[1]

Beginning at the age of five, Caley was ensconced in a zealous religious community. The idea that she lived with deprivation, without Jesus in her heart, had been driven in powerfully, so much so that she felt the need to affirm her triumph over this deprivation each week during the altar call. Most likely she was not alone in this. In fact, it would be fair to assume that this internal repeating dialogue was one many congregants experienced; for indeed, how many of the attendees of this small rural church at any one service had not already given their hearts and pledged their loyalty to Jesus? To have the idea of such personal depravation, a conviction of such depth of one's sinful nature, at the age of five is a commitment to the First Church of God that Caley, as is evident in her memoir, finds difficult to surrender. It left a permanent mark, especially after that same community banned her mother, and subsequently her family, from attending the church.

In 1965, while Caley was still five, her father, Dick Young, left home and traveled to Biloxi, Mississippi, to report for active duty in the army. The big problem, however, was that her father was retired from the army, and was somehow convinced that it was 1954. This delusional episode resulted in hospitalization for a brief period. Yet before he was able to return home, Dick was diagnosed with cancer, which required further hospitalization. With her father away for what had turned into months, Caley's mother, June, had to find work to support herself and three young children. She found a job waitressing, work that required her to serve alcohol. For the members of the First Church of God, this meant June was breaking their sacred covenant, rules the church members had agreed to abide by, which were written in black stenciled letters on muslin that hung behind the pulpit. A meeting was called around the time Dick was released from the hospital and a vote taken that excommunicated June from the church. Although both Dick and June likewise stopped attending in solidarity, June continued to drop the children off at the church for Sunday school, waiting in a car outside. Then one day Caley's Sunday school teacher made June the object of a lesson about hypocrites, telling the class that Caley's mother was a bad woman. After that, all the Young children stopped attending.

Looking back at the years that follow, Caley clearly sees herself as a child who was suffering a powerful loss. Who knows how well she understood her feelings at the time, but looking back, she writes in the pages of her memoir:

> [I]t was so hard to get used to the long, empty hours of Sunday mornings with no more church: no Sunday school teachers who loved me, no felt-board Bible stories, no take-home craft, and no sweaty coins gathered in my palm awaiting their clunk into the offering plate. Without our church service there was silence where my father and mother's voices had once melted together in victorious song above me.
>
> My Sunday mornings were quiet now. Empty. I was ten years old and longing for a way to find my way back to God.[2]
>
> Was there no one who noticed that I really, really missed church? That I was sad? Ate a lot? Slept a lot?[3]

From the first day of the vote Caley has seen her life as having been indelibly altered. Her symbols of ultimacy, a world that had been so carefully and passionately defined, had been taken away from her and her family. If she was seen by someone from the church in town, she was not spoken to or acknowledged. The sense of isolation was also reinforced by the fact that, soon after the vote, the Youngs purchased a farm outside of Moultonborough. The farm was for them an escape, which in Caley's mind was the only way the family could retake possession of their lives, to preserve and create their family in a place that no one but themselves could define and control. Caley regards the farm as "the landscape I would rely on all my life."[4] And yet the fact that her parents never made the attempt to find a new church still puzzles her. It was as if, in the attempt to find a safe place free from judgmentalism, they also exiled themselves from expressing their faith in a communal setting. Having agreed to the covenant themselves, it was perhaps all too clear to her father and mother that they no longer belonged.

For the family, we can speculate that the breaking of the covenant became a persecutory object of transgression. Not having met with forgiveness, support, and understanding, the vote left the Youngs to enter a conflict between their shame over having broken the covenant and the anger toward an environment that could be so cruel. As a result, their concern for group-defining rules and identity completely abandoned them; and in terms of their relation to their own God imagoes, the Youngs shut down, and in a sense, abandoned themselves. They were now left to fend for and care for their own spiritual lives, or at worst, deny any need for spiritual life at all. It was as if a child had been cast off by her parents, left to tend to her own needs for nourishment, growth, and development. As Caley reflects, the farm represented a place she could always count on as the place where she and her family's attachment to objects of ultimacy could suffer no further damage—and yet also a place that provided little opportunity for reparation. The farm was a powerful source of retreat and would remain one in her mind's eye. She writes:

[W]hen the lines get drawn, too often, I am on the other side. I'm the girl who was told, "Your mother is a bad woman," Or, more recently, "I would not want you to lead our Sunday school unless you sign this statement against homosexuality." It has been implied, over and over, "You really aren't one of us unless you use the same words we use to talk about God."

And what do I do with these stands that leave me out?

I get away from the crowd and try to be still and know God. I go back to the woods of my girlhood. I sit and stare at small, perfect ferns. Sometimes I sing. Or turn to words Jesus said when he was here among us. I read, "Come unto me, all you who labor, and I will give you rest." That's what Jesus said.[5]

What is the labor Caley is referring to in quoting this scripture? Could it be that she lives in her psyche with sharply drawn lines between good and bad symbols of ultimacy day after day, year after year?

Caley is quite aware that the vote cast by those church members so long ago made a lasting impact on her faith. In a conversation she has with her mother, in preparation for writing her memoir, Caley recreates the scene of the vote, finding herself growing angrier, not just at the congregation, but at her mother, who seemed unable or unwilling to recall the details Caley so hungrily sought. In Caley's view, her mother should be equally angered; instead, June appears distraught. Caley's anger at the First Church of God is being placed, in some significant part, on her mother. Yet Caley also points out that her mother was only in her twenties at the time, with three small children and a sick husband, and that no one offered her an alternative to the job she took:

I stared at her. I was incredulous as I watched my mother cry and heave that old shame. I didn't know what to say. . . .

I found myself losing my breath. It was not like I was sitting beside my mother in the house where she lives alone, years after my father died. It was as if it was thirty-five years ago and I was in the newly finished sanctuary of the First Church of God in

Moultonborough, New Hampshire. And I am there, as the woman I am now. I am my mother's protector. And I am not going to stand for any of this.

"God," I call out. "Mrs. Nichols, Ginny Muzzy, somebody—please, listen to me." I am crying. "Don't kick my mother out. Please. There are some things we are *never* going to find again."[6]

Here Caley relives the senselessness of being excommunicated, angrily pleading with God and the church members in her memory. The moment marks a turning point from persecution to pining when Caley envisions herself in the role of a mother to her mother, who is now a child, something innocent and good, that Caley must defend. Instead of living in withdrawn, self-recriminating numbness, she comes out fighting, and in so doing identifies and recovers, in the person of her mother, something of herself that she lost so long ago.

Identifying the people who instigated a sense of betrayal, moreover, is another illuminating piece in the recovery of faith. In Caley's mind, throughout her life she had always thought that those who voted her mother out were strangers. It was not until she probed and plied her mother for answers, and in soliciting details from some old friends of June and Dick Young—who likewise left the church after the Youngs had left—that it came out one night. The two women who June remembered motioning to ban her from the church were the same people with whom she had studied the Bible, knitted articles of clothing, and exchanged hours of childcare. They were women that Caley still sees from time to time even as an adult. "Two ordinary people took our church from us."[7] It was their simple, blithely committed acts of exclusion that makes Caley now wonder, "To how many generations do the actions of that one, particular winter extend?"[8] With the knowledge that the acts of those who kicked her mother out of church were the acts of friends, Caley's grief takes a further step, a realization that the hurt cuts deeper than an abuse by a stranger or someone who can be demonized and conquered in personal fantasies. The damage was done to the ability to trust, not just others, but to also the ability to trust one's own capacity to judge who can or cannot be trusted. It becomes a matter both of perceiving what is wrong with the environment and of what is wrong with the self, and understanding which perceptions are valid. Not only had Caley been implicated in the original transgression of her mother, and relegated in perpetuity to an outgroup, she had also been rendered—most especially by her self-recrimination—incapable of ever participating in a group.

In her teen years, during the early 1970s, Caley became involved in the Jesus Generation, going off to a group that met in a barn, sang Christian folk songs, praised God, and listened to prophecies. At first, she was glad to be back at church, enjoying the warmth of mutual fellowship, but then she began to observe power struggles among the elders of the group. She observes in hindsight that the struggles were typical in such grassroots movements, and yet at the time they felt so devastating. Again, for her the object of her faith began to disintegrate, the damage and the trauma resurfaced. Caley describes one service where she felt this disintegration personally. A speaker began prophesying, "I see a raven, a dark, dark raven. Circling among us. Circling dark. Circling low. There is a raven among us, here in this very room! It is looking for a place to land. Oh my people, don't let it land." She began to think that what the speaker was saying pertained just to her. She felt terrified that of the three hundred people in attendance, she was the one the raven would land on:

> I knew that at any moment that huge, black bird was going to land on my shoulder and everyone would be able to see. I was the *only* one in the place it would pick. I knew it.
> Having been kicked out before, I was ready to be kicked out again. . . .
> I wondered: *Why do I keep trying? Why do I keep thinking I can find a way to fit in?* There always seemed to be something about me that didn't get things right.[9]

Here we see the internalization of the negative environment, or in Freud's words, the shadow of the object descending upon the ego. Having felt the experience of rejection from a church that introduced her to fear images of the holy, Caley finds that her ability to seek God among others is damaged. To make a myopic conclusion that she should be singled out among all the participants—and one must wonder how many others felt the same way about such an eerie speech—bears evidence of self-blame and self-loathing. Making such a conclusion, however, comes as no surprise when considering the spiritual trauma she suffered at the tender age of five. Furthermore, Caley's ability to take satisfaction in such a group, to be able to play in the group, and creatively possess its symbols was tenuous at best, and likely remained an inhibition to her participation. As she mentions above, she had the feeling that she could not get things right: "I was too religious for some. Too worldly for others." Such an observation reveals her inability to take pleasure in such a group. More to the point, it demonstrates that anyone who has suffered such a breach of trust is left with an inability to feel at home in *any* group. A feeling prevails that one is an imposter, a pretender, as in Winnicott's false self, forever in fear that the true self will be exploited or obliterated. It is a two-sided fear that the true self belongs neither in the religious group because of deep doubt and unbelief, nor in a secular group because of a strong commitment to a way of life defined by religious authority.

Fortunately, the simple expression of Caley's frustration with not belonging also contains a scrap of anger, and the potential for the discovery of self-agency, which comes to the fore in the paragraphs that follow, where Caley describes the incident that led her to leave this group. At a meeting some months later, a woman who was an elder expressed a prophecy that Caley and her boyfriend were not meant to be together. What God had told this woman was that Caley was too outgoing for this young man, and that it was instead the woman's own niece that would best suit him. Caley writes:

It was almost laughable.
Enough, already. Enough. As much as I wanted God, I was sick

to death of His people. Of their incessant manipulations. . . .

I looked across the table at the elder's wife with her expression so earnest, stood from the table, and left the room.[10]

Here Caley discovers a measure of contempt for spiritual community, though unfortunately it is a rebellion that will only be met by further rebuke and aloofness rather than acceptance and love. In fact, it is an environment that is most likely the worst possible place for her to restore her faith within community.

Over time, Caley concludes and gains confidence in the fact that that she will not find sacred symbols within the confines of a church group, which seems an important step. In fact, she begins to see examples of God existing in people and places she had never thought—or been taught—to associate with God. There were the many people with whom her parents were friendly after the vote of excommunication:

These friends of ours did not call themselves the people of God but they were always *doing* the things God said to do; sharing what they had with those in need; not picking up the first quick stone of judgment; offering help but never needing for anyone else to know about it. They loved us, their neighbors, as themselves. Better even.[11]

After attending college, discovering the world of literature, traveling abroad, and eventually becoming married, Caley describes that she and her husband went looking for a church environment where they would both feel as though they were beginning something new:

[W]e needed a place where we could define and redefine who we were and who God was to us—not a place where our beliefs were already presumed and defined and cast.[12]

What Caley presents, in connection with what has been discussed here about Winnicott's transitional phenomena, is a piece written with a strong note of awe and wonder about both *finding* and *being found*, or in this case, being lured or compelled. In the busy streets of an urban Boston neighborhood Caley and her husband noticed a man dressed in a black, full-length cassock.

> The paradox of this man, walking slowly with his hands behind his back and the ease with which he made his way down the deteriorating avenue, caused us to slow the car to see where he might go. The way he seemed to float in that full-length cassock above the swarm of the city was something I needed to understand.
>
> He crossed the avenue, not waiting for the pedestrian light. We turned down the street where he was heading, feeling an unspoken urge to follow him.[13]

Caley describes that the man disappeared into an Episcopal church, a kind of church they had never attended. They noticed its Gothic Revival architecture, the old rose bushes growing out of the base of a castle-like tower, and heard the sound of the Vesper bells. When they attended the service the following Sunday, they took in the many sites of interest inside the church. There was dark lighting, stained glass, wrought iron stands of lighted candles, and heavy, tall, straight pews. A bell rang, an organ sounded, and a parade of choir boys walked in. Three men followed in procession carrying a cross. Caley and her husband navigated their way through that first Eucharistic service by mimicking what the other parishioners did. They noticed that the others in attendance came from a cross-section of life in the church's neighborhood. It seemed that no one was excluded from the service. Their experience of that day showed them that all they need do was "enter in" and take part in the liturgy. No one was asking them what they believed or what tradition they came from. No one was preaching sermons laced with fear and anxiety. All they were asked to do was to, "Be still. Watch and wait. Taste and see that the Lord is good."[14]

What Caley and her husband found that day was a place where

they could rediscover God and recreate who they were as people of God. They experienced in the Anglican liturgy and symbolism a freedom that allowed for their unspoken, undernourished mysteries of life and faith. The very embracing of uncertainty brought with it a feeling of opportunity, *both* the chance to possess and be possessed by the experience, which for the former absolutist borders on the exotic and intoxicating. Nevertheless, first and foremost this new church experience was a place where they could feel safe, protected from the "hardest things"—words used in the title of Caley's memoir. For Caley in particular, this church would become a place where she could return to her own primary images of the divine and let them play freely upon her imagination. Here she would begin the process of slowly rediscovering and reclaiming her initiative.

One of Caley's experiences that was particularly revealing of her effort to recover and stake a permanent, unassailable claim for faith and religion involves her time spent as a children's Sunday school teacher. When she attended Sunday school at the First Church of God, a great emphasis was placed on attendance, which would be rewarded with a gold star adhered to a chart. Looking back, Caley realized that the recognition given to regular students was likely matched by the shame felt by those who were not. Now, as a Sunday school teacher herself, Caley writes: "[I]t satisfies an old need in me to be especially generous to the ones who can't seem to get there." Sunday school is for Caley a new transitional ground, a field in which she may play with the very articles of faith that were so closely controlled and manipulated in her past. It is also a place of opportunity for reparation, of making amends for the spiritual darkness she used to carry by bringing light into the lives of the children she teaches. "I am here now to give the children who come my way some things that I didn't get when I was their age."[15]

In the Sunday school class Caley led, there was one student, Laura, who was not one of the regular attendees of the church. For a time of some months, Laura and her siblings did regularly attend, but were mostly unfamiliar with the stories of the Bible and the key events of the Christian year, which receive a special emphasis in the

Episcopal Church environment as compared to a fundamentalist church. Caley discovers one Sunday, as she is naming off the various events leading up to the Crucifixion, that Laura has no idea that Jesus was crucified. "They . . . killed . . . him?" The dumbfounded and shocked expression on the girl's face seems to equally surprise Caley. "*Stop the lesson Kate,*" she thinks to herself. "*Stop the cramming, the view of the whole thing as regular and rote, as something we all know already anyway.*"[16] For Caley, this becomes a moment to participate in the fresh discovery of the Passion story. In Caley's experience as a child, the dark, painful descent of the Passion story had likely been underplayed, as it is in some Protestant churches, in favor of the strong emphasis on the bodily resurrection. Caley finds herself in the position of both mirroring, or empathizing with, Laura's horror, and of reexperiencing that horror herself, and in some ways for the first time: "I looked across that Sunday school table at Laura, reached for her. 'You're going to love the way this story ends,' I said to her and told her what I know."[17]

The actual lesson of that Sunday covered the New Testament story of the woman who committed adultery, and who was about to be stoned. Again, Laura soaked in the story as the class made a play out of reenacting the scene. Caley could tell from Laura's reaction that Laura loved the story, and how Jesus answers the questions of the accusers in such a way that the woman is not unfairly stoned. "That story about Jesus' goodness became her own," Caley writes. "What she received the day we acted out the story of the forgiven woman nobody gets to take away." For Caley, Laura is learning these lessons from the Bible and about God in a supportive environment. She's not shielding Laura from the depth or severity of the story but delivering the story and allowing her student to take possession of it in a way that is meaningful to her, not just the teacher or the church. This good-enough mother role that Caley assumes as a Sunday school teacher not only encourages true spiritual discovery on the part of her student, but it helps Caley reclaim pieces of the spiritual imagoes that were "taken away" from her in her own childhood. Another healing moment in Caley's journey back to faith also comes in the interaction with a child; in this case, it is her own ten-year-old daughter who asks to hear the story of why Caley never received a mustard seed necklace. This story from Caley's past comes up the day her daughter receives a mustard seed during church services one Sunday. Caley proceeds to reveal the salient yet momentous details of how her family had been barred from the church of her childhood, of how at the time they stopped attending altogether, she had been just about to receive a mustard seed necklace for memorizing the names of the books of the New Testament. She had memorized all those names, but never received the necklace. Caley describes her daughter's sadness at hearing the story, who in turn, interestingly, comments on how it would be too sad a story even to tell her younger sister, a six-year-old. Caley had already decided not to relate this story to the younger daughter, no doubt fearing—perhaps more than was warranted—what it might do to the girl. What is most compelling for Caley, however, is what happens days later. Her ten-year-old presents her with a mustard seed necklace she had secretly purchased while the family was visiting the National Cathedral in Washington, DC. She gives her mother the necklace on Christmas morning—a time of celebrating a most significant birth and beginning. Instead of hurrying to see her own stockings and gifts as usual, the daughter rushes to give her mother a special box. Inside the box is a mustard seed necklace sized for a child. For Caley, it is the perfect size, and a wonderful gift:

> I imagined [God] wanting to say to me, *Listen, Kate. The way a mustard seed is like the kingdom of heaven is this: it takes a long time to find a place to grow well. But you are doing it. And now you help these daughters. Look at it all. I'm there.*
>
> Am I just putting words in God's mouth? That always worries me. Yet I want to pay attention to each layer of meaning as my own girl gives me the very thing I needed when I was a girl.[18]

Her daughter's gift is a significant healing moment for Caley, not just because of the significance for Caley's own past, but also because of the opportunity she created for her daughter to act out of compassion and do so of her own volition. For Caley it is a healing moment especially because she sees the pain of her past—and her anger toward the thoughtlessness of the adults in that past—is now being mediated by a child, one who holds unaffected and unmarked faith and trust in her hand.

There are other examples of mourning and rediscovery of faith to be gleaned from this sensitive memoir, but I will conclude by discussing one final observation Caley makes about her experience with church. She writes, again in reference to her own children, of her concern about whether they will come to know the same numinous feeling of the divine that she discovered at so young an age:

But at times I have feared for my children's relationship with God. How could they know Jesus if they didn't sing, "Just as I Am" at the end of the service each week? I know our relationship with God doesn't depend on how we set up our service. And yet. There are some moments—so vulnerable and precious and important—that seem only to happen in a church that has an altar call. There's a part of me that won't quite rest until God lets Billy Graham live long enough to do one more crusade in New England.[19]

For Caley, those imagoes of her early church experience still remain, but the difference now is that she can acknowledge them, making her pining for them a conscious dialogue. Note that this expressed concern for her children's faith comes near the end of her book, as perhaps one last homage to the authoritarianism in the religion of her past. She also observes: "Maybe I need to rely more on God and less on the ways I think we get to God. To stay clear of the trap that there is only one, exact way it happens."[20] Caley is bringing to conscious thought a brief observation on how she has new access to the most precious and powerful aspects of what is holy. In the past, the access was granted on the condition of her passivity and submission to a "right" way. This method was endeared to her, and she loved it and had made it a part of her. Now she is in the process of raising that love to a new ideal, wondering about its hold on her, and reviving her sense of possibility and hope for something new. Only a few pages later we find her describing a very different kind of resolution about the ultimate symbols of her worshiping experience. In her description of participating in a Eucharistic service, she writes:

I felt a physical sense of home. Of the holy familiar.

And I feel it each time I leave my seat to walk up the long aisle to the altar . . . I walk well-known steps to receive the earthly elements of bread and wine, which change in ways I do not need to understand, into the very presence of Christ.

I walk with others, like me and not like me, to answer another kind of altar call. The call to come. To taste and see. No one forces the gift. You answer by walking toward it. . . .

I bring myself and everything I have ever been to the altar.[21]

In just these few remarks Caley demonstrates the mechanism of mourning and the rebirth of religious imagination and faith. She reveals the transition from using up her attachment to her old, now dead imagoes, consciously acknowledging her love for them in a way that is free from self-recrimination or bitterness, toward a sweetness and trust for discovering something new. Rather than having that new sense of the holy driven into her—or enjoined by her own neediness—Caley finds herself walking toward it and receiving it as a gift. She is occupying Winnicott's transitional space, both finding and being found by the sacred. Although she consumes the elements, she is not simply consuming for herself, but sharing and participating with others in the presence of the ultimate.

The Episcopal service seems to offer Caley a more direct connection to what is sacred. Feeling closer to God in a liturgically mediated context is in itself an irony for a cradle fundamentalist such as Caley. One of the longstanding ideologies of Protestantism is that the individual has a direct connection to God, the chance to participate in a priesthood of all believers. Especially for absolutists, the Bible, as literally applied in every word, is the primary portal to God, and it is far less necessary, perhaps even heretical, to find God through ritual joined with, received by, and interpreted in concert with others. And yet, the liturgy is the solution for Caley. The Eucharist, or communal sacred meal, is the place where she can finally explore the meaning of God as if for the first time. It is a safe place, safer at least "for now," and free from the emotionalism of her absolutist past.

To conclude, Caley's journey of faith follows a course that exemplifies all the elements of trauma and loss, anger and aggression, the depressive position, mourning, the rediscovery of the numinous, and the interplay of the transitional space. Her struggle is one that has lasted throughout most of the decades of early and midlife and may well last much longer. She goes from discovering at an early age a potent sense of God, faith, and community, to losing it all, and then regaining it bit by bit in new and different ways much later in life.

Yet her story begs the question as to whether there is still more to come. Having gone from a place where "everything was all right" to a place that is "safe, for now," we can only wonder whether Caley is merely at some midway point in her journey of mourning. In the future, she may still explore new concepts of God and new forms of liturgy. Perhaps she'll even make her way to still another faith community or, perhaps just as likely, act as an agent of transformation for the Episcopal church in which she has raised a family and spent much of her adult life. To be sure, the closeness of an absolutist community, as distorted as it may sometimes be, provides an identity and worldview that is often missing in contemporary life. And Caley had experienced that closeness intensely. But to be content with a place that is merely safe does not necessarily challenge someone like Caley to the fullest possible resolution of her trauma and loss. Such a loss is, after all, a microcosm that represents spiritual loss throughout contemporary life. Certainly, the safety provided by the church environment Caley grew into was without qualification the key to her rediscovery of faith in community. It could also be argued that safety is all a faith community should provide. And yet play, as Winnicott would define it, contains an element of surprise, even of risk, confrontation, interaction, responsibility, and danger, which—through a facilitating environment—is overcome through a game where there is trust that all will survive and live with deepened understanding. We are thus left to wonder whether Caley has yet to enter still other places of spiritual risk and surprise, and what those places may reveal.

7
The Pilgrim's Journey:
Diana Butler-Bass

ONE OF THE MOST revealing features about psychoanalysis is the observation that we all live with pathology. In the life development of any one individual, there is always trauma, a feeling of loss, and the defenses that arise as a response. In the postindustrial society of the United States, with our tradition of placing a high value on entrepreneurialism, individual malleability, and mobility, we often look for the quick fix and pay little attention to the problems that lie below the surface. It is difficult, for example, for our health care system to understand the merit of a long-term counseling treatment like psychoanalytic psychotherapy. Even within professional psychology, psychoanalysis is commonly misunderstood as a mechanistic theory of the stages of psychological development and not as a therapeutic method of interpretation of personal narrative building and meaning making. The same may be said for the journey of faith: no matter how normal a journey it may seem on the surface, there is still a struggle with pathology, one that is just as mighty as for those whose lives are clearly in disarray. The same dynamics are still at work in any life, and it is quite possible that more of these dynamics are encompassed and tolerated by a situation that could be called healthy and progressive.

The religious journey of Diana Butler-Bass is one such example of someone who in many ways has adapted to the challenges of individual faith in our time as outlined in this discussion but is also someone who struggles greatly. Unlike the other accounts presented here, Bass reports never experiencing a clear or extreme break with her religious life or a long-term disillusionment and subsequent period of noninvolvement. In fact, she says, "Nearly every Sunday in the last forty years I have been in church."[1] In her memoir, *Strength for the Journey: A Pilgrimage of Faith in Community*, she introduces herself as a contrast to her fellow baby boomers. Instead of leaving organized religion, she has been a "stayer." When we generally look at those who have fallen away—some because of extreme difficulty—the dynamics of the loss of faith come forward in sharp relief. Turning to Bass's story, we will, on the one hand, have to hunt a little harder for the pathos she battles, but we will find that even though she has been a stayer, she has likewise struggled deeply with absolutism.

Before any summarizing or analysis is possible, it is important to clarify that Bass's memoir is a mixture of spiritual autobiography and ethnographic study of the changing mainline church during the 1980s and 1990s. Having earned a doctoral degree, Bass is a church historian, and has held academic posts in schools across the country. Her book is at once a chronicle of her own life of faith as well as a documentary of the ways mainline churches are working to reform their identities. How they struggle to regain their congregants in the wake of a mass exodus caused by the flight to suburbia, the religious experimentalism that began in the 1960s, and the tides of rationalism. Many memoirs are filled with rich internal details, but with Bass's book, they share center stage with historical, theological, and sociological descriptions of the various churches she attended in the early decades of her adult life. My discussion of her book, therefore, will also offer an opportunity to raise broader observations that support the sociological component of the arguments in previous chapters.

To begin, one thing that must be clear about Bass's story is that even though she considers herself a stayer, she has only done so amid her own journeys of social dislocation. Her story is different from many of her boomer peers in that as she moved from place to place, she always found a church in which she could become involved. Two important observations must be made to understand just what kind of stayer she was and was not. First, and most obvious, is that Bass's choice of vocation was to become a professional student of the church. She attended an evangelical college and continued to an advanced degree in divinity. Although many individuals pursue studies in religion and do not participate in religion, at least on the surface of things, Bass's trajectory through her education nearly required it. Her commitment to participation, however, contained much more than that. There is more than an implied message in her memoir that she is not just a single example of how not to fall away from faith, but rather a reformer and leader for the church today. I say this because it will become increasingly clear in the pages that follow that there is a highly charged personal struggle in Bass's pursuit of faith, one that is revealing both of a unique difficulty with her individual past and of a quite common social struggle.

Second, as alluded to, when it comes to Bass's connection to community, there is little about her life that you could call staying. Bass's story is a journey of moving from place to place, community to community, church to church that so many of us have experienced. She has stayed with church mostly because of her own aspirations for religion, both vocationally and personally, and done so only amid much experimentation and transition. Though she does not imply this, it would be misleading to suggest that we might discover the complete formula for fully and healthfully integrating the individual into church life by looking at Bass's story. There is a great battle going on in her life, one that further illuminates the problems outlined in this book. Yet there is also a triumph within that battle, one that will give us a fair measure of insight into the discovery of faith and religion in our times.

Bass's story begins with growing up in a working-class neighborhood in urban Baltimore in the 1960s. She describes it as a place where she could walk the streets alone, knowing that the adults in the community were looking out for the children. It was a place where everyone read the same codebook of morals, norms, and values, even though there was some mixture of religion—Lutherans, Methodists (her tradition), Catholics, and Jews. She writes:

> We all knew our place in this world. It was a world of boundaries, rules, and roles. Social class, race, ethnicity, birth order, and gender determined everything. We believed that God made it that way.[2]

It was a community that provided Bass with a primary identity and life plan. There was some talk of the children going off to college, but for the most part she would have been someone to marry her high school sweetheart and go to work in her uncle's flower shop that was handed down only to first-born sons.

She says that her fondest childhood memory is standing next to her mother in the balcony of their Methodist church singing "Holy, Holy, Holy" one spring morning. Here Bass reveals in the image of her mother what is clearly one of her most primary objects of faith:

> At that moment, she embodied God to me—joy and hope incarnate in a yellow dress and pillbox hat. Nothing, I was convinced, could ever go wrong with her by my side.[3]

Yet things did go wrong. The community she knew began to change, and the image of the homogeneity began falling apart. There were protests in the streets. Women were questioning their assigned roles. Children were going off to college and not filling the posts at the family businesses. There was a growing number of single people. Bass's parents felt that the world no longer seemed safe, and decided to flee to the suburbs, which meant that they joined the Sunbelt migration in the 1970s and moved to Scottsdale, Arizona. The impact of that community environment, however, left her with a lasting impression of loss:

> The village vanished. And even though I am only in my mid-forties, I feel ancient when I return to Hamilton's haunted streets.

Everyone I knew is gone; we have all become wanderers in a different world. On the streets of Hamilton, only the buildings remain. I can look through the windows of my grandfather's shop—the windows that I looked out of as a young child and first began to see the world—and gaze into the sterile office supply store that has taken its place. Someone ripped out the beautiful azaleas that graced my mother's yard and paved over the entire lawn. The bakery, the movie theater, the drug store soda fountain, the Kresge's department store—all gone.[4]

The Hamilton neighborhood was for her an example of Homans's common culture, or Wuthnow's dwelling cultures. It was not, however, a world that could adapt to the massive movement of the second half of the twentieth century: to claim access to one's own destiny, to ride on new superhighways to find an education and a job, and to possess single-family homes on newly developed land.

Upon moving to Arizona, Bass decides she does not like her parents' traditional Methodist church. It is as if the congregants of that church are trying to preserve the 1950s. As a young teenager, Bass picks up on its irrelevance and stagnation, and feels dissatisfied. At her new high school, and at the age of fifteen, she meets friends

who convinced me I was a sinner going to hell and I needed to be saved. Perhaps I was just scared and lonely, missing my childhood home. But I believed them and the Bible they preached. I got "born again" and joined their church. For the next six years, that congregation formed me and served as my home church while I attended an evangelical Christian college. I studied the Bible and theology, attended prayer meetings, went on mission trips, and usually attended church on Sunday. I dreamed of being a missionary or Bible teacher.[5]

What is unique about Bass's faith trajectory is that it began in an environment that made faith a natural part of everyday life. She felt acceptance, love, and a sense of home. When she entered adolescence, she had lost that sense of belonging, and, at a time when the formation of individual identity and ideology is most fertile, she became embedded in the exclusionary evangelicalism of the 1970s. Thus, we find in Bass two warring yet quite powerful primary images of faith: a loving sense of belonging and a fear-based, boundary-setting ideology. This dichotomy runs throughout her memoir, showing up often in her work to reconcile *her own* conservative views and evangelical zeal with *her own* liberal-minded, liturgy-focused, mainline Episcopalianism. These two vitally potent poles to Bass's faith are often conflicted, and both cause her personal and professional trouble; however, when she discovers ways to reconcile the two, they bring solutions for her and perhaps some important answers to the changing nature of communal faith in our world today.

Having become indoctrinated in evangelical subculture, Bass decided that the college for her would be Westmont College in southern California. She continued to attend a nondenominational evangelical church through her junior year, but then became increasingly discontented. The architecture of the building and the worship services seemed sparse. The revivalist hymns did not imbue a sense of wonder, and the theology seemed to contain fear and condemnation rather than grace and love. Together with some like-minded friends at Westmont, she began meeting weekly for singing old hymns, Bible reading, theological sharing, and feeding each other bread and wine. During this time, she had the opportunity to travel abroad, experiment with missionary work, and tour Europe.

While in London, at the door of Westminster Abbey, her friend said, "Let's go. I've not taken the Eucharist all summer and I feel as if I'm starving." Inside, Bass joined others in prayer, kneeling in church for the first time. She writes:

As we prayed, the most decrepit and rumpled-looking Church of England minister came through the sacristy door. He stood in front of us, looked warily at his tiny congregation, and opened the Prayer Book. . . .

Finally, we stood. The priest turned toward the table and

started speaking to God: "It is very meet, right, and our bounden duty that we should at all times and in all places give thanks unto thee, O Lord, Holy Father, Almighty, Everlasting God.

"Therefore with Angels and Archangels, and with all the company of heaven, we laud and magnify thy glorious Name; ever more praising thee and saying, 'Holy, Holy, Holy, Lord God of hosts, heaven and earth are full of thy glory; Glory be to thee, O Lord most High.'"

I felt like crying but do not remember if I did or not. I do remember that I was stunned. Completely and utterly. Years later, I would understand the dimensions of the moment much better. The words of the Prayer Book were those from which the Methodist liturgy of my youth had been drawn; I am sure I felt at home with my Methodist childhood God.[6]

This liturgy in Westminster Abbey struck Bass not just because of the liturgical parallel with her Methodist youth, but also because, in this instance, it contained the words, "Holy, Holy, Holy," the very words she associates with her "fondest childhood memory." This moment in Bass's spiritual journey marks a transition point between her evangelical, nondenominational, "spiritually austere" worship and its conservative theology and her entry into a more tradition-bound, richly liturgical worship with its liberal theology. She began attending an Episcopal church with a friend once back at college. Although it at first seemed too exotic for her, by the time she was to graduate, she had become committed to that tradition so much so that in her search for a graduate school she chose a school that would have a thriving Episcopal congregation nearby.

From Southern California she moved east to New England to attend Gordon-Conwell Seminary, which had gained a reputation for being progressive despite being rooted in evangelical Protestantism. According to Bass, the school had, at the time, attracted many students like herself that were from mainline Protestant churches—Methodists, Presbyterians, Congregationalists, Episcopalians, and American Baptists—but had been "born again" during the Jesus

Generation of the 1970s. Bass writes of this group of students: "We wanted to infuse traditional Protestantism with evangelical zeal."[7] To students in their middle to late twenties, the mission seemed clear, and yet as they discovered, the timing was far from perfect; the next two decades would see the emergence of the Religious Right. At Gordon-Conwell, the professors who encouraged these progressive students would be increasingly marginalized. Even the church she attended, Christ Church, was at the time quite conservative on issues like changes in the liturgy and women's ordination. It was at this time, in 1984, that she married Buck Butler, who she describes as a man of "intense theological certainty," and who preferred to attend a fundamentalist Presbyterian church. It was here that she realized how much she missed the liturgy.

> Whenever I attended this church—which met in an ugly, ramshackle sanctuary—I would weep. The Calvinists of that congregation thought I displayed a remarkable spiritual sensitivity to the preaching of God's word. But I was sobbing because I missed the Eucharist and all the heartbreaking beauty of the liturgy. I missed stained-glass windows. No matter how illogical, I missed the *via media*. I tried, but I could not return to spiritually austere Protestantism. I begged to go back to Christ Church, where we might combine [my husband's] Calvinism with my need for a more mystical, mysterious sense of God's presence. He eventually agreed.[8]

For Bass, the liturgy had become like a "lighthouse" and a "beacon pointing the way." The worship experience was rewriting what she now calls her internal theology. No longer was she as interested in creeds, Christology, or predestination. She was curious about the experience of worship, the power of the Easter Vigil, and the solemnity and the texture of both the ritual and the sacred spaces. She was discovering that theology is not only defined by the logic of apologetics, but also by the nonlinear, embodied center of the worship service. Leaving the epistemological elaboration of her experience to another discussion, psychologically speaking, we may speculate that the experience of the liturgy had opened for her a world of new and loving objects, ones that pay homage to the God she discovered in her childhood and yet led her to overcome the absolutism of the groups she experienced in adolescence.

Even in this honeymoon with the liturgy, Bass began to discover a struggle in each of the churches: a struggle between conservative, establishment Episcopalians and a new, progressive, sometimes openly liberal group. There were also the "country club" members for whom church seemed merely a manifestation of their social status, a place to formalize life passages, and a source of comforting affirmation. Bass, however, wrote: "God wanted me to become an Episcopalian so that I might help save the [mainline] church."[9] In what was no doubt a carryover from her evangelical days, she wanted the church to stand at odds with culture, to be an element of change, and to create an environment of both committed piety, weekly ritual observance, and a place of community solidarity and social action.

Bass often describes herself as feeling caught between these various poles at work in the Episcopal Church. She spars with some of the more liberal aspects growing within the Episcopal Church while simultaneously running directly toward them. This comes as no surprise considering the powerful evangelical imprinting that had come in her identity-shaping years. At St. Stephens, the church she attended while pursuing a Ph.D. at Duke Divinity School, the rector was working toward change, incorporating liturgical innovation, and attracting new, younger members. The southern establishment members, however, were not pleased. Internal pressure and even false accusations were levied against the rector, and he eventually resigned. In an obvious statement about the grief involved in faith, Bass writes:

On his last Sunday at St. Stephen's, in an overly dramatic protest, I wore a black dress and a black hat to church. I mourned my friend's defeat, the failure of his dreams. Even more, perhaps, I mourned the loss of what I hoped could be. Chip and Carol envisioned a spiritual synthesis between evangelicalism and Episcopalianism, a place where I could put the pieces of my theology and spirituality together. Part of me died that day. I did not know, however, what part. I felt terrible.[10]

We must be careful to understand that Bass saw this as a struggle between the decades-long laissez-faire liberalism that supposedly caused a hemorrhaging of members through the 1960s and the commitment, theological zeal, and piety of evangelicalism—what she was calling "intentional" Episcopalianism. Again, we see Bass's inclination to view the issues strictly as conservative and liberal, defining faith around positions on social issues or beliefs, but throughout her memoir it is sometimes unclear where she stands. Looking at things from a perspective of power, Bass was protesting the economic conservatism of old-money southerners in a North Carolina church and their eschewing of church as a place of personal and social transformation for all classes—or in her case, financially-strapped graduate students in religious studies. What we see emerging in Bass is a quest-driven spiritual journey, but not that of the average boomer. Hers was not designed for endless seeking and consumption but had a specific destination that would deliver both a new sense of personal faith and a community in which faith could be expressed, nourished, and sustained. She was intentionally seeking a new spiritual home that could house both the zeal of her adolescent identity formation and the embodied spirituality of her early childhood but would do so creatively and with elements of discovery and surprise.

Bass eventually left St. Stephen's, her experience there having left her feeling rejected and emotionally exhausted. She and her husband visited various churches, and almost settled on the Duke Chapel, a Methodist church. "The chapel's high church Methodism, especially the Wesley hymns, tugged nostalgically at my heart." They felt lost, however, in the large number of people the church attracted, and she was averse to the "Methodist sentimentality" she perceived there.[11] She writes that she "craved the Eucharist," which is a statement sounding almost like the infant crying for the warmth and nourishment of mother's milk. The Eucharist had become for her a ritual through which she was spiritually (and physically) fed. The Episcopal service gave her a sensory experience as well the assurance that she was safe and bound to something much greater.

What we observe here is one of the major keys to the rediscovery of faith, namely, the simple hunger that Bass describes. It is linked to Klein's concept of pining, where once we have detected our separateness from the object, as an aftereffect of our spent aggression toward the object, we come to seek its presence and succor. After having expressed so much of her anger toward her experience at St. Stephen's and having gone through a grieving process that included a return to some of her earliest religious objects, Bass had rekindled her desire for ultimacy.

Bass and her husband traveled from Durham to Chapel Hill and to Holy Family, a place she describes as gentle and accepting. In fact, it was a church without dramatic conflict. Along with a few other graduate students like herself, Bass saw a blank canvas on which to paint an emerging faith. She writes that it was her experience at Holy Family that "would ultimately form the foundation" for her renewal of faith.

She found renewal, for example, in her participation in an evening Bible study. She complains that even though she considered Bible study "deeply ingrained in [her] spiritual consciousness," and that it was a venerable practice of Christian faith, she considered it tedious. She reports that it was also a time when she "was suffering from depression and feelings of failure and self-doubt," though she does not elaborate as to why. The Bible study was the only small group meeting that Holy Family offered, and her sense of piety affirmed that she must be committed beyond regular Sunday service. Even though she was a graduate student in divinity, Bass noticed that the Bible was being read differently here than in any other study group she had been in before. In college and seminary, she had been taught to explain away contradictions in the text, whereas this new group took different passages of text, however contradictory with each other, and looked for the particular and unique theological points each passage offered. She explains that:

Through the arguments and insights of the group, I began to understand that the Gospels were not history books—they were theology books and were to be read accordingly. As theology, my friends at Holy Family read the Bible and trusted it. It was possible to read the Bible seriously but not literally. . . . Through the months, I found myself wanting to go on Thursday night. No one read the Bible in ways I expected. . . . Eventually the Thursday night Bible study changed me.[12]

Before she had attended this group, the one passage that provided a lens through which she viewed all others was John, chapter three, where Jesus says that "no one can enter the kingdom of God without being born of water and Spirit. . . . You must be born from above." Through all her experience as an evangelical, Bass understood this to be the ultimate test of Christian faith, namely that of being "born again." In one month of her attendance at the study group at Holy Family—and she still recalls the exact date it happened, like any conversion experience for an encultured evangelical—she came to understand that the text of Matthew 22:34-36 undermined the born-again shibboleth:

A lawyer went to Jesus and asked, "Teacher, which commandment in the law is the greatest?" As a Jew, he was asking what to do to be a faithful follower of God—in contemporary parlance, to be "saved." In the parallel passage in Luke 10:25, this emphasis is more obvious when the lawyer asks, "Teacher, what must I do to inherit eternal life?" In both cases, Jesus replied, "You shall love the Lord your God with all your heart, and with all our soul, and with all your mind. . . . [Y]ou shall love your neighbor as yourself. On these two commandments hang all the law and the prophets." He did not say, "You must be born again."[13]

A lawyer, a person who participates in enforcing and defining the law, brings forward without equivocation the central tenet of Jesus' teaching, that which is known as "the greatest commandment." For

Bass, it was a sudden experience of freedom from what she had associated as the ultimate center of meaning for her faith and a simultaneous discovery of something new to put in its place:

> I had read Matthew's words hundreds of times, and I do not know why they hit me with such force that night. Perhaps it was the disciplined study of reading scripture for a year; perhaps it was the safety I felt with the group. As I sat there and listened to the discussion, I realized that John had been written much later than Matthew, and was, historically, the least reliable of the Gospels. Yet I had pinned my whole understanding of Christian faith on a single chapter from its pages. Now, looking at the words recorded closer to Jesus' own ministry, Jesus said something I never really heard before: Love God and love your neighbor as yourself.[14]

This group proved to be a significant place of therapy for Bass's faith; it provided a supportive environment in which she could work through the details of her personal theology piece by piece. She experienced little concern over whether her musings would be met with shame or manipulation, knowing instead that she would be constructively challenged and encouraged. She was reworking a key identifier of the absolutist mind—a profession of faith that one has been born again—and putting in its place the commandment of love. Faith was no longer a question of status but a matter of process and behavior.

> I wanted to shout, "No this cannot be! Jesus told us the point of the whole thing? Love? How do you love God and your neighbor? How can I love myself? Have I gotten it wrong all these years? The point was not scaring someone into heaven or saving them from hellfire. The point was not about what you believe about Jesus but what you do in his name? The point was love. Loving God and my neighbor. That simple? That complex? The Gospel turned me inside out. I felt sick. I felt like I had been cheated by pastors and teachers and professors my whole Christian life. But at that moment it changed. Indeed, the Bible has

never looked the same to me since.[15]

Bass is on the threshold of discovery, of taking her faith and striking out against the object to which she had pledged allegiance, either by choice or by coercion. In that aggressive impulse, she is coming into a new relationship and new objectivity. With her realization that salvation is about loving herself, but also about loving others in Jesus' name, she is discovering self-agency. Her initiative that grew within the Bible study group allowed her to do this reworking and made it possible to see her faith and religion in a clearer light, perceiving more of its outline, depth, and texture.

In the weeks following, I spiritually ran to that Bible study. Passage after passage sounded brand new. Bible stories that I had known since youth seemed freshly written—intimate and personal words from God—refreshing and renewing my entire sense of Christian faith. Faith was not about fleeing something. It was about joyfully running toward something.[16]

Bible study itself had become for Bass a place for exploration and, suddenly, a *tabula rasa* upon which to be joyful and creative, and through the rules of biblical criticism to employ her own industrious desire. Bass was showing all the markings of returning to childhood developmental tasks and to childhood objects, reusing and reincorporating them once again. Her experience also paralleled her encounter with liturgy, where she discovered a new set of rules for approaching the sacred. Ironically, she had truly begun again, been "born again" amidst the fight to rebuke the evangelical definition of being born again. This conversion was not so much a change to a new faith, but rather a new sense of access and ripeness. What she didn't quite realize at the time was that she had awakened a self-agency that would eventually lead to significant personal changes: a divorce from her religiously conservative husband, her departure from professional evangelicalism, and her claiming of a role—despite her beliefs in the Apostle Paul's admonition against women preaching in church—as a member of the clergy.

After completing her graduate studies, Bass returned to West-mont, the evangelical school where she received her undergraduate degree, to accept a position in teaching. This return would deeply test her resistance to the evangelical demons that haunt both her internal world of religious objects but also the external connection to the evangelical community. Her relationship with her husband seemed to become increasingly strained, particularly as she began work with a spiritual mentor and embarked on personal journal writing. One significant point of departure with her husband was on the issue of women's ordination. He was adamantly against it, but she had grown to accept it, even wondering whether that was the path she was meant to be on all along. Despite the important changes she was ex-periencing, she kept her views to herself, and describes herself as be-coming "a different woman inside than the one who appeared on the outside."[17] She was discovering "a voice of my own" by reopening her interest in medieval Christian mystics that she had discovered the last time she had been at Westmont. Through the journaling and the spiritual counseling, she became less "disconnected from [her] emo-tions." Whatever was repressing those emotions began to lose its control over her:

> As the fear abated some, anger took its place. I felt as if I had been a caged animal for years, never able to be myself and always living into the expectations of those around me—husband, teach-ers, employers, colleagues, clergymen. But now I wanted out.[18]

We know of course that this is not the first time she experienced anger toward all those who had shepherded her faith. She expressed it in her revolutionary new understanding of scripture mentioned above. Only now the anger is coming more to the surface, even while she is working at her evangelical alma mater, where her thoughts and emerging behaviors meant that, as in the spirit of Klein, "I was biting the hand that fed me."

One telling scene she describes occurred while she was teaching her doctrine class on "Anthropology: The Doctrine of Man." In a lesson on original sin, she asked her class what the book of Genesis says about humanity. After a long reluctant pause, one student said, "The book of Genesis says that God made me evil through and through." In Bass's state of discovering her anger toward her religious background, this student's comment became a watershed moment for the new spiritual self that was emerging. Anger, irritation, but also an assertive impulse took her over.

> I stared at her, barely believing what I had heard. She had repeated some mantra learned at her home church about original sin. She was eighteen years old, had long dark hair, clear eyes, and delicate skin, was a nice girl, a beautiful young woman, really intelligent, with a polite and gracious demeanor. Evil? Who told her she was evil? . .
>
> I must have been quiet for one second too long. The whole class was looking at me, waiting for me to respond. Instead of thanking her, however, I blurted out, "Does the Bible really say that? Does the Bible teach that you are evil? Pick it up. All of you. Pick up your Bibles. Pick them up. Turn to Genesis, chapter one."
> The startled students obeyed. I actually startled myself.[19]

Bass proceeded to walk the students through verse by verse, accentuating the places where God deems the work good. She reports that her students all seemed to her as being "awake," and perhaps seeing this passage as if it was the first time. She knew that much of evangelicalism is firmly posited on the idea that people are ultimately sinners, evil through and through, and, in the words of Calvinistic doctrine, totally depraved. To go to the very beginning of the Bible and with such force emphasize the goodness of creation as the ultimate precedence of humanity, and not as a simple warm up act for the story of Adam and Eve's transgression, challenged the primacy placed on original sin. The location of this outburst meant that Bass had more fully discovered her rage at her own wholesale acceptance of depravity, especially, we may add, as a woman. She is emerging from her silent, self-resentment, even for resenting herself—a key and particularly difficult challenge for those emerging from evangelical absolutism and patriarchy—and instead claiming goodness. Moreover, she is exercising her self-agency within the confines of an evangelical college classroom, and, like the Sunday school teaching of Kate Young Caley mentioned in the last chapter, she is both reclaiming her own faith objects while also striving to be an agent of change in developing the faith objects of those around her, mainly the coming generation. The only problem for Bass personally is that, in her effort to destroy the object that purports her depravity, she is not going to find that the object will survive her outburst and still care for and support her; instead, it would be vengeful and retaliatory. In reality, she insisted with her department chair that she not be asked to teach doctrine, and remain mainly with church history, which was her specialty. Nevertheless, her days at Westmont were now numbered. She could not muffle her new voice, and she moved on to Rhodes College in Memphis, Tennessee.

Over the next three to four years, Bass describes her continuing adventures in the Episcopal Church. In Memphis, she continued to struggle with old guard Episcopalianism and the theological liberalism she often encountered, but mostly insofar as it encouraged apathy and a relaxed attitude about participation. Her own evangelical piety led her to envision a church of members who attended every Sunday and volunteered in and lived intentionally within the surrounding community. Bass continues through most of her memoir to give evidence to an internal battle that was attempting to marry her conservatism—defined by her Jesus Generation years—with her involvement in a liturgically grounded, ecumenical faith community. She experienced, in more than one of the many churches she attended, the "caught between" feeling that can be observed in those who are in transition. She felt as though she was an imposter, duplicitous to herself and her environment. Fortunately, some of this struggle with a false self would abate later when she left academia and accepted a position as a theological educator at Christ Church in

Alexandria, Virginia, having remarried and followed her second husband to a new job in Washington, DC. This urban, history-laden Episcopal church is the last ecclesiastical stop in her memoir, and she mentions how she is glad to be there, is tired of moving, and wants to provide a place of stability for her daughter.

Bass summarizes her book by saying that much of her personal adventure in faith has paralleled what is happening to the mainline church. As the bulk of the populace moved to the suburbs and abandoned the mainline churches in urban environments, many churches died, and others are in the process of dying. Yet at the same time, there are mainline churches that have found new members in the baby boomers—professionals who inhabited the gentrified city areas. They started having children and brought their philosophical views from the 1960s into the 1990s. The Episcopal churches she experienced were becoming less and less homogeneous and were no longer social country clubs for the upper-class elite. They were increasingly being populated by "citizens of meritocracy," by people who had been through college and discovered their own way of life, one not defined by where or to whom they were born—as in the days of the Hamilton neighborhood of Bass's youth. She counts herself among those whose lives led them out of the old common community. She made her home wherever her education and job required, and moved from church to church seeking, no doubt, some fashion of symbolic connection that she experienced in her early years.

Reading through Bass's memoir, one can also sense that there is much more at work than a mirroring between her faith and the changes going on in mainlines churches. The work of finding the common community that she caught a glimpse of in her childhood encompasses much of the two conflicts we find throughout her book: her internal and external struggles with both conservatism and liberalism, and her desire for commitment and relational engagement in the context of a growing desire for liturgy and the Eucharist. Yet, there is an additional personal element we see at work. As mentioned, the memoir includes various moments of lament about those who do not take church seriously, and a clear attraction to the "overt piety" and "serious practices of faith."[20] This attraction is revealed in what she relays about her mother in these later pages:

> In the late 1960s, my mother, increasingly disenfranchised with the Methodist Church, used to complain that the sermons were not "religious enough." Preaching had become an exercise in political protest; biblical interpretation seemed to disappear from the pulpit. "Why go to church?" she would mumble. "It's just not the same as when I was a girl. There's no purpose to it anymore."[21]

When Bass offers this quote from her mother, she explains that in the 1960s the urban clergy were becoming more political and were challenging middle-class values. There was less emphasis on biblical interpretation, spiritual comfort, and working for charity. The fashion in mainline theology had become philosophically secular and began to lose touch with the laity. When Bass's family moved to Arizona, they discovered another church that better resembled the staid Methodism—though with some evangelical and fundamentalist shadings—they had lost in urban Baltimore. When Bass joined a nondenominational church as a teenager, we may consider it her own rebellion against her parents' traditionalism. Instead of joining the secularists, as many fellow boomers did, she ran headlong into a highly devout absolutist subculture. Her rebellion ironically led her into the very piety her parents were also seeking at the time, only in a more extreme form—and this makes the trajectory of her mourning unique. It becomes all the clearer that her evangelical quest was an attempt to reclaim the very community cohesion her family had lost. Yet her attempt to completely conquer and act out against her parents' faith was ultimately unsuccessful. Bass's experience with absolutism forced her to seek ways to recover what she had lost from her days living in Baltimore.

As Bass matured, she rediscovered the joy of her early spiritual life with her parents through the solemnity of the structured ritual in Episcopalianism. She understood that evangelical salvation and theological rightness were not a substitute for the aesthetic experience of transcendence. And yet she does not altogether abandon the claims of faith she purchased in her ideologically formative years, particularly clinging to the desire for spiritual camaraderie that comes in group participation such as Bible study. This very study of the Bible leads her to a modern, textually critical love of sacred scripture. Over time her views of religion become blended with her evangelical background, and, as a final denouement, she embraces the new streams of what in the past she would have called secularism; that is, she accepts women's ordination, sees the church as a social equalizer, not an economic buttress, and is cool toward divisive discussions around abortion and biblical inerrancy. For Bass, church must remain in tension with the culture around it, but in no way separate or exclusionary.

The religious rules Bass came to accept and demand, she admits, do not come easily. Spiritual play is flexible, open, and indebted to handed-down frameworks, but always adapting to the particularity of its participants. Protestant evangelical churches cannot do both in her view. The high creedal and participatory commitment they demand bring a rigid ideological and ritual structure that does not permit the openness she finds necessary. Moreover, some of the religious distinctiveness of the evangelicals of the 1970s had dissipated while their subculture moved into the mainstream in the 1980s and 1990s, even into the world of national politics. Instead, as Bass writes, "it is hard to be a mainline churchgoer."[22] The truly strenuous journey takes on the weight of spiritual confusion and powerlessness, dispenses with pretense, and directly involves itself in community, which is for Bass the very mainline churches that have been losing members in recent decades. On the one hand, it is sometimes difficult for Bass to feel God's presence, but on the other hand, the sense of authenticity—the full acknowledgement of the other who survives our own hubris—within community is much stronger and more accessible. Spiritual play for Bass contains danger and struggle, where the stakes are high, not because they involve her personal salvation for the hereafter, but because they engage her in the overall wellbeing of those around her in the present. With this more engaged spirituality also comes a greater need for creativity to realize the potentially greater rewards it brings.

Through this work of faith in community, Bass seems to capture more than ever that sense of the common culture she experienced as a child in Baltimore. There she lived among a variety of ethnicities and the faith traditions each upheld, yet there was a sense of living in a shared space, and all things were equal. Decades later, after the major changes in the urban environment and the creation of suburbia, she had been forced to seek that community in a more abstract form. Although the Episcopal church in Alexandria, Virginia, where she became "director of faith formation," does not always resemble her ideal of a faith community, it is nevertheless a coming together of a variety of perspectives, more within the faith community itself rather than in the extended neighborhood of her childhood.

Pilgrim is a word Bass stresses toward the end of her memoir. For Bass's life of faith, being a pilgrim means taking a long, difficult journey. But it is also a journey of adventure that embraces openness to the new and a taking leave of the past in favor of the possibility of a new life. What we find striking in her calling herself a pilgrim is that it is qualitatively in contrast to that of the seeker. Bass is seeking community. She sees herself as setting out on a strenuous journey in search of community and very much intends to find it rather than questing endlessly. Even though answers are hard to come by, she is determined to reach a destination and starting over in that new place. She seeks a physical location, though one that is spiritually defined and sacralized. It would be a place where centers of value and meaning are not set in stone but are stable and an integral part of everyday life.

We also may observe that what is taking place for Bass personally is not adequately described by faith stage development. Without a doubt, a progression has been taking place, and Bass has built a wider world of understanding and universality, yet such a progression is historically, socially, and psychologically located. These contours of her development point toward the broader problems she helps solve for us all. In this case, Bass's mourning parallels how today's faith community can adapt to meet identity needs in a mobile, culturally blended world, disconnected from its past.

8
The Search for Grace: Randall Balmer

WHERE DIANA BUTLER BASS'S STRUGGLE could be summarized as
an attempt to recover the common culture of her mid-twentieth century Baltimore neighborhood, Randall Balmer's can be understood
as a mourning of the rural farm life that is the lost birthright of so
many in the United States heartland. With that social change comes
a similar set of mourning issues, but with different manifestations.
Once again, we will observe a deep rebellion, an ongoing battle with
self-recrimination, sadness, longing, and ultimately a fight to reclaim
the lost spiritual imagoes of the past. In Balmer's case, however, we
may speculate that the loss is perhaps more broadly shared with the
deepest core of American evangelical culture, as that culture is born
from the individualistic, self-made farmer or homesteader image that
is deeply embedded in our consciousness.

In his memoir, *Growing Pains: Learning to Love My Father's Faith*,
Balmer locates his beginnings with his paternal grandfather, who emigrated from Switzerland and started a farm in the Nebraska prairie.
During the Depression, this grandfather left his wife and five children in Nebraska to find work in the West, and never returned. The
struggle of farm life in a family without its father is the backdrop for
the life of Balmer's father, Clarence Balmer. One night as a young
adult, however, Clarence heard a sermon on Jesus' salvation and de-
liverance, and from there he began the lifelong commitment of an
evangelical adherent. This conversion experience was his ticket out

of the penury and hardship of farm living in the 1940s and 1950s. Clarence Balmer imagined a world of assured and glorious destiny, well-defined and supported. He went to Trinity Bible College and Seminary in Chicago and then to Wheaton Graduate School. Consequently, Randall Balmer grew up in the home of a devout, evangelical, Bible-preaching pastor in the Midwest. From the earliest possible age, his life was immersed in a strict, pious, clean-cut existence, where he lived "in a tiny world where every question had an answer."[1] The style of living was carefully defined from the day he was born through childhood, adolescence, and early adulthood:

No cards, no dancing, church three or four days a week and at least twice on Sunday. And no premarital sex. I had to sneak off to my first motion picture at the age of sixteen, feeling dreadfully guilty the whole time. We didn't have a television until I was nearly ten, although I'm not sure if that was because of religious conviction or relative poverty. Probably a bit of both.[2]

A life-defining moment in Balmer's introduction to this world came early in his preschool years, a fact that cannot be underestimated in its importance for his religious development and struggles in later life:

I was "saved" at the age of three at the kitchen table in the back of a parsonage overlooking the Minnesota prairie. After breakfast and our family devotions, my father asked if I was ready to invite Jesus into my heart. For some reason, I have a vivid mental image of the toaster, its brown fabric-covered cord trailing off the table. Yes, of course I would renounce my sinfulness and ask Jesus into my heart, and from that moment on I was saved. I had been born again.[3]

Not until much later in his life did Randall see just how impossible it would be to appropriate and understand for himself the faith his father was handing him, and how much he was instead simply creating imitative behavior that would please his parents, or in his own words, creating "a ratification of the beliefs and regimen that had been drilled into me since birth."[4] Years later, as a professor of American religion researching a book on fundamentalism, he observed adolescents around a campfire at a Christian camp in upstate New York. They were giving their "testimonies" and recommitting themselves to Jesus and a born-again faith. Balmer was reminded of his experience as a young person doing the same. His private incredulity as he watched the young campers, trying so hard to convince themselves of their depravity and sinfulness to make believable their public confessions, reminded him how much his life of faith had been committed to pleasing something external to him rather than himself. Balmer writes elsewhere in the memoir of "ritualized rebellion," the way so many teens feel compelled to manufacture a rebellion, to fabricate a sinful self, for the sole purpose of creating an acceptable conversion experience. For Balmer, this desire to bring credibility to his sinful nature began at the earliest possible age. Yet even in an environment that sanctioned mental self-flagellation, there is an artificiality and, particularly among clean-cut preacher's kids such as Balmer, an inability to understand or appreciate one's own sinful nature. The false self, in this case the "sinful false self," has complete control, inhibiting even the remotest initiatives of the true self and exploiting the mistakes that one naturally makes.

Balmer's story raises here what for many children of born-again culture is the pervasive, lifelong theme of inadequacy brought on by the expectation of parents who want spiritual metamorphosis in their preschool aged children. Such children are asked to embrace the denial of the self, and to take on the me/not-me/former-me duplicity of their parents. Erikson's stage-specific schema is particularly suggestive of what is happening here for the child of a born-again and the spiritual indoctrination they endure. Erikson, somewhat like Klein, argues that the play age is when good and bad find more complex and elaborate representations on the stage of a child's imagination. A divided self emerges and the guilt that results can be managed in the identification with the hero—elaborated in playing and storytelling—who vanquishes weak and evil "others."[5] The danger comes in identifying too strongly with the hero, or alternatively, giving up on the hero, finding it too burdensome a task. A rigid identification becomes what Erikson calls the ritualism of impersonation, which is reminiscent of Winnicott's false self. In this ritualism, play becomes stilted and uncompromising; it loses a sense of adaptability, creativity, and innovation. As a result, the play loses its luster, becomes difficult to make happen with others, and takes on a quality of "dead earnestness."

In the case of the child of the born-again, an ideological decision is placed before a child that should only be asked of those in adolescence, early adulthood, or beyond. The "decision" to invite Jesus into one's heart and take on the status of "saved" is presented as the same no matter what age. Such children are given permission, warranted or not, to skip through various developmental milestones and bypass participation in the construction of their identity. The child no longer has the opportunity or the need to *identify* with the hero, where his own individuality is preserved, suspended, and articulated in socially acceptable ways. Instead, the child *is* the hero as defined externally by the absolutist group. He or she has now stood outside of evil and gained permanent entry into existential and eternal goodness—without having needed to earn it, or to understand the consequences of not engaging it. The child is denied the expression of frustration and anger, the chance to diffuse aggression, and to experience the survival and love of the other, because the child has taken on the idealization of the other and denied the self. There is little chance to understand how to incorporate both good and bad internal feelings. There is only good—hence the prominence of the acensive position in absolutist groups. At this point ritualized play is shut down or seriously impeded, particularly regarding the content of faith and religion. Now, however, too much has been asked of the child, and he or she will always fail and fight internally to live up to their hero status. The child becomes an impersonator, always lacking self-agency and struggling, as Balmer has, with inadequacy even though he is victoriously and joyously saved and part of the fellowship of like-minded believers. In numerous instances throughout his memoir, Balmer testifies to his feeling of not measuring up:

> Why did my life seem empty, despite all of my achievements? . . What happened to the triumphant Christian life that I was supposed to experience, moving from victory to victory until I tasted sweet union with Jesus? . . "Happiness in Jesus" was so elusive that I gave up on the quest.[6]

> My spiritual life, I recognize, is only a dim reflection of that of my father, although it is something I struggle over mightily.[7]

> Still, some days I am overwhelmed by a sense of inadequacy; I wonder how the Almighty could possibly make any use out of a flawed vessel like me.[8]

In Balmer's case, the emasculation of his boyhood spiritual development was even more difficult because he was the first-born son. He felt the pressure to continue the family business, namely, his father's calling in ministry. Moreover, as the child of a preacher, Balmer dealt with the pressure of helping his father maintain a certain image. Living that life not only meant having to abide by the rules and standards of their cultural group, but it also meant giving up some boyhood dreams, initiative, and the desire to pursue his own interests. It was his father's ministry that took center stage in their family life. Parenting apparently seems to have been left to the mother, even though Balmer, as the first-born son, no doubt would need much more guidance if he was to fulfill the expectation of following his father's vocation. As Balmer writes: "The Lord's work left little discretionary time for his [Clarence's] family."[9] Subsequently, it would be his father who would come to represent all that he would be struggling against, particularly in the spiritual area: "[M]y struggle to claim the faith over the last several decades has involved a titanic struggle with my own father."[10] That struggle would not just involve finding a new path to faith over and against his father's path, but also to garner his father's love and acceptance in the process.

Early in his memoir Balmer describes how much he loved baseball as a child, even though his father took no interest in sports. When one day his father returns from town with a ball and a bat to play for the first time as father and son, Balmer "couldn't have been more excited." He writes:

> After swinging wildly at a couple of pitches, I decided to let a few go by. Somehow, even in first grade, I had learned enough about baseball to know that four balls constituted a walk and, perhaps to save myself the embarrassment of swinging and missing more pitches, I elected to draw a base on balls.
>
> "What's the point of all this?" my father huffed. "If you don't swing I'm just wasting my time." He tossed the ball in my direction, turned, and headed back to his study.
>
> We never played ball again.[11]

Balmer lost a piece of his childhood that day, unfortunately at the hand of a father who was "distant and austere, disapproving and abandoning," excellent words to summarize what transpired in the only instance father and son played baseball. As Balmer relates in these pages, his perception of God bore similarities to his perception of his father.

The expectation of Balmer to take on the identity of his father remained ever present. Such expectation could not have been made clearer than at the Christmas following his fifth birthday when Balmer was presented with a three-foot-high replica of his father's pulpit. A picture of Balmer standing behind the pulpit, at the age of seven, is reprinted on the flap of the dust jacket of the memoir. In the opening chapter of the book, he describes placing this photo on his desk in New York, at the suggestion of a friend, no doubt to better recall what it was like to be that child. He mentions that at first this image made him laugh, seeing his short-cropped hair and awkward glasses. Then the image brought on the memory of the incident with his father playing baseball. The desire to please a distant father, and the impossibility of finding satisfaction is a reminiscence brought on by the picture, and a theme that Balmer seems to have carried throughout his life. Over the years, Balmer's parents held on to that small pulpit, bringing it with them wherever Clarence had accepted a new preaching post. Balmer speculates that the pulpit symbolized an "overwhelming nostalgia" but also "dashed hopes and expectations, not to mention unanswered prayers."[12] The pulpit had become for his parents, in essence, a memorial, though perhaps one that was no longer truly alive. The pulpit signified their unfulfilled wish to see their first-born son carry on their evangelical identity and piety in a way only they could define it. Yet to Balmer, the pulpit had come to symbolize his early experience with the loss of a nurturing, mirroring, developmental environment. "The pulpit for me was a reproach; I winced whenever I saw it. It also represented everything I found co-ercive and stultifying about evangelicalism."[13]

The pulpit cuts to the core, primary religious imagoes of Balmer's spiritual life. It is an exploitation he experienced at the hands of his own parents, one that will not be easily named, which will require tremendous psychological work to overcome. Indeed, the tone of Balmer's memoir at certain places rings with anger, acrimony, and self-recrimination. It seems a constant lament, though marked with sadness and hints of forlornness. Balmer's self-agency with faith had been relinquished to his parents and the absolutism they participated in, and much of his faith from there forward would have a quality of something that had been lost or misplaced. Rediscovering it would no doubt be marked with many difficult moments of frustration, un-ease, and confusion.

Growing Pains is an unusual memoir in that it is a collection of essays Balmer had written on different occasions or presented in sep-arate speeches. There is not a clear linear direction or historical pro-gression, and some events are repeated. Even the choice of words to describe the events shows repetition. Such a book almost demands that the reader step back and look for the overall connections or themes that emerge despite the stated purpose of the book. In sum, Balmer spends the bulk of the time expressing his misgivings with his evangelical background, often exercising a tone of sadness, bitterness, resentment, and an equally significant amount of self-reproach. He omits virtually any discussion of his current involvement in church—also Episcopalian—and whether it brings him solace or a new way of articulating his faith. Instead of the stated message of the book's subtitle, *learning to love his father's faith*, it appears Balmer remains frustrated by religion. When he makes a point of saying that no one would recognize him as an evangelical, it makes one wonder if he is worried over the matter. He writes in a seemingly confident tone, "There was a time when I mourned that, but no longer."[14] In a memoir lamenting personal and cultural background, such an evaluation seems unconvincing. Intellectually, Balmer may be sure that he no longer need worry about whether he could be identified as an evangelical, particularly in his professional role as an academician of religion at an Ivy League university, but psychologically speaking, the struggle remains with much melancholy, perhaps even *because* his university life gives the illusion of distance from his childhood. We can surmise that much of the work of distancing himself from his past remains, especially when he makes statements such as that below. In speaking of his sons' religious upbringing, he writes:

> It weighs heavily on my conscience that Christian and Andrew can't recite the books of the Bible and don't know the words and motions to "Zacchaeus was a wee little man, and a wee little man was he."[15]

Yet despite Balmer's inability to come fully into the work of mourning, we also find him offering provocative pieces that connect his struggle to broader forces, essays that bear evidence to an emerging if only nascent hope for something new. Although the book is directed at his father's faith, many essays in the memoir seem totally unrelated, and a reader might wonder why they were included at all, if not to extend the book to a publishable length. Nevertheless, when applying an eye to the overall themes the book presents, such essays are perhaps the very place where we find a potent recognition of loss, although now in a more social and cultural context rather than personal. From the standpoint of the argument I am presenting in this study, Balmer's memoir appears as perhaps one of the most perceptive, though perhaps most unresolved, of both personal and collective loss than all the others. Allow me to briefly summarize each of these seemingly unconnected essays.

"Postcards" is about a collection of postcards, much of which were given to Balmer by his grandmother, that date to the middle decades of the twentieth century, a time "before instamatic cameras made us a nation of shutterbugs and before interstate highways, fast food, and television obliterated regional distinctions and transformed American culture into something as bland and sterile as a Big Mac."[16] To Balmer, postcards speak of a world when people were in awe of the country's landmarks and placed value in visiting them almost as if they were pilgrimages to enchanted holy sites. From the postcards Balmer also observed that people seemed more candid in their communications with each other, and correspondence demanded "clarity and perspicuity" unlike the instant, thoughtless babble of cell phone talking or twenty-four-hour news networks.

"My Father's Cars" describes Clarence Balmer's passion for large, beautiful American cars, despite his limited pastor's budget. When Balmer writes "I'm sure I cannot fathom all that a 1929 Model A Ford symbolized to a poor farm boy," he assigns to cars what seems to be the same significance he assigns to the evangelical faith that was his father's "ticket" out of the farming way of life. "As it turned out," Balmer continues, "a call from God, not a carburetor, liberated him from the Nebraska soil."[17] As an aside, one must wonder about the connection between financial opportunity and evangelicalism, if not also the mobility and consumerism cars represent. Nevertheless, Balmer's father's love for big cars continued throughout his life, unabated even by the oil crisis of the 1970s. This reminiscence on his father's cars represents a way for Balmer to create a desperately needed ideal of his father, one that is playfully free from the evangelical persona of his father.

"The Passing of an Era" is a tribute to Balmer's grandmother, who was born and spent most of her life on the family farm in southeastern Nebraska. During the Depression, her husband, Balmer's grandfather, left the family and never returned, eventually settling in the Northwest. This abandonment left Balmer's grandmother to raise her six children on a hundred-acre farm. Years after his grandmother had been convinced to live the final decades of her ninety-eight years in a nearby town, the farm fell into disrepair. Balmer writes, "The farmhouse itself is old and dilapidated and uncared for. The huge red barn, once the showplace of the entire community, recently collapsed beneath the ravages of time and neglect." Underlining his point, Balmer continues, "Grandma's death marks the passing of an era. All of her children have opted out of farming, and there is no one left to carry on the tradition."[18] Through time, neglect, and the dislocation that came with a postagricultural, postindustrial society, Balmer and his family lost the world that gave them definition and identity.

In "Some Thoughts on Attending a Fifteen-Year College Reunion" Balmer describes a reunion at an un-named Bible college in the suburbs of Chicago. He takes a few pages to describe how the very place that was supposed to ensure his enculturation as an evangelical, and cement his destiny as a preacher's eldest son, was ironically a place that caused him to challenge his own thinking, thanks in large part to a college president that, during the 1970s, pushed the boundaries of acceptability and hired a free-thinking faculty. But in the years since, that president was replaced with one that pandered to the conservative agenda. At the reunion, people were applauding the conformity, the improved foundational giving, the new buildings, and increased enrollments. Balmer, however, was stricken with sadness: "I felt a tragic sense of loss throughout an evening of self-congratulatory speeches and breathless soliloquies about God's faithfulness." Further on, Balmer offers an explanation that it is the loss of "creativity and critical engagement" that he misses. The result, he writes:

leads to personal despair, as I was reminded in poignant

conversations with several classmates who still struggle with feelings of guilt and inadequacy because they cannot affirm the right doctrines or conjure the requisite piety for full acceptance by the subculture.[19]

Here we once again encounter the self-recrimination that comes with failing to uphold the sacred symbols of the absolutist group, a turning in upon the self instead of an outward directed assertion against the failures of the absolutists. It is a melancholic sadness turned inward in the failure to join a group denial of loss.

"Eyes on the Fencepost" is the speech Balmer gave at his father's retirement. In it he writes that, when thinking of his father's sermons throughout a long career of preaching, it was the farm stories that he remembers best:

You shivered with him on the walk to the one-room school house, stopping in the corn shocks along the way for shelter from the wind. You felt the blistering sun in the summer, the dust in your teeth at the end of a long day of planting, cultivating, and harvesting.[20]

So convincing were the farm illustrations that "[e]ven the junior-high kids in the back . . . stopped their wiggling to pay attention to the preacher."[21] Balmer's favorite story of his father's was one about plowing a straight line by keeping "your eyes fixed on the fencepost at the far end of the field." Indeed, it would be a metaphor for his father's life, even through and perhaps especially in his seminary education. This story would likewise be the one thing that, ironically, represented all that Balmer chafed against in his father. Yet, even in the complimentary context of the speech, his closing words contained another, perhaps openly ironic and playful meaning when he said, "The furrow he had plowed is straight indeed. It is very, very straight."[22]

There are not one, not two, but three brief essays on life in California. More than any of the others, these seem at first blush the most out of place because they have little to do with either a discussion about his father or faith in America. In each of the essays Balmer laments the tragedy he sees in California, once an Eden but now a place that lives on borrowed water, allows unchecked, senseless development, and demonstrates a devaluation of humanity. To Balmer, California represents one of the most fluid and promising places for the American Dream, and yet is also perhaps the most depraved and barren in what it offers as a center of meaning and value. In two of the essays, he quotes the very same line from Joan Didion, "The future always looks good in the golden land, because no one remembers the past." Simply, Balmer is struck by the loss going on in California and the abject disregard for regional particularity and the natural environment that seems attacked most brutally.

Two additional essays turn the focus from California to Balmer's experience of living in New York. The first essay is about all the challenges and aggravations of living in a city, which he finds bearable only because of its evidence of belief in common grace and redemption. Balmer finds in this city that has so much history, so much of its own brutally leveling forces, and so much of its own human tragedy, that collective grief, forgiveness, and compassion become an absolute necessity forced upon its inhabitants. Indeed, the entire section in which these extracurricular essays fall is entitled, "Glimpses of Grace," though it is only in his essays on New York that we find some explanation of what Balmer means by grace, which seems to be encapsulated in the concept of common humanity. Other essays in this section seem only to touch upon the topic of grace, revealing what seems to be Balmer's slow movement into mourning. The other essay on New York relays Balmer's occasioning upon a group of mourners gathering at the Imagine memorial to John Lennon in Central Park. Once again, we are struck by the strong sense of loss coming from the words and subjects Balmer writes about:

When the news of his assassination spread a decade ago, radio stations played Lennon's song "In My Life," which began, "There are places I remember in my life, though some have changed," and I recall being overcome by an ineffable sadness. Sadness at Lennon's death to be sure, but also because I was reminded of the places and people in my own past that I could never recover.[23]

Surely for someone raised in America's heartland and now living in Manhattan, the change in going from the homogeneity of his evangelical past to the melting pot of one of the largest and most complex cities in the world would bring what must be a very palpable sense of loss. Moreover, like Lennon and the lyrics from his song "Imagine," Balmer can only agree and bemoan along with Lennon who seemed to know that "something was terribly wrong with Western culture—its materialism, its vapid religion, its easy resort to violence."[24] Balmer's awareness of materialism, vapidity, and violence is made all the more acute by their various manifestations in the absolutism of the culture in which he was raised.

Having reviewed Balmer's variegated autobiographical pieces, we must ask whether it is not without significance that in a book about the struggle and the negotiations with a father's evangelical faith, we find so much discussion of broader changes in society during the last several decades. Understanding the changes, even lamenting them, as Balmer does the degradation he perceives in California, is for Balmer an act of mourning. If we assume that evangelicalism represents for Balmer an evasion of the changes, then "loving his father's faith," that is, creatively reincorporating it, may only be possible through understanding and facing the very problems these changes bring. Moreover, we should take care to recognize that facing the ultimate, Oedipal other found in these broader contexts, likewise helps Balmer heal, or in the words of Klein, repair his primary objects as defined by his relationship to his father. The constellation of his essays, then, represent a dialectical working through of the social and the personal. Where society has become abandoning and distant, Balmer looks for instances of grace that simultaneously repair his relationship to his father and help him recover the wonder lost at the hands of his father during boyhood.

Even among these revealing entries in Balmer's memoir, perhaps the strongest insight he offers, regarding his struggle with his father, and subsequently his father's faith, comes in the reflections about his grandfather. Balmer's grandfather, Fred Balmer, was a Swiss immigrant who settled on a homestead in Nebraska, early in the twentieth century. When the Depression hit, as mentioned, Fred left his wife and children in the effort to find work. Fred never returned, and eventually divorced his wife and left the family to fend for themselves. It was out of this environment that Balmer's father Clarence, the youngest, fled to the vocation of pastor in an evangelical tradition, while his other siblings likewise moved on to careers that permanently removed them from the family farm. Balmer's father seemed especially estranged from his father, driven deeper by his faith's doctrinal position on divorce and alcohol, two moral points on which the grandfather had failed grimly. Having never forgiven Fred for his desertion, few opportunities ever arose for Clarence Balmer's son Randall to see his grandfather.

The tone of the words Balmer uses to describe his handful of experiences with this grandfather expose an enigmatic reverence for the man. Balmer seems taken aback by the great differences in temperament between his father and grandfather. The former seems brooding and distant, whereas the latter seems to be "a contented and peaceful man."[25] Having emigrated from Switzerland, Fred Balmer was the outcast of his family, a characteristic with which Randall finds affinity—perhaps especially now that he himself had likewise committed the unpardonable sin of divorce. Balmer made only one visit alone to his grandfather's small farm, and there is an undeniable note of hope and joy in Balmer's description of this memory, even of a playfulness that he never seemed to experience at the foot of his own father:

Grandpa drove me in his 1965 Mustang to the Oregon coast, where we sat wordlessly for a long while taking in its incomparable beauty. Along the way he turned to spit tobacco juice out the window, but he had neglected to roll it down. Thinking I hadn't noticed, he discretely wiped it with a handkerchief, stealing a glance in my direction. We shoveled manure from a local farm into the back of his pickup truck for redistribution in his garden, and when we came in from our chores he offered me some home-made elderberry wine. He also took me by the Helvetia Tavern down the road, where he proudly introduced me to his friends.[26]

How different this grandfather must have seemed, and still seems, to Balmer. Balmer briefly departs from the forlorn tone that we find through much of his memoir and shows glimpses of freedom and self-agency. In Balmer's explanations and evaluations of his evangel-ical past, much of his cool headedness seems to come from his aca-demic persona, what is perhaps, at least in part, a construction of a false self. The voice he speaks with as an academic lacks the winsome initiative and uniqueness that we find in his pining for his grandfa-ther. The grandfather seems in fact the negative image of Balmer's own father, and more importantly, a father-figure in whom the bad coexists with the good. For Balmer's own father, as with much of the Protestantism in which Balmer was reared, there is little room be-yond victory in Jesus and the strict living. Incorporating the bad with the good is an impossibility. As a child, Balmer could never assume the depressive position, and find the room to mourn the loss of the good object—as evidenced by the abandoning father who walked away from the batting practice. The father rebuked him and would not be there to receive the boy's disappointment and anger. Subse-quently, Balmer would find difficulty in enlarging his world beyond the good object he had constructed thus far, to say nothing of en-gaging more of his world beyond his "father's faith."

Balmer himself, ironically, had become in many ways a prisoner of "victory in Jesus," never knowing what had been won, where the battlefield was, or why there had been a fight. Balmer was a recipient of the victory, and not a participant. The grandfather, however, made no pretension about salvation, and yet, at least in Balmer's mind, had found grace. Such contentedness amid one's own failings becomes a fascination and enchantment for Balmer, which he never experi-enced in the platitudes of his Sunday school teachers. We may speculate that to the extent Balmer can engage the memory of his grandfather, and a feeling of being loved and accepted by that man, he will better incorporate his anger at both his own father and also himself. Now that both his father and grandfather have died, that task is more of a necessity than ever before. Assembling a collection of writings about his father, his upbringing, and the world that the father's faith was responding to in fact creates a memorialization of his father, even an act of play. We should expect that writing the pieces in the book was a step in expressing his feelings of nostalgia and melancholy.

Like his grandfather who found his ticket out of Switzerland and subsequently the failure of an American dream in Nebraska by going to the West coast on his own, and like his father who found his ticket out through evangelicalism and the sometimes peripatetic life of a pastor, so too must Balmer find his ticket out. Perhaps to demonstrate Balmer's own new direction, in his *Thy Kingdom Come: An Evangelical's Lament*, he takes the absolutist approach within evangelicalism to task, expressing his desire to claim a new way of being evangelical, one free of the recent political accretions it has been assigned:

As an evangelical Christian, someone who takes the Bible seriously and who believes in the transformative power of Jesus, I want to reclaim the faith from the Religious Right. I also want to protest that most of the Religious Right's agenda is misguided, even ruinous, to the nation I love and, ultimately, to the faith I love even more.[27]

9
Freedom and Discovery: Carlene Cross

LOSS OF FAITH SOMETIMES COMES because of some imperceptible agent in our lives, such as exposure to alternate worldviews or social mobility. Other times it may come through action in the face of real threats and dangers. In the case of Carlene Cross, as she describes in *Fleeing Fundamentalism: A Minister's Wife Examines Faith*, removing herself from her life as the wife of a fundamentalist pastor became a matter of personal survival. For Cross, the work of mourning meant not mere theological jousting and fading away from a toxic church environment, but literally running for dear life from the very thing she had loved, in which she had invested her livelihood, and where she thought she was comfortably placed. While all the psychological elements of suffering through loss are present, Cross's more extreme situation asked her to face the feelings of loss head on. Some of these feelings may be mastered quite successfully, while others must necessarily be driven underground to be dealt with later once everyday life has moved to a safer place. Cross's story illustrates just how starkly these mourning issues may be confronted and how an individual can creatively address a loss that is personal, social, historical, and cultural.

Cross's upbringing took place in a remote region of Montana where her father was a farmer. Cross's father was a nonpracticing Catholic who emigrated in 1910 from Bohemia (Czech Republic) to the United States and was a man who distrusted preachers of any kind. Her mother was from a more sophisticated background, that is, "an impressive lineage of French sea captains, Revolutionary War Heroes, and poets."[1] Unlike Cross's father, her mother properly enunciated her words, liked to read widely, and enjoyed the philosophical conversations she could have with a Bible college evangelist who would occasionally pay them visits.[2] Seemingly desperate for cultural activity, her mother became interested in the evangelical culture that was growing at the time, and read books like Hal Lindsey's *Late Great Planet Earth*, which predicted an imminent apocalypse.

Due to the remoteness of their farm, there was no nearby church that Cross's family could attend. However, she herself was able to attend a vacation Bible school every year, and there she came to believe that she was a sinner and at age eight asked "the Lord to come into my heart and clean it up." In comparison to some other stories we have reviewed, Cross was not attending any type of church group on a regular basis and the impact of this childhood conversion experience lacked the type of encompassing community reinforcement that others often experience. In Cross's high school years, religion did, however, become a regular component of her household once a church formed nearby and her mother, even her father, began to attend regularly. Cross offers few details of this experience other than that it was the result of efforts by the same Bible college that brought the vacation Bible school and Hal Lindsey to their area "preaching that the Bible represented the exact words of God."[3] It was finally at the age of seventeen that Cross describes what became for her a moment of primary acceptance of this fundamentalist brand of Christianity:

That evening in 1975, I sat in the kitchen of our old farmhouse and listened to the rainsquall move over the Rockies and into our valley. I felt the air grow heavy and oppressive, almost purple, as off to the east leaped platinum branches of lightning, momentarily suspended in silence until thunder shook the windowpanes with a great crash. A second lightning bolt flickered in the alfalfa field outside, illuminating the page open before me: "And I stood upon the sand of the sea, and saw a beast rise up out of the sea, having seven heads and ten horns, and upon his horns ten crowns, and upon his heads the name of blasphemy."[4]

She continues describing her reading the book of Revelation while the storm rages outside:

I thought of the desperate future of the world and how Mom said that Jesus was coming back to rapture all the faithful Christians to heaven and leave all the unsaved behind to live through the Great Tribulation and wear the Beast's brand. It was in that moment that I stepped from the pathway of my normal life and detoured into another world—that of serving God rather than indulge my own sinful flesh, which, until that instant, I had always been happy to do.[5]

For Cross, her religion dictated that the world was near its end, that strife and suffering for unbelievers was imminent. The violent nature of her religious worldview would even cause her nightmares about the impending doom. And she reflects that "[my] attraction to fundamentalism was not out of quiet reflection but cold fear."[6]

One of the key psychological features of Cross's memoir is the nature of her opposite attachments to her mother and her father. She describes her mother as learned, intelligent, and cultured, and her father as her family representative of everything backward that one finds in the desolate prairie. She believed that her father saw her as a willful, independent child, like a wild horse that, needed to be broken. Her mother, however, "who had buried a life that might have been," took an interest in Cross's development, driving her eighty miles to dance lessons, piano lessons, and orthodontia appointments. Cross no doubt loved her father and his sense of tireless devotion and knew that she had become a "snobbish child," one who was "embarrassed to be from the country." She would imagine herself as Kathryn Hepburn, "self-assured and witty—not plain and coarse." And she would hide out in the local library's alcove reading glitzy magazines and dream of living in big cities.[7]

Cross's way out of the world of the Montana prairie, however, would not come through the glittering life of a Hollywood actor, but through the world of an absolutist and separatist subculture. She had enrolled in a small Christian Bible college 500 miles away from home, where her brother had matriculated the previous year. There she felt affirmed in her commitment to a tangible, right way of living, sure that she would be putting a sinful past behind her.

I had a strong feeling that a chapter of my life was ending and another one about to begin. . . . This was the *real* world, not the carnal one. . . . It was exciting to be inducted into this new family that had taken the mantle of 'defender of the faith' . . . leading the fight against the Catholics, who worshipped icons, the Jews, who didn't believe that Jesus was God, and the liberals, who didn't acknowledge the Bible as inerrant . . . I decided to take the Bible seriously right from the start and follow its teachings to the letter.[8]

Cross's ideological hunger of young adulthood, seemingly thwarted by the barrenness of Montana prairie farm life, now met with an ideologue's feast. Learning doctrine, memorizing scripture, even abiding by strict dress and behavior codes at this small college of 250 students gave Cross an impenetrable identity, seemingly strong and safe from any outside influence. In a manic-like under-taking, she transferred her desires and good objects onto the isolated group of which she was now a part. Cross had found her release from a backward world, but at the cost of substituting Bible study and strict social codes for a love of literature, glamour, and glitz. By going to college, she had discovered a way to embrace her mother's lost dreams, even if now she, like her mother, was entering a world that was far from her original ideals.

Cross's transition into the world of fundamentalism was made even more complete when she met David Brant, the man who would become her husband. He was the small college's star student and a witty and compelling preacher. The campus's "most eligible bachelor" and "the most impeccable Christian scholar" was all the more renowned on campus because he had come from a background that included a violent, alcoholic father, where Brant himself had learned to abuse alcohol as a teenager. Brant's personal story could be used to enthrall his listeners and convince them of the power of faith to turn any life around, making him "a real catch for the team" and giving concrete evidence of a God that is active in the world today. For Cross, his allure couldn't have been stronger because he sounded so intelligent:

> I took my notebook and pen and quickly wrote down all the astonishing phrases and new religious vocabulary he was using: complicated words like *Eucharist*, *Soteriology*, and *Septuagint*. He had a genius for language, and it occurred to me that he sounded worlds apart from the Montana cowhands I'd grown up listening to.[9]

Yet even as Cross's commitments to this world grew and became more involved, her memoir demonstrates a continued duality in her desire for independence as a woman of the world and her efficient devotion to integrity and self-reliance, an extension of the combined influence of her mother's desire for knowledge and her father's individualism. While evangelizing Hutterite women (interesting in itself) in a secluded community in eastern Montana, Cross worried over their lack of opportunity, though marveled at their "unguarded tenderness." When smuggling Bibles to Poland during the final years of the Cold War era, she was given time to travel to France, where "Paris enticed me into a warm lust for life. For a brief glimpse, the city illuminated the dark lens of pessimism that I had faithfully worn as prescribed."[10] On the surface, she sees her struggle as one between the pious prescriptions of the fundamentalist world she inhabits and her "lustful," sinful nature, which despite her every effort she cannot suppress. Even her dreams represent this core struggle between the authority she submitted to and her yearnings for glamour and independence:

I started having nightmares about my wayward mind, dreaming that I was making a distressing journey through a succession of hostile landscapes. I was a dazed wartime nurse, lost among the rubble of London in 1945, running through a labyrinth of bombed out multistory buildings; then a bewildered Puritan, shaking in a dank prison and waiting to be examined by the magistrate for the devil's mark. In the final dream I am fleeing a German inquisitor (a man who had the same mailbox mouth as Mr. Foreman), hiding in a barn loft and peering out into the quiet snow that whispered softly down to earth.[11]

In each sequence, Cross is playing the role of someone running from catastrophe, defined at least in part by the apocalyptic obsessions of her subculture. Her role within the dreams evokes a theme of nobility amidst ruin, either as a wartime nurse, one who ministers and helps others despite risks to her own safety, or as a "bewildered Puritan," one who strives to live an exceptional, pious life, but nevertheless is capriciously accused of wrongdoing. She does not identify herself in the third sequence except to say that she is once again a runaway, but this time from a German inquisitor, one who resembles a particularly hostile professor with a "mailbox mouth" at her Bible college, but finds protection in a barn loft, nestled in a peaceful snowstorm, which may be a recollection of her Montana prairie home. The metaphors of these dreams represent both the collective fundamentalist view that the world is an evil place on a path of self-destruction and her own struggle to reclaim independence amid that worldview. The nightmares showcase the unconscious working through of the dissonance of her current life, and bear evidence on how the good internal objects of her childhood years are making demands on her present, early adult experiences of conscious self-organization.

Unfortunately for Cross, the dualities of her life would only worsen in the coming years, and her struggle to overcome them would become greater and more entrenched. After she graduated from the Bible college, Cross married Brant, and immediately began having children, the first being born when she was twenty-one. Brant went on to earn two master's degrees at two different seminaries, one in Washington and then one in Chicago, bringing his family with him to each place. After seminary, Brant was asked to pastor a church in Washington. During this time Cross eventually realized that she was being asked to suspend her interests in Bible study and intellectual engagement and instead assume the role of a quiet pastor's wife. At the same time, Brant seemed to become more concerned with control over Cross, focusing on her image and on how clean she was keeping their home.

To explain the new role she felt compelled to assume, Cross relates two experiences in which she went for training to be a minister's wife. One was a seminar given at the Bible college while she was still a student there. Entitled "Being a Godly Addition to Your Husband's Ministry," the seminar was given by seven women who sat behind a table and offered advice on what to expect. One speaker, who Cross defines as "a lifeless face that looked like a waxwork in candlelight," admonished the listeners to remain soft-spoken and nonthreatening. Another speaker advised that as a minister's wife one should not make friends with any of the other women in the congregation, as it will spark jealousy, or result in a private comment about one's husband and become grist for the rumor mill.[12] The other experience occurred years later at a church conference in the Northwest. Pastors' wives were competing about their husbands' programs and building proposals, and they were not actually interacting with one another. In the evenings, they would wander through the camp pathways alone "with poker-faced politeness." During a lecture about maintaining professional distance, one woman broke down in tears, revealing her failures to maintain such distance and how she had possibly jeopardized her husband's ministry. All the comforting comments the woman received seemed insincere to Cross:

I stepped back, and suddenly the crowd looked like a herd of sheep, like those my Uncle Bud raised on his ranch back in Montana. "Blah, blah, baaaaah," they bleated. "Sheep," I remember my uncle saying, "are the damnedest critters. Cattle will spook and stampede, squeeze past a broken fence, or push through a pole gate to freedom—but not sheep. They'll stay happily corralled and easily made into mutton without one single protestation." I turned and fled the room, closing the gate behind me.[13]

Cross leaves the room and heads down to the lake where the conference is being held and admonishes herself saying, "You. You have come to accept your own subjugation."[14]

The revelation in the memoir of her husband's controlling behavior, and Cross's full realization of the role she was being required to fulfill, mark a turning point in her narrative. A few pages later Brant admits to her that he had been sneaking out of the house to go to strip clubs. His habit, in fact, is an addiction, evidenced by an admission that he even did it when Cross was in labor with their third child. From this point forward their relationship began to deteriorate. There was an attempt at counseling, but it was sabotaged by Brant. Her husband became more severe in his behaviors, recruiting two other couples in their congregation to join them both in alcohol-soaked nights out, then to return home and bathe nude together in a hot tub. On one occasion, Brant, the dynamic pastor of a rapidly growing church, attempted to dance on stage during an amateur night at a gay bar. Cross increasingly thought of separation and divorce but was terrified at going it alone as a single parent with no credentialed education or work experience, not to mention that she was unprepared to face the fact that a divorce meant ruining her husband's ministry.

Yet despite her fears, Cross began laying the groundwork for leaving her husband and the religion she had adhered to so carefully. Cross applied her skills as a student and began devouring books on Christian history. The books became one of her lifelines, even though she hid them in a closet so as not to aggravate her husband or raise the judgmental interest of parishioners visiting their home.

They affirmed her earliest intellectual ambition:

> As I studied, I felt as if I were following a light far in the distance, breaking its way through the fog. The more I read, the more I discovered that most of what I was taught in Bible college was refuted by historical record.[15]

At the end of this flurry of independent study, which included study in biblical criticism, Cross had an acute experience of reorientation in her worldview. It occurred while driving in a car during a rainstorm, not unlike her conversion experience as a teenager:

> Suddenly I saw myself at seventeen, sitting in our old farmhouse kitchen while that wild rainsquall beat against the windows, sending rivers of water down the glass much as it was now doing on the car windows. . . . *When you're a child, everything is simple*, I thought—*you know it all.* You leap into a boat and begin rowing without hesitation, without shame, without reflection. . . . Tears filled my eyes, and I turned my head to the Cascade Mountains, obscured in fog. I cried, not over my loss of faith, but because I didn't have the guts to pick up the oars and save myself from the catastrophe ahead, to leave the church or my marriage.[16]

What this period represented for Cross may seem in some respects just a simple shift from one theological worldview to another. Alternatively, it may more properly represent the creation of a new worldview. Beyond the doctrinal and codified coercions of her subculture, she was discovering a more reality-driven, although largely undefined, life beyond. Cross's biblical study signaled that the rules surrounding her sacred symbols were changing. Moreover, by describing her discoveries in her memoir she is creating a text that others can read and objectify and, in some fashion, participate in the culture creating it offers.

Despite this new set of rules emerging internally, Cross's external circumstances had not yet shifted. Her mourning process had only begun. Cross's acquiescence to her husband's duplicity and that of the fundamentalist subculture made her feel as if she herself was now being duplicitous. Even within the discoveries she was making about religion through her own study, she still experienced a high degree of self-recrimination, bordering on the edge of melancholia, primarily because of the initiative she had taken. Her strong adherence to whatever new discoveries she was making were infused with spite and unresolved anger, which likewise contributed to the self-recrimination. The new worldview she was constructing as a means of survival was in danger of remaining quite rigid. In Winnicott's terms, the potential space she inhabited had not enlarged or become more fluid; rather, it was still encapsulated in a limited, marginally functional set of confines. At night's end of one particularly drunken excursion with her husband and another couple, Cross was nauseous and vomiting and describes the experience as follows:

> I hung my head over the toilet and threw up again, trying to expel the cesspit of self-loathing that festered inside me. *You are as hypocritical as the worst of religious charlatans*, I told myself, *if the wolf in front of you is David, the precipice at your back is your own deceit.*[17]

Just like the person who becomes angry with the loved one that has died yet directs that anger inward because he or she feels guilty over their anger, Cross was at war with her own guilt over not being strong enough and aware enough to direct her anger toward the rigid ideals and the people who propagate them, including her husband. By and large, Cross had already detached herself from the situation she was in, found new symbols to structure her world, but had not yet put herself physically in a place where she could fully detach the past and live out those new symbols.

Not until the day when Cross's husband had become especially abusive verbally did she determine that she must leave him and the life they had built. She decided to stop home-schooling her children, to take on a waitressing job, quit attending church regularly, and begin taking classes to earn a bachelor's degree. She adopted a mantra of "job, education, emancipation." True to the experience of many who have finally stopped identifying with an absolutist group, Cross felt liberated. "In the days that followed, I felt excited, almost giddy. . . . No one was going to get a chance to talk me out of it. Even God, if He did happen to exist, wouldn't be able to sway me."[18]

As her new life began, she started coming face-to-face with the slow process of mourning. While waitressing at Seattle's Space Needle, she became friends with LGBTQ coworkers, and felt shame over her past ignorance in condemning people she knew little about. A new critical self-agency was emerging. Then, during a church Bible study led by Brant, a question was posed by a member of the group about whether hell was a literal place. Brant's response was an unequivocal affirmation of hell, based on Jesus' mention of it in the New Testament. But Cross spoke up, saying she was not certain she agreed. There was only an embarrassing silence, followed by an outright reprimand from one of the other women of the church after the meeting. Cross's mere raising of the question bore evidence to her emerging self-agency, a good object for which she had developed strengthening affect. Alternatively understood, the question she posed was an aggressive act of dispensing with the idealized object within; it represented a courageous step for an ego, or a true self, affirming itself in a hostile environment. Cross survived the attack. In yet another sense, she was ministering to herself without external help. What on the surface seemed a futile act, was in fact on the inside a therapeutic moment.

After a final act of reckless behavior by her husband—in the wintertime he had left the children alone in their house with no heat for hours when he was supposed to be caring for them—Cross told him to leave, beginning their separation. When he apparently came to their house late one night some days later and slashed her tires, she decided to purchase a gun, upon the unofficial recommendation of a police officer who cautioned her that a restraining order would only further aggravate a man like her husband.

While these external struggles progressed, Cross continued with her self-directed study of religion. She explored the patriarchal

accretions of the Old and New Testament, feeding her desire for independence from dogma. She discovered research on the moments
in ancient history when goddess religions existed and when their creation myths were rewritten by conquering groups, a process called
"remything." Again, we see her describing these turning points in her
thinking during experiences with water, no doubt a marker to the
reader that they were conversional moments, like a baptism. Some
of this study took place on the shore of Lake Washington, as she
relaxed while her children played in the sand and the water. After one
day on the lakeshore, she writes:

> I was still thinking about this ancient remything event when I
> stepped up the porch stairs and into the house that evening, tak-
> ing off my sandals and walking barefoot across the soft carpet and
> upstairs into the bathroom. I undressed, turned on the shower,
> and stepped in.
> *So what if Genesis three is simply a remything event?. .*
> I stepped out of the shower and went back downstairs in my
> bathrobe, leaving wet footprints on the carpeted steps. . . .
> I thought maybe that was why Yahweh told the Hebrews to
> annihilate the people of the land: to eliminate the female threat
> found in the goddess worshippers. . . .
> One summer evening, after hours of reading, I felt angry and
> exhausted, my thoughts beginning to bunch up in a corner of my
> mind. I needed some air, so I closed my book, threw on my over-
> coat, and began walking up the street while a fine mist covered
> my face.[19]

She also read carefully through the letters of Paul, evaluating his
restrictions over women in church and weighing those against the
overall message of Jesus. Such observations, along with her experience with her husband's illicit behavior, and upon hearing similar
stories about the husbands of two of her fundamentalist friends—
one about a husband who had been visiting prostitutes and another
about a husband who had been hiding a large box of violent

pornography—led Cross to wonder about whether the brand of Christianity that she had been a part of actually contributed to a problem of male sexual domination and abuse.

Balancing work, school, and children, Cross ran into a period of financial trouble, and she applied for welfare. Her sense of isolation grew, and her mental state took a turn for the worse. She describes a dream at this point in her memoir where she is standing at a train station, self-assured, reading *Cosmopolitan* and just as she's about to board an elegant train, she realizes that she doesn't have her ticket. As the train pulls away from the station, she is left alone and standing naked. The dream manifests her desperate fear that her goal may not be attainable. At this time, her religious cynicism grew, driven even deeper through an intellectual history course she attended in college where she was exposed to the thought of Friedrich Nietzsche. She had reached a new emotional despondency. Spite for her past grew, but was also perhaps more conscious and objectified, and was better externalized rather than self-directed:

> To me, simple literary criticism made it clear that placing the Gospels in the same text as Paul's letters was like attaching *The Bhagavad Gita* to *Mein Kampf*.
> It was time to take Christianity and send it to the morgue.[20]

Cross's desperation seemed complete. She had begun to question if life had any meaning whatsoever. She started running "for hours every day." Then her husband delivered what she thought would be the final blow. Brant ran up a credit card debt that showed up on Cross's own credit report and prevented her from receiving a necessary student loan. The night she learned this news, she retrieved some gin from her freezer and became drunk. But amid her tears, one of her daughters approached her and hugged her, saying, "It's okay, Mom. We're going to be okay." She describes what is a clear turning point:

> My mind said back to me, "This is your evidence of the divine."

In my little daughter's indomitable spirit was mirrored the Hebrew meaning of her name, Micael: one who is like God. . . . It was the only faith I held, the only truth that remained, the only sign of God I trusted. My job was to finish the journey for them.[21]

Cross came out fighting, called up Brant and demanded he clear the debt. She realized at that moment that "something inside me could not close off the universe, reducing all truth to a narrow string of empirical operations, cold as a razor's edge." The credit incident was the final abandonment, coming at a moment when all self-persecutory thought had been spent, and the daughter represents the new God, the new-yet-old goodness that Cross can now reactivate and for which she can now pine. Her transitional space began to widen. "I had to acknowledge that stubbornly rejecting all possibility of God displayed the same intolerance I had found in Fundamentalism. Dogma, religious or empirical, ended the pilgrimage of discovery."[22] With her student loan back in place, Cross resumed her coursework. In her classes, she enjoyed expressing opinions whenever the occasion called for it. She formed a crush on one of her professors. She felt as if the future "was starting to weave a hopeful pattern." After she received her bachelor's degree, she even found the opportunity to attend graduate school.

One of the final chapters of the book, entitled "Going Home," describes times when Cross brought her children to Montana to show them their heritage. The irony of returning to the roots she had spent so much energy deriding did not escape her. She had worked hard at keeping her rural background a secret, and yet now she was enjoying introducing it to her children. She was returning to the world of her childhood "without hesitation." This returning represents a regression to Cross's past in service of the ego, an adaptive maneuver that allows her to rediscover her childlike trust and hope, then to have capacity to create new ideas, new structure, and growth. Her reactivation of the world in which she first overcame the depressive position is now complete. She now can recognize her sorrow over her mistakes and losses and is free to form an identification with an emerging sense of home and family. The very ambitiousness that had driven her into a life of fundamentalism, insofar as it was an object attached to her mother, had run its course in the rebuking of her life with Brant, and now she was pining for the quiet, lonely prairie that her father had embraced all his life. "It was the same calm loneliness that renewed my soul," she writes. Moreover, she recalled the words of her father: "'Some folks find God in a church,' Dad would say, 'but I find him here on this prairie, all around me, everywhere.'"[23] On her return west to the Seattle area from one of these trips she stopped by the church where her husband had been a celebrated pastor. The church was quiet, empty, and abandoned; weeds had overgrown its grounds:

> At that moment the great mystery that hides behind our tears, behind our exhausted, browbeaten days, seemed to shine through the clouds and let me know that grace had always been there, watching over me, watching over my children. I cried over my own bitterness—the anger that I'd clung to like a tattered blanket for years. It was time to let it go. It was time to separate the concept of spirituality from the aberration of Fundamentalism.[24]

New psychic structure had formed. Cross had grown spiritually, but only through leaving the religion that used to define and mediate her spirituality. Cross at this point begins to delve into Buddhism, following the path of many who find it necessary to turn inward for their connection to something sacred. She also reads through the Gnostic Gospels of Jesus. She quotes the Gnostic Jesus as saying, "If you bring forth what is within you, what you bring forth will save you. . . . He who has known himself has simultaneously achieved knowledge about the depth of all things."[25]

A word that succinctly describes Cross's spiritual rebirth is *discovery*. In the concluding remarks of her book, she once again uses that word, writing that "spiritual growth is a road of discovery—not of submission to a rule book."[26] Without a doubt, this realization for Cross is just what she needed to regain her trust in the world and find a new relation to ultimacy or what matters most. We must ask at this point, however, whether her looking into Buddhism, or her interest in Jesus' secret gospels, will remain useful to her and continue to provide her with a sense of discovery. This more mystical alternative gives her reprieve from the dogmatic confines of her absolutism and adds a dimension to her religiosity that was no doubt missing. Yet now that she has found grace and freedom, widened her transitional space, and developed new psychic structure, will she develop as a self in relation to others, and ultimately engage the socially constructed symbols of the world she lives in?

10
The Yoke of Rationalism:
Margaret McGee

BY MANY ACCOUNTS the spiritual journeys discussed to this point have each borne evidence of deep social and personal loss. In each memoir, while in some ways the loss has been engaged, denial and avoidance of the loss remains a problem. In each narrative there is always a sense, at least from an observer's point of view, that there is so much more to come for each of the storytellers. The story, in most cases, has not yet reached its third act, much less its denouement. The freedom from the trauma of loss, while found only when the trauma is confronted, comes in glimpses and shattered pieces. The internal struggle continues. The first narrative discussed—that of Kate Young-Caley—seemed to embody sadness. In the midst of the struggles, the hope of resolution and reparation seemed palpable. Caley's story was a clear, open, and powerful illustration of the mourning process at work. The other accounts all had their moments of working through as well, each in their own contexts and according to their needs. The final memoir that follows, however, shows someone on a journey that from many angles seems to be operating in the world of postmourning. It at first looks as though a self-agency works unhindered and can function and explore at will the possibilities of the diverse spiritual landscape around it. This person's journey appears, in comparison to the others, highly creative, well embedded in tradition, and far from the stereotype of the seeker on the perpetual spiritual quest, never really engaged in community. Yet in reading this memoir one must work hard at finding *any* signs of loss and mourning, either individually, socially, or culturally. Without a doubt they are there, but this story is one of relatively little trauma, and to a degree represents the path of those who have not come from extreme situations. This person is part of the larger group of spiritual travelers who perhaps have experienced little acute absolutism yet nevertheless are living with the broader social and cultural strokes of loss. This position includes its own set of challenges, some that are just as problematic, beginning with the fact that they are all that much harder to name—proving more than ever that it is difficult to mourn an ideal.

Raised in Ohio by parents who were both the children of ministers and strong believers in good grades, Margaret McGee reports that "We worshipped equally at the dual altars of church and school. . . ," and she was good at both.[1] Her father was the superintendent of both the school district and her church's Sunday school program. Her parents' fathers were both ministers in the Evangelical United Brethren Church, which merged with the Methodists in 1968, and which became the denomination of the church where she experienced her early spiritual life. McGee describes her early church participation in a few broad strokes throughout her book and, other than relaying a few perceptions of God and faith, offers little indication that she found religion rigid or stultifying. There are no appearances from angry church leaders, disenfranchising distant parents, or overbearing ritualizations. In fact, McGee's exposure to religious tradition seemed to have a rhythm in which she found solace and stability, and even a little age-appropriate boredom. McGee also conveys that in church she could be a star, serving as an acolyte and even a reader of scripture when her church held a children's service.

At the age of twelve, however, her mother drove her to a Christian camp in West Virginia. Here her narrative takes a marked turn toward a feeling of aloneness and coldness. Not unlike many preadolescent children who are taken to a summer camp and left there by their parents, McGee felt alone and unhappy. She does not mention the word homesickness but does write about not being able to find a single friend while she was there, which is reminiscent of Carlene Cross's experience at a pastors' wives conference.

The camp was the place that exposed her most clearly to the more severe and far-reaching vagaries of absolutist religion:

> At camp I had my first up-close experience with hell and redemption, which changed my relationship to Jesus and drew me temporarily closer to the church. And yet it was that same experience that sowed seeds for my later desertion.
>
> That's because I was saved at summer camp, and it was only after I was saved that I could know for certain that I was going to hell.[2]

McGee notes that in her upbringing she was saved three times: twice at summer camps and once in front of her parents at a church revival. She appears well aware that the more extreme forms of her experience with religion provide for her the objects of her later disenfranchisement. She does not elaborate specifically on these experiences elsewhere in the book, but does lament religion's exclusiveness, male-centeredness, literalism, and historicism, as well as its vulnerability to personal and social corruption. However, alongside these commonplace experiences with absolutism, the world of education and the pursuit of knowledge soon began to have an equally powerful influence. Consider for example an experience she relays about a high school science project:

> In the ninth grade we took general science from Mrs. Harris, and I had a conversion experience there much more long-lasting and profound than any that had happened to me in church.[3]

McGee goes on to describe that her teacher offered extra credit to anyone who created an insect collection with a display case and included scientific identifications. McGee became fascinated with insects, "especially iridescent and colored ones," and decided to take on the project. One of her main tasks was to create a "killing jar" using an empty mayonnaise jar, cotton balls, and ammonia. She would capture an insect in the jar, watch it die, pluck it out with tweezers, pin it inside a cigar box, and include a label with the scientific name she had found in a book from the library. As someone who was once afraid of insects, she describes her sheer delight in bicycling to fields around her home, capturing insects with a net—sometimes even with her hands—killing them and collecting them until she had a tower of cigar boxes of classified and categorized insects. She describes her experience in good detail and with enthusiasm, even relaying for example her observation of how stubborn wasps were at dying, insects that "won my respect."[4] Yet after so much work with insects, McGee began to lose interest:

> Gradually, the joy drained out of insect collecting. The insects I loved the most, the bright butterflies and the iridescent dragonflies and beetles, lost what I loved about them in the process.[5]

Here McGee comes up against a great world of wonder and fascination. In her encounter with and in her effort to get close to nature, she finds herself an aggressor and killer. After her work at getting close to insects, she finds she is destroying the very thing she loves and admires. There is a parallel here to the infant's first encounters with the mother that Klein describes. To come into relationship with the mother, the infant learns to differentiate subject and object, the me and not me. In so doing, the object becomes split between good and bad, the good breast and the bad breast. Acting out against the bad, which is also the good, and yet seeing the mother survive the aggression and still love the infant, creates an object that the infant, in Winnicott's words, can *use*. The infant's sense of participation in externality brings about its growing personal investment and faith in the external world. In McGee's attempt to encounter objects of complete wonder, she acts out against them, witnesses the consequences of her quest to conquer the world of insects, sees that world survive despite herself, and gains a new respect and love for it.

Most importantly, she has found an object she can use that has opened a space for play and discovery:

> At the time, it didn't feel like conversion: I didn't cry, and I didn't sense God at work in my cigar boxes. But I had walked through a door, and the world on the other side held more chances for the divine to show through.[6]

McGee's basic trust and faith, her ability to play, and her feeling of awe are at work here through an individualized, relatively unstructured, and seemingly unspiritual content, and yet her experience packs all the power and hope that the most social, highly structured, and deeply symbolic content is supposed to elicit. The mere inclusion of her bug stories in a memoir about faith is revealing. More to the point, the drama she plays out in her insect collecting is truer to the words *conversion, transformation,* and *change* than any experience she had with being "saved" three times.

McGee offers little of her ensuing teenage encounters with religion, other than to say that "what faith I had became more brittle, more absolute." On the one hand this rigid turn exemplifies the stage-appropriate response of most teenagers whose task it is to establish a clear ideology. On the other, however, McGee's embrace of this ideological stage seems particularly potent. She speculates, for example, that her personal piety was so bound by rules that the youth group in which she played a leadership role must have been relieved when she graduated from high school.[7] From this point forward her memoir speaks of twenty-five years where she supposedly pays little attention to the spiritual side of life, beginning with college, where "the change came all at once." Courses in literature and philosophy opened her up to Mark Twain's biting satires of religion and as well a certain professor's "elegant proof that God could not be proved."[8] At this point in her life, McGee viewed religion as distorting truth and working against critical thinking. She concluded that the two pillars of her upbringing mentioned earlier—religion and education—were mutually exclusive, contradictory, and toxic to each other.

These conclusions are by and large commonplace, yet that does not preclude the observation that McGee is deeply defined by both the worlds of religion and education. Could it be, in fact, that McGee had become caught in her own rigid dualism, now transferred to the world of enlightenment and rationalism? McGee's first steps back to communal religion will further suggest the conclusions we may make.

Feeling trapped by mistakes she was making as an adult, McGee decides that she wants to grow beyond her current self and become a better and kinder person. This decision came at a time in her life when she was in a "mess" in her relationship with a group of people with whom she worked. She had found herself in crisis, and felt a need for something stabilizing, yet knew there was much work to be done. She knew, also, that she could not do it on her own. Like a team of software developers, about whose programs she wrote technical manuals for her financial income, she observes about her spiritual life, "I needed a team to work with me on this."[9] In her ensuing search, McGee sets for herself the goal of attending groups of every religious affiliation in her area. Yet almost as quickly as she makes this resolution she abandons it, realizing that "Like it or not, my spiritual roots were in the Protestant Christian church."[10]

What begins as a seemingly logical and well-meditated experiment quickly unravels in the face of the primary attachments of her religious upbringing. Citing the Methodist Church as "too close to home," she eventually decides to alternate between two churches, one Episcopal and the other Unitarian Universalist. In the former, she felt a thrill in the liturgy as though she was part of a theater production, only now as a participant. In the latter she found herself pleased that there was no mention of God and that she was surrounded by "overeducated thinkers who like to talk about ideas" who reminded her of herself. McGee's experience with both congregations is summed up in her respective reactions to the Nicene Creed in the Episcopal church and the Seven Principles in the Unitarian church:

I understood the Unitarian principles with one reading and agreed with them. In contrast, I disagreed with every word in the Nicene Creed and wasn't sure I knew what it was talking about in the first place. But I was curious.[11]

McGee's dual attendance continued in this fashion for nearly two years. One week she would immerse herself in the majesty and mystery of the Eucharist, even while struggling with its doctrinal background. The next week she would enjoy a completely noncreedal experience, where there was freedom to entertain sacred symbols in any fashion, including those from other religions. In the Unitarian church, she participated in a "build your own theology" workshop where she was encouraged to write her own credo, while she also finally found herself able to say parts of the Nicene Creed in the Episcopal church, without blushing, and with the ability to "mean what I said."[12] Recovering a feeling of ownership and creativity in the one also brought her an appreciation for the tradition and normativity of the other. However, over time McGee realized that she was missing things in her respective churches by only attending them every other week. Even though her level of commitment to each church was admirable, the flaws in the approach were growing more evident. She felt torn and realized that the only solution was to quit one of the churches. She decided that:

> [M]y issues with Christianity were too engaging; they were what I thought about, both inside and outside the church. . . .
>
> I was trying to discover my relationship to the myths and images of a religion I once thought I knew well, but now found as new and surprising as it was familiar. I had to be there, on the battlefield, to keep the discovery process going.[13]

She decides to downgrade her membership in the Unitarian church and deepen her commitment to the Episcopal church. McGee's earlier statement that she was brought up in a household that worshipped at the dual altars of religion and education appears to capture a theme that carries through her adult life as well. She creates a dualism in her approach to religion and rationalism as a young adult and continues to do so even when she returns to corporate religion, with the Episcopal church representing her religious roots and the Unitarian church representing her rationalistic side. The dualism she creates, that religion is unreasonable and reason is irreligious, that sacred and secular are mutually exclusive, is one that is of course not unique. McGee's struggle with dualism comes to the fore more than once in her memoir, showing that she maintains an awareness of it. In her renewed approach to the Bible, for example, she concludes that there is more to scripture than a literalist view offers, whether that is through the lens of religious fundamentalism or secular atheism. Either way, it loses the idealization of literalism for McGee:

> Stories in the Bible became more interesting to me after I realized that they were trying to get at something other than historical fact. Before this, I had thought of Bible stories in one of two ways. Either I "believed" in a story, meaning I thought it was based on a historical event . . . or I *didn't* believe in it, in which case it was untrue and irrelevant.
>
> Now I was on a different wavelength. Could these stories be part of *my* myth?[14]

The stories in the Bible now became relevant and potent for McGee insofar as they could bring new ways to understand her life and help her discover the contours of her spiritual journey. The historical events on which the biblical stories were based, while important in how they locate the events in a certain place and time, became secondary in comparison to the personal meanings they contained. The dualistic polarity of fact and not-fact became more fluid, and less prominent in comparison to how it could be *used* to transform her consciousness. Elsewhere she writes:

When I saw the virgin birth as proof of Jesus' divinity, I was looking at it through my post-Enlightenment eyes—the only eyes I've got. Nobody in the first century had post-Enlightenment eyes. Back then, hyperbole was a more acceptable literary device than it is today. . . .

For me the question had changed from this: "How could Mary have possibly been a virgin?" To this: "*Why* a virgin? In bringing God to earth, why did an angel's visitation take the place of the sex act? Could Mary's virginity possibly have anything to do with me?"[15]

Over several paragraphs she explains that the virgin birth is essentially a story about letting God inside, about being a virgin ripe with potential and opening oneself to the holy and the possibilities of making that holiness incarnate in the self.[16]

The above example describes quite succinctly the personal transformative act of reexamining the articles of an inherited religious tradition that is losing its luster—that is, a rationalist approach to faith—and finding new ways to make use of it. As previously argued, this turning point is socially and historically located, and is not a simple matter of faith stage development. McGee's transformational work takes place both in her personal developmental trajectory but also in that of the world around her. In her case, the work is a matter of reencountering the pieces of the past, rejecting the accretions they had been assigned, and finding new ways to make meaning of them. McGee's is a pattern that in most respects appears postmourning, long past manic denial, and as already having expended most aggression. Instead of taking long detours through a paranoid-schizoid position, McGee is actively engaged with the depressive position. She seems more readily able to enter the transitional space and exercise her creativity with ultimate symbols, finding ways they can be *useful*, a word she herself employs in her evaluation of the Trinity:

When I first returned to Christian churches, I had little use for the Trinity as a description of God. I thought it smacked of

THE YOKE OF RATIONALISM

committee work. A few hundred years after Jesus lived and died, a bunch of clerics got together to describe what was new about God in their young religion. In my judgment, they had compromised on a description that contained a little of what was most important to each of them, without, unfortunately, making much sense.

So I asked myself, could the Trinity be useful to me?[17]

She begins with the Holy Spirit, to which we'll limit our discussion:

At first, I was mystified by the Holy Spirit. . . . After listening to the language about the Holy Spirit in the liturgy for a while, eventually I did hear patterns that struck a chord. The Holy Spirit was often connected to God's presence, God's *spirit* that suffused creation. Okay. When I prayed, I prayed to a God who was *right here*, not far off looking down at me. I could use the Holy Spirit as a metaphor for God's immanence.[18]

McGee's concept of the Holy Spirit takes her negative evaluation of the Trinity and turns it into something she finds useful. Mentions of the Holy Spirit in creeds, sermons, prayers, or liturgy now take on a feeling of something more than a sterilized cultural artifact. She has come into a relationship with the object of her faith and is now engaged in a game to see what it will do, and what it can offer to her personally.

In the example of McGee's reappropriation of the Trinity, we detect a clear theme of faith and spirit as something that is close and internal. She seems to join the many boomers who likewise seek divine immanence in their religious questing. Eschewing any concept of an "angry God," and the autocratic institutions that uphold it, many rediscover their "spiritual" side by seeking ultimate symbols of immanence. McGee does a good job of seeking this immanence; however, she does so in a way that also reveals a genuine struggle with externality. She rediscovers her sense of the divine in the natural world around her, for example, echoing the "conversion" she describes in her ninth-grade insect-collecting project. Tellingly, she begins to keep a nature diary. She would write short, detailed descriptions of singular objects around her house, whether it was the movement of a cloud across the sky, the sound of a snake slithering through gravel, or even in the feeling she experienced in turning her compost pile. By reflecting carefully on these objects, as a discipline of "paying attention" and contemplation, McGee discovered transitional space, liminality between sacred and profane, where she was neither inside, nor outside, but at the borders of meaning. From objects of nature to the symbols of religion, everything to her seemed connected in the immanent divine, which was at the same time transcendent and transforming. Her dualism, consequently, would fade:

> The dichotomy I had seen between science and religion, between rationality and belief, broke down. It was all religion. Paying attention to the natural world around me, listening to a talk on the historical Jesus at the Quimper Fellowship with my fellow Unitarians, singing the Gloria at St. Paul's with my fellow Episcopalians: it was all religion.
>
> I even came to terms with the primary descriptions of God used at both my churches, descriptions that had bored and annoyed me when I had first come back to church.[19]

McGee's narrative brings us to a key pattern we discover in those who can re-approach the life of faith and the ultimate symbols of religion, namely, the ability to discern the wholeness between fact and not fact, good and bad, sacred and profane, literal and representative understanding.

Yet McGee's journey remains, for the most part, an internal, often intellectual one. Interaction, sharing, and especially confrontation with other people take up little space in her book. If the return journey to articles of faith includes consistent engagement with externality, then that means engaging the challenging and sometimes messy experiences of personal relationships, especially in a religious community. In fact, what we discover in McGee's epilogue is that, after having decided upon just the one church over the other, her attendance even in that church fell to only Christmas, Easter, Ash Wednesday, and Good Friday. She remarks that her relationship with religion is not over, but nevertheless lets it go fallow after the events she describes.

Could it be that, after making so much peace with her religious past, even rebirthing her individual faith and discovering that religion can indeed be something in which she finds meaning and discovery, she nevertheless remains stalled in an adolescent ideological position? Or has she assumed a dystonic position of the conjunctive stage of faith, paralyzed by paradox and unable to take risks that might make her objects of faith once again appear rigid or worst of all, unthinking? Or, finally, has she embarked on finding symbols of ultimacy that can be shared in communities not defined by the contemporary institutions of American religiosity?

One final example from McGee's memoir provides a clue to where she resides in her mourning process with religion. The priest of the Episcopal church encouraged McGee to join a spiritual support group that met in the priest's home. This suggestion came, interestingly, as a follow-up to McGee meeting with him to explain her position on doctrine and whether it would be appropriate to receive communion. In the support group, each person was required to share the events of their week and relay something about how he or she felt about them. One person in the group, Janet, a woman who had lost her son, annoyed McGee. The woman would, in McGee's perception, list the events of her week mechanically, without giving much indication of how she really felt about them. McGee writes:

I could never figure out how she *felt* about what happened to her. It all seemed so mechanical. She skimmed the surface and never found any meaning other than the easiest and least threatening.[20]

Even when Janet would describe the time when she and her family scattered the ashes of her son's body among the misty San Juan

Islands in the Pacific Northwest, she seemed to do so with little sadness or depth. All she could offer was that it was "really neat." McGee felt it her responsibility to help Janet get in touch with her feelings, and that her duty was to do more than "nod mindlessly at Janet week after week." McGee's presenting concern is with mindlessness or taking an unanalytical approach to anything she was encountering in the support group. Ironically, it is perhaps her own inability to feel that is at issue here. Her reasoning, rational mindset led her to anger and had become a block against finding a way to relate to Janet. Contemplating this problem, McGee decides to look at it from a Christian point of view, that is, to love Janet as she loves herself. Even though McGee finds it difficult to love Janet, this was her job, she tells herself. McGee then asks herself whether this means that she is supposed to feel some emotion, or instead change her behavior. "I told myself to forget about love as *emotion*. Think of love as *behavior*."[21]

For McGee the idea of love being a behavior was a breakthrough. To relate to another in love, especially in Christian love, means acting in a way that is compassionate, rather than something coercive that is motivated by her annoyance. In her thinking through of this problem, McGee admits to herself that she does not know how to love herself any more than she knows how to love Janet. Perhaps this realization is a mere overgeneralization, or perhaps she is also returning to a primary faith object. McGee's struggle over her concern with Janet is just as likely a struggle with the idea of a God imago that acts lovingly toward her. Her next few paragraphs take up this very subject, resulting in a poem that she composes on God in nature and the love that she perceives there. After composing the poem, she decides to give it to Janet, the experience of which left her with a feeling of compassion, and a conclusion that she was blessed in her relationship with Janet after all. While this episode marks a turning point for McGee, it illustrates in general the often-seen difficulty of those who are struggling with a loss of faith in their ability to relate to others in a sacred community. Coming into relation with others, such as the spiritual support group, means encountering others who are bringing different sets of needs and perceptions. In McGee's case, she singled out someone who apparently could not express feelings, which was a part of her own faith struggle, that is, that she herself worried over whether she was supposed to base her religious faith on feeling, something she was not inclined to do because of its mindlessness or unthinking nature. What she instead discovers, at least in her experience with Janet, is that faith is not just feeling, but also action and behavior, which precedes the feeling.

McGee's approach, in general, was to link thought or belief as a precedent to feeling. Here she discovers that action, with thought present but in check, can be the precedent to the feeling that brings her into relation with others. McGee's ongoing discussion about doctrine throughout her narrative demonstrates just this exact struggle with her analytic approach that keeps her from feeling. Consequently, we find very little description, other than the episode with Janet, of her relationships in rediscovering religious community. Faith remains, by and large, a matter of belief and doctrine. It is little surprise then that McGee first chose two congregations to attend, and then having settled on just one, has trouble remaining committed, though that is never the whole story.

Unlike most of the other memoirs discussed, McGee's denial is not so much embedded in the imagoes of fundamentalist absolutism, but rather in the enlightenment absolutism that is equally common to our time. The advantage of her position is that she is comparatively free of acute trauma, her self-agency and independence remain intact, and subsequently one finds little of either self-recrimination or manic anger toward her religion. The disadvantage, however, is that the loss she struggles with is that much harder to name and mourn. Her experience contrasts with those, like Randall Balmer, who testify that if it were not for their strict evangelical college education, they would never have been led to confront so thoroughly their religious upbringing. The exigencies of McGee's inability to mourn are evidenced by the absence of close contact with others in her faith community. Nevertheless, it is worth being reminded that McGee's journey is not unlike the journey of many others, and in her case in particular, the journey is perhaps the most universal to the North American experience of all that have been discussed here so far.

Conclusion

THE GOAL OF THIS BOOK has been to describe the individual, psychological components to overcoming a disconnection from a community of shared symbols. I have argued that we cannot discover these components solely through sociological analysis or cognitive developmental psychology, both of which are often the preferred methods by which to do so. Instead, what is also necessary is a recognition and analysis of unconscious, lifelong psychological dynamics. I have nevertheless also argued that unconscious symbolic life is linked and profoundly affected by social and historical forces, many of which are defined by the loss of common culture, or a lack of a clearly articulated identity. The dislocation, diversity, bureaucratic, and technocratic social structures of our time create tremendous pressure on us to establish a healthy, creative use of symbols of ultimacy that can and must, as a psychological necessity, be shared and celebrated in community.

What I have proposed as the solution to discovering the keys to a successful return to religious community is the understanding that the individual both personally and as part of a broad social whole suffers a loss, one that is often more difficult to name and overcome because it is a loss of an ideal, or a set of ideal objects (relationships). If we view those who have fallen away from their faith as individuals undergoing a loss, then we may look to theories of mourning by which to understand that loss. I have relied on psychoanalytic theories of mourning that take into consideration how loss is overcome both on the conscious and unconscious level. I have explored the psychoanalytic language of mourning and melancholia in the work of Freud, the depressive position given by Klein, and the transitional space, play, and creativity offered by Winnicott, to show the path back to ultimate symbols shared in community. The psychoanalytic theory of mourning tells us that the keys to return to faith experienced in community involve embracing feelings of sorrow that leads to pining that leads to play, and by doing so finding an ascent and a way forward. Not to do so is to remain in suspended animation and be chained to the ghosts of loss. In the "madness" or religious mourning, not melancholia, we find the ability to thrive within paradox, to eschew the primacy of logic, to discover surprise and have a chance at experiencing hope and joy. Finally, what I have additionally argued is that by entering the process of mourning, we discover both the steps of overcoming loss individually as well as socially and historically. What we find in the memoirs discussed above, for example, are not only the personal successes that the individual has attained, but also how those successes are socially significant and how they participate in and represent a larger change. Such successes go beyond solving developmental tasks and instead create new culture and new ways of expressing and relating to what is considered ultimate and divine.

Having presented five case analyses of individuals who have revealed their sometimes extreme struggle with religion, I am better able to summarize some of the prevailing characteristics both in the struggles of the loss and in the work that brings about gain. I suggest here that separate these characteristics by using the words *dystonic* and *syntonic*. When originally employed by Erik Erikson, the former were thoughts and behaviors that represent failures to complete a stage-specific task within the life cycle, and the latter represent the completion of that task. I have chosen to use them here because they intone the ongoing, two-sided, or bipolar dynamic between melancholia and mourning. Dystonic elements may be described as the overall regressive, inward states that are mostly consumed by and often propagate pathology, whereas syntonic qualities connote a forward motion and a resolution of pathology. Offering such a summary may help us better understand the negative manifestations of the loss of faith and religion, as well as ways to encourage and protect the triumphs that emerge. I will also offer, by way of my final concluding statement, a few words about what came as a difficult lesson in this study and what it offers in terms of a new discovery for the psychoanalytic language of mourning.

Before proceeding, however, I wish to add a word of caution that I have been providing all along but is now more important than ever. What follows is a general outline of the dynamics of mourning faith. Although these dynamics are placed more or less in an order from beginning to end, what is at the beginning is not mutually exclusive from what is at the end, or vice versa. One may have succeeded in recovering the connection between their faith and community, but they may remain stymied with uncompleted tasks that keep them from fully engaging that community. Conversely, one may remain disconnected with any form of community but may also be doing some truly creative work in rediscovering that connection. While there is always a developmental, life-cycle progression taking place, and while much of what is summarized below could be placed within the young adult stage, that progression is always in relationship to the traumas and pathologies of individual temperament and family upbringing, as well as socio-historical forces, and is not exclusive to any one stage of life. In overcoming the loss of common culture, a task which those emerging from an absolutist mindset must solve, the progression becomes less a function of life cycle development and more an ongoing dynamic of personal healing and cultural change. Consequently, each of the characteristics I summarize below is in relationship to all of the others. An individual may have progressed through the earlier ones and found resolution in the later ones, but it is a resolution that remains embedded in the loss. The difference, I would suggest, based on the memoirs above, is that the individual becomes better at the daily overcoming of inherited existential pathologies. Theologically speaking, we become better at discovering grace despite our failings. This dynamic is a function of the fact that mourning an ideal is extraordinarily difficult, and takes

LOST FAITH AND WANDERING SOULS

tremendous effort and time, a factor I will discuss one last time below.

Dystonic Characteristics of Faith Loss

One of the most obvious signs of loss of faith and religion is undoubtedly an inability to find joy in thinking about shared faith. A lack of interest may come through a sense of being neglected or abused, as in the case of Carlene Cross, who suffered immense hardship at the hands of a nearly cultlike environment. Here we find notable moments of psychological *numbness, withdrawal,* and *paralysis.* The world these women once knew and idealized is no longer there. It had been annihilated and permanently placed outside of their reach despite painful longings to retrieve it. Caley describes how as a young child she slept and ate more and felt particularly empty on Sunday mornings. In her memoir written as an adult, she recognizes that she was at times an unhappy child solely because of her family's loss of their church community.

Accompanying and perhaps following numbness and withdrawal are more intense unconscious processes of turning the feeling of loss back upon the self. As Freud stated, in normal mourning the world has become colorless, but in melancholia it is the ego that has become colorless. Because mourning a cultural loss—and the ideals and relationships that represented the loss—creates an enormous task, falling into melancholia is an ever-present danger and is characterized by ongoing bouts of *self-recrimination* and *inadequacy.* Caley suffered moments when she felt as though there was something inherently wrong with her, that she would never get things right. She was mired in shame, not guilt that she had done something wrong that can be fixed, but that she herself was wrong. Although she was making her self-recrimination known and conscious by describing it in her book, we can certainly detect a hubris in the thought process that she is alone in her depraved state. She is, as Freud describes, the melancholic who complains incessantly and is unaware that the complaining is directed at the lost object that one cannot retrieve and yet is the unattainable ideal that is the source of the shame. So many of those who are struggling with faith loss likewise feel an ongoing sense of loneliness, and likewise can't seem to stop talking about their former religious life. Similarly, there is much self-recrimination in Randall Balmer's memoir, though there he describes it more as a general feeling of inadequacy. The intent of his memoir is to learn to love his father's faith, but there is a clear sense that he will never live up to the expectations of his father. Learning to love his father's faith, therefore, is likewise upholding an ideal that cannot be attained. Balmer suffers a spiritual version of chronic fatigue syndrome, where the symptoms of disillusionment linger indefinitely, as long as they are connected to idealization and inadequacy.[1]

Along with self-recrimination and inadequacy come feelings of *duplicity, fraudulence*, and of being *caught between two worlds*. Cross was at the beginning stages of creating psychological distance between her emotionally abusive husband and yet felt as though she did not have the courage to live out her conviction that the life she was living with her husband was wrong. She hated herself for it, concluding that remaining with her husband was acting just as deceitful and hypocritical as him. Creating distance from one's ideal life of faith nevertheless will bring about the notion that one has failed as a member of a group and will make it difficult to feel worthy in any group setting. This struggle is especially difficult for those who have emerged from an absolutist group that encourages exclusion of outsiders and sets up a division between the "chosen" and the "damned." The ex-absolutist now must live among those who are forever lost. Diana Butler-Bass's attempt at infusing mainline Protestantism with evangelical zeal serves as an example of overcoming this feeling of being caught between two worlds. Those outside the evangelical-fundamentalist world somehow lacked zeal, were not pious enough, and needed her sense of enthusiasm, and yet time after time she encountered difficulty.

Duplicity and fraudulence make it difficult to form attachments, as in the case of Margaret McGee. As she worked her way back toward a participatory faith, she attended two congregations at the same time and was reluctant to commit to just one. Such ambivalence is reminiscent of the infant who fails to see that the mother who is providing is also the mother who withholds. In the life of faith, the individual who feels ambivalent toward a religion that has been lost is also likely one who is unable to see both the good and the bad in the church community, which is now seen as either all good (yet unattainable) or all bad (and therefore undesirable). This view of faith is largely dualistic, as in the case of McGee who saw religion and science as antithetical rather than as pieces of a larger picture.

These dystonic characteristics each represent a basic rigidity in the individual's approach to the life of faith, even though it is the existential reality of loss. The loss experienced remains somewhat hidden from view. Attempts to discover it become easily mired in repetitive thoughts and actions that affirm negative, persecutory objects. Idealization of the negative objects results in numbing and a general lack of interest in relating to oneself or others with articles of faith. Manic denial is likewise at work here, cutting off any chance at discovering good, benevolent objects by over performance, rigidity, and embracing the bad, dictatorial objects. True anger at the life of faith has yet to be realized and is prevented by a bullying mind or superego.

Syntonic Characteristics of Faith Loss

Although it may seem to be taking things in a negative direction, outward *anger* directed at what has been lost in the life of faith is just the response that opens the door to newness. Confrontation especially with those who have propagated a rigid, suffocating life of faith will bring to the surface the pain and sorrow of the loss. Often, however, this is not possible, and reasonable substitutes, such as one's current pastor, must take their place. In the case of Caley, one such moment of anger arose when she felt incredulous at her own mother's inability to indict her friends for their blithe maliciousness in her ex-communication. Likewise, we hear of several moments between Balmer and his father when they engaged in epic battles about Balmer's choice of vocation—battles which, unfortunately, seemed to end in bitterness. It comes as little surprise that what we see in some of Balmer's continuing work is an aggressive act: to retake evangelicalism from the Religious Right, an attempt no doubt to reinhabit his anger toward his father and strike out on his own.[2]

As with Balmer's lament against the Religious Right, it's also common to feel *betrayal* at the hands of those who helped us cut our teeth in the life of faith. Bass reports feeling betrayed by a religious authority that misled her from the true doctrine of salvation of Jesus' teaching, as well as betrayed in that she was encouraged not to pursue the ministry because she was a woman. Cross, likewise, in her research of religious and biblical history discovered that the stories and doctrines that had been tersely impressed upon her were often no more than remything events that bore the mark of conquering patriarchal tribes and not divine inspiration.

Provided that the feelings of anger and betrayal are given their due and allowed to be expressed in a facilitating environment, an *acute feeling of loss* finally has the chance to become known. The person who can enter into the sorrow of the loss is the one who will reactivate their earliest and most powerful experiences of doubt, confusion, and disappointment, and how they were overcome through guilt, reparation, and the restoration of the creative, playful relation. All the accoutrements of the false self, that is, the objects that are not truly owned and inhabited, are stripped away, and a feeling of emptiness ensues. The absence and death of the lost object, against which all anger has been spent, however tragically, becomes more real and conscious than ever before.[3] The true self, such as it is, finds a moment to come forward; or in other words, there is a freedom to rediscover the hope of something sacred and divine, however defined, and fill the emptiness. Amidst the loss there is gain. Arising from the sorrow comes a pining for goodness. Cross describes the moment when she was on her living room floor weeping and feeling as though she could feel no worse and then her young daughter approaches her and tells her that everything will be well. The daughter's presence, love, and simple insight represented for Cross the facilitating environment that held her and would survive her despondency.

With the freedom that follows in the wake of anger and emptiness comes the rediscovery of *initiative* and *self-agency*. The loss has by degrees been incorporated and one feels a certain level of peace. There arises a new confidence that one cannot be so easily manipulated by religious authority, and yet is able to engage that authority and perhaps even participate in it and change it. Caley's experience of becoming a Sunday school teacher and providing to her students the love and acceptance she never received demonstrates what can happen when self-agency emerges. An observation worth underscoring at this point is the fact that teaching children in the life of faith can be a powerful tool in rediscovering one's own love of ultimate symbols. Here the life of faith may develop a feeling of *playfulness* and *discovery*. Caley likewise experiences a moment of playfulness when one of her daughters takes it upon herself to give Caley the much-coveted mustard seed that she never received from the church that ex-communicated her mother. Ironically, Balmer discovers moments of playfulness when he visits his grandfather, the man who his father had scorned, and perceives a peace about his grandfather.

With renewed initiative, self-agency, and a sense of discovery also comes the desire to engage others and put the new confidence to the test, to *share* it. Here the individual has entered the transitional space, and now perceives the sacred symbols and ideas and rituals as a playground to express what represents the things most dearly held. Bass appears vitally interested in sharing her faith, making it participatory, despite the failures and imperfections she encounters. McGee eventually discovers that she cannot alternate her attendance between two churches, and that she should instead become invested in just one. In addition, entering a playful space likewise means taking a fluid approach to doctrine. For McGee, doctrine becomes a question of what she can use to better understand herself and the world around her. The doctrine of the virgin birth, for example, becomes less a question of right belief and more an entertaining puzzle where the solution comes in finding the powerful meaning in the story that is significant in the moment of its telling. Along with such discovery and initiative comes the chance to perceive new richness in the articles of faith that now seem to have endless depth and ongoing power, not trapped in time or space.

Final Remarks

Two further observations will answer questions that have been posed earlier in this book. First, they key question of the broad inward turn in the life of faith was answered by the acknowledgment of the loss of common culture that continues to show itself in American society. An implicit hope in this study is to discover what it will take to get people to return to communities of faith, even though it is difficult to fully conjecture what those communities of faith should be. What we can be sure of is that a great longing for community exists in our world today, and the disconnection and dislocation many people suffer is quite palpable. Psychologically speaking, community is a must, and that is especially true for the life of faith. Although the inward turn of faith has been an inevitability, even at times a saving grace, one must wonder about our ability to create deeply shared symbols even in "sacred community," not just the sacred self. Although it is beyond this discussion to identify mandates for community in today's culture, we may at least look to the memoirs discussed here and observe moments when community has once again become possible. Wherever the inward turn has been the result of absolutist culture, be it fundamentalism or rationalism, we have also found a desire to strike out and rediscover the articles of faith anew, even among baby boomers who so acutely experience the loss of common culture in the United States. Consequently, the inward turn is not the last word or the death knell of religion. Instead, what we find is a new interest in the mystery of faith, even in its beauty, as something to behold, rather than just something to believe in. Interestingly enough, most of the individuals discussed above found themselves attracted by more liturgically constructed, rather than didactic, forms of faith.

The second question left unanswered asks whether we learned anything that would augment what we know about the language of mourning, particularly as it is applied to faith. What surprised me the most in analyzing the above memoirs is that there is more to the painstakingly slow process of mourning than Freud acknowledged; that is, it is even slower than he imagined. When it comes to mourning an ideal, as I have argued, infinitely more complex challenges exist. The ideals and the relationships connected to them run deeper and are at least equally as powerful as attachments to immediate family members in our lives. They hearken to our earliest, most formative moments as well as point forward to our greatest dreams and desires. They are the very building blocks of language, thought, and behavior. When our use of symbols becomes broken, however, we are woefully ill equipped to make repairs, and the recovery process is much longer than one might think. There is no simple regimen or treatment that will apply for all and will bring about resolution within a prescribed time frame. What should be made clearer in the theory of mourning is that mourning an ideal means accepting moments of the confusion and darkness of melancholy. As Paul Ricoeur once mentioned, we live in melancholic times, in which we feel immense pressure to perform on our own all the functions of the community.[4]

Despite what may seem like bad news, the psychoanalytic language of mourning indeed appears to resonate strongly with the life of faith and religion in today's world. Through this lens I was able to detect in the lives of the above memoir writers' moments of overcoming the past and being creative in the present. Moreover, these moments were anything but insignificant. One of the gifts of great sorrow is the opportunity for an equally great joy. In examining these memoirs, we saw people who have suffered greatly the broken symbols of our time. They found moments of transcending the brokenness that were bright, shining, and filled with hope. As Kate Young Caley would say, no one gets to take that away. Amid our melancholy, we can realize transcendence, not just for ourselves individually, but for those around us as well, even for society as a whole. There may be no simple healing process to follow from beginning to end, one that leaves us free from the brokenness of our time, but we can surmise that it is possible to become better and more practiced at a new desire to love, despite that brokenness. This proficiency of creative

CONCLUSION

transcendence, I argue, is the crux of rediscovering faith in community.

Acknowledgments

I am deeply grateful to the teaching, mentoring and life of Dr. Johan Noordsij, who helped me find the original avenue for creating this book. Thanks as well to Michael Christensen and Bill Rich, early readers of this manuscript. I will also be forever grateful to my interdisciplinary graduate school education at Drew University, which gave me opportunities to read widely and even discover key theoretical content that wasn't on any syllabus at that time. That education has stayed with me and provided a healthy dissonance between a scholar's mindset and the faith of the everyday people I've served professionally.

There have been many family members, friends, and acquaintances along the way who have encouraged me to publish this book and when I thank them here, I hope they know who they are. I'm grateful to my parents, Paul and Patti, who have been supportive of this work. Above all, I dedicate this work to Elena and Addie, who inspired me to keep working, and most especially to Lisa, who not only helped proofread the final pages, but has also been on her own similar journey, yet also with me every step of the way.

About the author

David Morris, PhD, is a lifelong student of psychology and religion. He has served professionally for major national publishing brands, working with bestselling authors and books. He is the publisher of Lake Drive Books (lakedrivebooks.com) and literary agent at Hyponymous Consulting (hyponymous.com), two innovative ventures working together to specialize in authors and books that help people heal, grow, and discover.

He received his doctorate at Drew University, and his publishing positions included executive roles at Zondervan Books, part of HarperCollins, and the books division of *Guideposts* magazine. He lives with his wife in Grand Rapids, Michigan, and they have two daughters. Visit davidrmorris.me.

Notes

Introduction

1. Kate Young Caley, *The House Where the Hardest Things Happened* (New York: Doubleday, 2002), 1-2.
2. Kathleen Norris, *Amazing Grace: A Vocabulary of Faith* (New York: Riverhead, 1998), 63-64.
3. Karen Armstrong, *Through the Narrow Gate* (New York: St. Martin's Press, 1981).
4. Karen Armstrong, *Beginning the World* (New York: St. Martin's Press, 1983).
5. Karen Armstrong, *The Spiral Staircase: My Climb out of Darkness* (New York: Knopf, 2004), xviii.
6. Karen Armstrong, "The Freelance Monotheism of Karen Armstrong," interview by Krista Tippett (speakingoffaith.publicradio.org: American Public Media, May 8, 2008), accessed June 1, 2008.
7. Julia Scheeres, *Jesus Land: A Memoir* (New York: Counterpoint: 2005), 360.
8. Douglas Coupland, *Life After God* (New York: Pocket Books, 1994), 273-274.
9. For a sampling of this literature, see Robert Altemeyer and Bruce Hunsberger. *Amazing Conversions: Why Some Turn to Faith and Others Abandon Religion.* Amherst (New York: Prometheus Books, 1997); Edward T. Babinski, ed, *Leaving the Fold: Testimonies of Former Fundamentalists* (Amherst, New York: Prometheus Books, 1995); Fred Cornforth, *Ten Who Left: People Who Left the Church and Why* (Boise, Idaho: Pacific Press Publishing Association, 1995); William D. Hendricks, *Exit Interviews: Revealing Stories of Why People Are Leaving the Church* (Chicago: Moody Press, 1993); Ruth A. Tucker, *Walking Away from Faith: Unraveling the Mystery of Belief and Unbelief* (Downers Grove, Illinois: InterVarsity Press, 2002); Stefan Ulstein, *Growing Up Fundamentalist: Journeys in Legalism and Grace* (Downers Grove, Illinois: InterVarsity Press, 1995); Marlene Winell, *Leaving the Fold: A Guide for Former*

Fundamentalists and Others Leaving Their Religion (Oakland, California: New Harbinger Publications, 1993).

10. Erik H. Erikson, *Young Man Luther: A Study in Psychoanalysis and History* (New York: W. W. Norton, 1958); idem, *Gandhi's Truth: On the Origins of Militant Nonviolence* (New York: W. W. Norton, 1969).

11. Erik H. Erikson, *Childhood and Society* (New York: W. W. Norton, 1950), 247.

12. James W. Fowler, *Stages of Faith: The Psychology of Human Development and the Quest for Meaning* (New York: HarperCollins Publishers, 1981), xi-23.

13. James W. Fowler, *Faithful Change: Personal and Public Challenges of Postmodern Life* (Nashville, Tennessee: Abingdon Press, 1996) 56.

14. Lucy Bregman, "Defining Spirituality: Multiple Uses and Murky Meanings of an Incredibly Popular Term." *Journal of Pastoral Care and Counseling* 58 (Fall 2004): 157-167.

15. Erik H. Erikson, *Toys and Reasons: Stages in the Ritualization of Experience*, (New York: W. W. Norton, 1977), 110.

16. Robert Lifton, *The Broken Connection: On Death and the Continuity of Life* (New York: Basic Books, 1979), 298.

17. Figlio, Karl. "The Absolute State of Mind in Society and the Individual," *Psychoanalysis, Culture and Society* 11 (2006): 129.

Chapter 1: The Sociology of Religious Participation

1. John Wilson and Darren E. Sherkat, "Returning to the Fold," *Journal for the Scientific Study of Religion* 33 (June 1994): 148-161.

2. Wade Clark Roof, *A Generation of Seekers: The Spiritual Journey of the Baby Boom Generation* (San Francisco: HarperCollins, 1994), 161-169.

3. C. Kirk Hadaway and Wade Clark Roof, "Disaffiliation from Mainline Churches," *Falling from the Faith: Causes and Consequences of Religious Apostasy*, ed. David G. Bromley (Newbury Park, California: Sage Publications, 1988), 12-13.

4. Paul Tillich, *Dynamics of Faith* (New York: Harper and Row, 1957), 50.

5. See Christopher Bader, et al., *American Piety in the 21st Century: New Insights to the Depth and Complexity of Religion in the U.S.* (Waco, Texas: Baylor Institute for Studies of Religion, 2006); Luis Lugo, et al. *U.S. Religious Landscape Survey* (Washington, DC.: The Pew Forum on Religion and Public Life, 2008).

6. David G. Bromley, "Religious Disaffiliation: A Neglected Social Process," *Falling from the Faith: Causes and Consequences of Religious Apostasy*, ed. David G. Bromley (Newbury Park, California: Sage Publications, 1988), 11.
7. One exception is Anthony Giddens, who contends that even among instances of social disintegration, there is always new integration being wrought by the counterforce of the human agent, and that it is invalid to argue that social forces are not malleable. See Anthony Giddens, *Modernity and Self-Identity: Self and Society in the Late Modern Age* (Stanford, California: Stanford University Press, 1991).
8. Roof, *A Generation of Seekers*; Robert Wuthnow, *After Heaven: Spirituality in America Since the 1950s* (Berkeley: University of California Press, 1998).
9. Roof, *Generation of Seekers*, 3.
10. Robert D. Putnam, *Bowling Alone: The Collapse and Revival of American Community* (New York: Simon and Schuster, 2000), 22-23.
11. Roof, *Generation of Seekers*, 252.
12. Christopher Lasch, *The Culture of Narcissism: American Life in the Age of Diminishing Expectations* (New York: Warner Books, 1979).
13. Donald Capps, *The Depleted Self: Sin in a Narcissistic Age* (Minneapolis, Minnesota: Augsburg Fortress, 1993).
14. Wuthnow, *After Heaven*, 162.
15. Ibid., 163.
16. Ibid., 162.
17. Ibid., 184.
18. Ibid., 188.
19. Ibid., 197.
20. Robert Wuthnow, *Growing Up Religious: Christians and Jews and Their Journeys of Faith* (Boston: Beacon Press, 1999), 167.
21. Roof, *Generation of Seekers*, 251.
22. Ibid., 235.

Chapter 2: Deepening the Field of Analysis

1. Lifton, *The Broken Connection*, 296.
2. Ibid., 296
3. Ibid., 297
4. Robert Jay Lifton, "Protean Man." *Partisan Review* 35 (1968): 13–27.
5. Charles B. Strozier, *Apocalypse: On the Psychology of Fundamentalism in America* (Boston: Beacon Press, 1994).

6. Martin Jay, "The Apocalyptic Imagination and the Inability to Mourn," in *Force Fields: Between Intellectual History and Cultural Critique* (New York: Routledge, 1993), 84-98.

7. Peter Homans, "The Decline of Mourning Practices in Modern Western Societies: A Short Sketch," in *Symbolic Loss: The Ambiguity of Mourning and Memory at Century's End*, ed. Peter Homans (Charlottesville, Virginia: The University of Virginia Press, 2000), 2-3.

8. Peter Homans, *The Ability to Mourn: Disillusionment and the Social Origins of Psychoanalysis* (Chicago: The University of Chicago Press, 1989).

9. Philip Rieff, *Triumph of the Therapeutic: Uses of Faith After Freud* (New York: Harper and Row, 1966); Lasch, *The Culture of Narcissism*.

10. Peter Homans, *Symbolic Loss*, 11-17.

11. Alexander Mitscherlich and Marguerite Mitscherlich, *The Inability to Mourn: Principles of Collective Behavior* (New York: Grove Press, 1975); Wolf Lepenies, *Melancholy and Society*, trans. Jeremy Gaines and Doris Jones (Cambridge: Harvard University Press, 1992); Henry Rousso, *The Vichy Syndrome: History and Memory in France Since 1944*, trans. Arthur Goldhammer (Cambridge: Harvard University Press, 1991); Jay Winter, *Sites of Memory, Sites of Mourning: The Great War in European Cultural History* (New York: Cambridge University Press, 1995).

12. Homans, *Symbolic Loss*, 16.

13. Capps, *The Depleted Self*, 9.

14. Erik H. Erikson, *Toys and Reasons: Stages in the Ritualization of Experience* (New York: W.W. Norton, 1977), 147-156.

15. Capps, *The Depleted Self*, 136-145.

16. Ibid., 11.

17. Ibid., 29.

18. Ibid., 74.

19. See Capps's discussion of Kohut's concept of mirroring in Capps, *The Depleted Self*, 29-31, 67; Capps draws from Kohut's discussion of mirroring in Heinz Kohut, *The Analysis of the Self: A Systematic Approach to the Psychoanalytic Treatment of Narcissistic Personality Disorders* (New York: International Universities Press, 1971), 115-118; idem, *How Does Analysis Cure?* (Chicago: The University of Chicago Press, 1984), 143-144.

20. Ibid., 7.

21. Robert M. Bellah, et al. *Habits of the Heart: Individualism and Commitment in American Life* (New York: Harper and Row, 1985), 243; quoted in Capps, *The Depleted Self*, 118.

22. Capps, *The Depleted Self*, 160-161.
23. Ibid., 162.

Chapter 3: The Uses of Faith Stage Theory

1. Erik H. Erikson, *Childhood and Society*, 262-263.
2. Fowler, *Stages of Faith*, 14.
3. Ibid., 17.
4. Richard Norman Shulik, "Faith Development, Moral Development, and Old Age: An Assessment of Fowler's Faith Development Paradigm and Aging" (Ph.D. diss., University of Chicago, 1979); Fowler, *Stages of Faith*, 107.
5. Philip M. Helfaer, *The Psychology of Religious Doubt* (Boston: Beacon Press, 1972); Fowler, *Stages of Faith*, 286.
6. Fowler, *Stages of Faith*. 132.
7. Ibid., 182-183.
8. Ibid., 183.
9. Paul Ricoeur, "The Hermeneutics of Symbols and Philosophical Reflection," in *The Philosophy of Paul Ricoeur*, ed. Charles E. Reagan and David Stewart (Boston: Beacon Press, 1978), 36-58; Fowler, *Stages of Faith*, 187.
10. Fowler credits this phrase to William F. Lynch, S.J., *Images of Faith* (Notre Dame, Indiana: University of Notre Dame Press, 1973); Fowler, *Stages of Faith*, 198.
11. William W. Meissner, *Life and Faith: Psychological Perspectives on Religious Experience* (Washington, D. C.: Georgetown University Press, 1987), 134.
12. James W. Fowler and Sam Keen, *Life Maps: Conversations on the Journey of Faith* (Nashville, Tennessee: W Publishing Group, 1985), 36; Fowler has also written, "The stage level of aspiration for a public church, it seems clear, is Conjunctive faith." James W. Fowler, *Faith Development and Pastoral Care* (Philadelphia: Fortress Press, 1987), 97.
13. For a criticism of Fowler's overlooking of the emotional dimension of faith, see also Walter Conn, *Christian Conversion: A Developmental Interpretation of Autonomy and Surrender* (Mahwah, New Jersey: Paulist Press, 1986), 83-89.
14. Fowler, *Stages of Faith*, 285-286.
15. Lewis Rambo, *Understanding Religious Conversion* (New Haven: Yale University Press, 1995), 165-170.

16. See Gordon T. Smith, *Beginning Well: Christian Conversion and Authentic Trans-formation* (Downers Grove, Illinois: Intervarsity Press, 2001); Scot McNight, *Turning to Jesus: The Sociology of Conversion in the Gospels* (Louisville, Kentucky: Westminster John Knox Press, 2002); Richard V. Peace, *Conversion in the New Testament: Paul and the Twelve* (Grand Rapids, Michigan: William B. Eerdmans, 1999).
17. Romney M. Mosley, *Becoming a Self Before God: Critical Transformations* (Nashville, Tennessee: Abingdon Press, 1991), 68.
18. John D. Barbour. *Versions of Deconversion: Autobiography and the Loss of Faith* (Charlottesville: University of Virginia Press, 1994), 3.

Chapter 4: The Psychoanalytic Stance

1. Erik H. Erikson, "The Galilean Sayings and the Sense of 'I'," *Yale Review* (April 1981): 333.
2. Sigmund Freud, *The Standard Edition of the Complete Psychological Works of Sigmund Freud* (hereafter *SE*), ed. James Srachey. vol. 21, *The Future of an Illusion* (London: Hogarth Press, 1981), 43.
3. Freud, *SE*, vol. 13, *Totem and Taboo: Some Points of Agreement Between the Mental Lives of Savages and Neurotics*; idem, *SE*, vol. 23, *Moses and Monotheism*.
4. See especially Peter Homans, *Theology after Freud: An Interpretive Inquiry* (Indianapolis, Indiana: Bobbs Merrill, 1970).
5. Paul Ricoeur, *Freud and Philosophy: An Essay on Interpretation* (New Haven: Yale University Press, 1970), 534-536.
6. For a full discussion of the functional vs. substantive approach to religion from a psychological viewpoint, see John McDargh, *Psychoanalytic Object Relations Theory and the Study of Religion* (Lanham, Maryland: University Press of America, 1983), 6-14.
7. See especially Hetty Zock, *A Psychology of Ultimate Concern: Erik H. Erikson's Contribution to the Psychology of Religion* (Amsterdam: Rodopi B. V., 1990).
8. Erikson, *Toys and Reasons*, 90.
9. Ibid., 89-90.
10. Ibid., 17.
11. Erik H. Erikson, "Ontogeny of Ritualization in Man," *Philosophical Transactions of the Royal Society of London; Series B. Biological Sciences*, 251, no. 772 (1966): 338.
12. Erikson, *Toys and Reasons*, 100.

13. Ibid., 110.
14. Ibid., 110-112; idem, *The Life Cycle Completed: A Review* (New York: W. W. Norton, 1982), 64.
15. Brian Koldodiejchuk, ed., *Mother Teresa: Come Be My Light* (New York: Doubleday, 2007).
16. For a striking example of how depression can strike the religiously devout, see Kathleen Norris's discussion of her struggle with melancholy in Kathleen Norris, *Acedia and Me: A Marriage, Monks, and A Writer's Life* (New York: Riverhead Books, 2008).

Chapter 5: Mourning and the Faith Journey

1. The problem of whether psychoanalysis replaces religion receives a fair amount of attention in the literature. The position I have taken here is summarized in Isaac D. Balbus, *Mourning and Modernity: Essays in the Psychoanalysis of Contemporary Society* (New York: Other Press, 2005), xviii-xix.
2. Freud, *SE*, vol. 14, "Mourning and Melancholia," 243.
3. Freud, *SE*, vol. 14, "On Transience," 307.
4. Freud, "Mourning and Melancholia," 244.
5. Ibid., 248.
6. Ibid., 246.
7. Freud, *SE*, vol. 18, *Group Psychology and the Analysis of the Ego*, 98.
8. Ibid., 133-135.
9. Freud, "Mourning and Melancholia," 254.
10. For a discussion of the connection between melancholy and religion, see Stanley W. Jackson, *Melancholia and Depression: From Hippocratic Times to Modern Times* (New Haven: Yale University Press, 1983), 325-331.
11. Freud, "Mourning and Melancholia," 256.
12. This summary is drawn primarily from Melanie Klein, "Love, Guilt, and Reparation" in *The Writings of Melanie Klein*, vol. 1, *Love, Guilt and Reparation and Other Works 1921-1945* (New York: The Free Press, 1975), 306-317; and also from Hanna Segal, *Klein* (Glasgow: William Collins Sons, 1979), 78-79.
13. Melanie Klein, "Mourning and Its Relation to Manic Depressive States," in *The Writings of Melanie Klein*, vol. 1, *Love, Guilt and Reparation and Other Works 1921-1945* (New York: The Free Press, 1975), 352.
14. Ibid., 362-363.

15. Ibid., 355-369; see especially the analysis of the dreams of Mrs. A and patient D.
16. Ibid., 361.
17. Peter Shabad, "The Most Intimate of Creations: Symptoms as Memorials to One's Lonely Suffering," in *Symbolic Loss: The Ambiguity of Mourning and Memory at Century's End*, ed. Peter Homans (Charlottesville, Virginia: The University Press of Virginia, 2000), 207.
18. Susan Kavaler-Adler, *Mourning, Spirituality and Psychic Change: A New Object Relations View of Psychoanalysis* (New York: Brunner-Routledge, 2003), 65.
19. This analysis of Bowlby can be found in Kavaler-Adler, *Mourning and Psychic Change*, 69; it draws on John Bowlby, "Pathological Mourning and Childhood Mourning," *Journal of the American Psychoanalytic Association* 11 (1963): 500-41.
20. See especially C. Fred Alford, *Melanie Klein and Critical Social Theory: An Account of Politics, Art, and Reason Based on Her Psychoanalytic Theory* (New Haven: Yale University Press, 1989), 57-103; Isaac D. Balbus, *Mourning and Modernity: Essays in the Psychoanalysis of Contemporary Society* (New York: Other Press, 1992), 65.
21. James Dobson, *Life on the Edge: A Young Adult's Guide to a Meaningful Future* (Dallas: Word Publishing, 1995), 75–76.
22. Patricia H. Davis, "Melanie Klein, Motherhood, and 'The Heart of Darkness,'" in *Religion, Society, and Psychoanalysis* (Boulder, CO: Westview Press, 1997), 98-100.
23. Figlio, "The Absolute State of Mind," 126.
24. D. W. Winnicott, "The Manic Defense," in *Through Pediatrics to Psycho-Analysis* (London: Tavistock Publications, 1958).
25. Ibid., 132.
26. Ibid.
27. Ibid., 133. Winnicott does not leave much room for the person who recognizes the self-agency in their abilities, but also sees their strengths as coming through the help of others, a community and the shared symbols that create avenues through which those abilities may flourish. The notion of a transitional space that is spread across the entire "cultural field," would be an entity that impacts the individual in such a way as to nurture and develop personal gifts. So it is not necessarily an indication of denial that positive contributions are attributed to God, a mentor, parents, a school, or a community. Nevertheless, the statement that denial may also

encompass a reinforcement of a feeling of worthlessness, a diminishment of ego, and a devaluation of the self remains true.

28. See Robert Webber, *Evangelicals on the Canterbury Trail: Why Evangelicals Are Attracted to the Liturgical Church* (Waco, Texas: Word Books, 1985).

29. For a full description of these three Winnicottian concepts and their connection to mourning see Susan Kavaler-Adler, *Mourning, Spirituality, and Psychic Change*, 74-80.

30. D. W. Winnicott. "The Use of an Object and Relating Through Identifications," *Playing and Reality* (New York: Routledge, 1971), 86.

31. Adam Phillips, *Winnicott* (Cambridge, Massachusetts: Harvard University Press, 1988), 132-133.

32. Winnicott, *Playing and Reality*, 91.

33. D. W. Winnicott, "The Development of the Capacity for Concern," in *Maturational Processes and the Facilitating Environment* (Madison, CT: International Universities Press, 1965, 1963).

34. Winnicott, "Transitional Objects and Transitional Phenomena," *Playing and Reality*, 2.

35. Winnicott, "The Place Where We Live," *Playing and Reality*, 104-110.

36. Winnicott, "Location of Cultural Experience," *Playing and Reality*. 97.

37. Winnicott, "Transitional Objects and Transitional Phenomena," *Playing and Reality*, 5.

38. Winnicott, "Playing: A Theoretical Statement," *Playing and Reality*, 38.

39. Ibid., 47.

40. Ibid.

41. Ibid., 48.

42. Ibid., 51-52.

43. Ibid., 51.

44. Winnicott, "Ego Distortion in Terms of True and False Self," *Maturational Processes and the Facilitating Environment*, 140-153.

45. Ibid., 147.

46. Ibid., 151.

47. Ibid., 150.

Part II: Biographical Analysis

1. Wuthnow, 38.

Chapter 6: Finding A Safe Place: Kate Young Caley

1. Caley, *The House Where the Hardest Things Happened*, 151-152.
2. Ibid., 22.
3. Ibid., 91.
4. Ibid., 14.
5. Ibid., 37.
6. Ibid., 12-14.
7. Ibid., 108.
8. Ibid., 105.
9. Ibid., 42.
10. Ibid., 43.
11. Ibid., 120.
12. Ibid., 56-57.
13. Ibid., 57.
14. Ibid., 65.
15. Ibid., 89.
16. Ibid., 93.
17. Ibid.
18. Ibid., 139.
19. Ibid., 153.
20. Ibid.
21. Ibid., 157.

Chapter 7: The Pilgrim's Journey: Diana Butler-Bass

1. Diana Butler-Bass, *Strength for the Journey: A Pilgrimage of Faith in Community* (San Francisco: Jossey-Bass, 2002), 3.
2. Diana Butler-Bass, *Christianity for the Rest of Us: How the Neighborhood Church is Transforming the Faith* (San Francisco: HarperSanFrancisco, 2006), 17.
3. Butler-Bass, *Strength*, 12.
4. Butler-Bass, *Christianity*, 18.
5. Butler-Bass, *Strength*, 13.
6. Ibid., 37.
7. Ibid., 61.
8. Ibid., 74.
9. Ibid., 12.
10. Ibid., 119.

11. Ibid., 123.
12. Ibid., 135.
13. Ibid., 136.
14. Ibid.
15. Ibid., 137.
16. Ibid.
17. Ibid., 165.
18. Ibid., 170.
19. Ibid., 181-182.
20. Ibid., 217.
21. Ibid., 213.
22. Ibid., 281.

Chapter 8: The Search for Grace: Randall Balmer

1. Randall Balmer, *Growing Pains: Learning to Love My Father's Faith* (Grand Rapids, Michigan: Brazos Press, 2001), 28.
2. Ibid., 27-28.
3. Ibid., 26.
4. Ibid., 31.
5. Erikson, *Toys and Reasons*, 102.
6. Balmer, *Growing Pains*, 19.
7. Ibid., 38.
8. Ibid., 71.
9. Ibid., 75.
10. Ibid., 46.
11. Ibid., 18.
12. Ibid., 48.
13. Ibid.
14. Ibid., 104.
15. Ibid., 80.
16. Ibid., 88.
17. Ibid., 93
18. Ibid., 98
19. Ibid., 105.
20. Ibid., 107-108.
21. Ibid., 108.
22. Ibid.

23. Ibid., 124.
24. Ibid.
25. Ibid., 84.
26. Ibid., 84.
27. Randall Balmer, *Thy Kingdom Come, An Evangelical's Lament: How the Religious Right Distorts the Faith and Threatens America* (New York: Basic Books, 2006), xii.

Chapter 9: Freedom and Discovery: Carlene Cross

1. Carlene Cross, *Fleeing Fundamentalism: A Minister's Wife Examines Faith* (Chapel Hill, North Carolina: Algonquin Books of Chapel Hill, 2006), 5-6.
2. Ibid., 13.
3. Ibid., 15.
4. Ibid., 1.
5. Ibid., 1-2.
6. Ibid., 16.
7. Ibid., 3.
8. Ibid., 21-29.
9. Ibid., 34.
10. Ibid., 62.
11. Ibid., 64.
12. Ibid., 82-83.
13. Ibid., 115.
14. Ibid.
15. Ibid., 131.
16. Ibid., 137-138.
17. Ibid., 150.
18. Ibid., 164.
19. Ibid., 200-201.
20. Ibid., 226.
21. Ibid., 237.
22. Ibid., 238.
23. Ibid., 250.
24. Ibid., 259.
25. Ibid., 263.
26. Ibid., 273.

Chapter 10: The Yoke of Rationalism: Margaret McGee

1. Margaret McGee, *Stumbling Toward God: A Prodigal's Return* (Philadelphia: Innisfree Press, 2002), 24.
2. Ibid., 27.
3. Ibid. 33.
4. Ibid., 35.
5. Ibid.
6. Ibid.
7. Ibid., 36.
8. Ibid., 37.
9. Ibid., 40.
10. Ibid., 50.
11. Ibid., 57.
12. Ibid., 79. McGee's "mean what I said" phrase is reminiscent of Erikson's "meaning it," where he observes the connection between faith and ideology. See Erik H. Erikson, *Young Man Luther*, 208-210.
13. McGee, *Stumbling*, 163.
14. Ibid., 128.
15. Ibid., 137.
16. Ibid., 137-138.
17. Ibid., 113-114.
18. Ibid., 115.
19. Ibid., 112-113.
20. Ibid., 63.
21. Ibid., 67.

Conclusion

1. For a discussion of spiritual fatigue, see Hendricks, *Exit Interviews*, 152.
2. Balmer, *Thy Kingdom Come*.
3. For a fuller discussion of reaching a "death place," a feeling of religious death, loss, and emptiness, see Ann Bedford Ulanov, *Finding Space: Winnicott, God, and Psychic Reality* (Louisville, Kentucky: Westminster John Knox Press, 2001) 140-141.
4. William B. Parsons, Diane Jonte-Pace, and Susan Henking, eds. "Conversations on Freud, Memory, and Loss: Paul Ricoeur and Peter Homans," *Mourning Religion* (Charlottesville, Virginia: University of Virginia Press, 2008).

www.ingramcontent.com/pod-product-compliance
Lightning Source LLC
Chambersburg PA
CBHW032053020426
42335CB00011B/310